Northern Lights
and Shadows

In memory of
Charles Tamboer, Jr.
from his beloved son
February 2006

Northern Lights and Shadows

Sixteen Years in the Alaska Bush

Lee Basnar

Printed in 2005.
Printed in the United States of America.
10-digit ISBN: 1-59113-778-0
13-digit ISBN: 978-1-59113-778-8
Published by Booklocker.com, Inc.
www.booklocker.com

Front cover photo
Moonrise over the Talkeetna Mountains viewed from the Basnars' cabin.

Back cover photos
Upper left: Joan Basnar with Alaska Range in background.
Upper Right: Lee Basnar.
Lower Left: Ravenhead Pond viewed from the Basnar cabin.
Lower Right: Lee and Joan Basnar's cabin in September 1981.
All photos by the author.

Cover design, interior design, and maps by Lorraine B. Elder.

TO JOAN,
WHOSE PARTICIPATION
AND SUPPORT
MADE THE DREAM
A REALITY.

Alaska

NOTE: MAP NOT TO SCALE

Basnars' Cabin Site

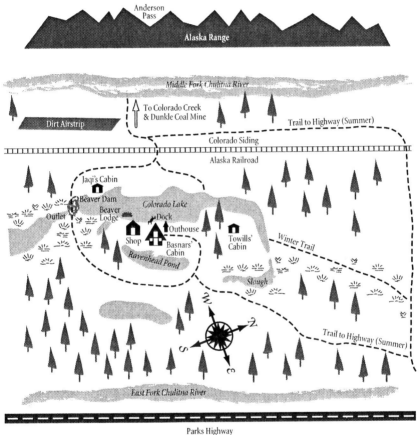

NOTE: MAP NOT TO SCALE

Contents

Breaking Trail

The storm began in the morning; snow fell throughout that day and night. When I peered from our cabin's living room window the next morning, the effect was that of staring into a vast swarm of white mosquitoes. Huge snowflakes swirled and collided in their rush to the ground, obliterating the outside world a few feet beyond the window.

I shoved a piece of split spruce into the stove, adjusted the damper to arouse our sole source of heat and raise the cabin temperature a couple of degrees, and selected a book from the bookshelves. A snowstorm offered an excuse to read books and write letters. During snowfalls of a foot or more, we hunkered down for a day or two, awaiting better weather.

"Lee," Joan said, "When is Russ due to arrive?" My wife, sipping her coffee, lingered at the kitchen window, staring out at the monochromatic world of a subarctic blizzard.

"Friday. Why?" I slumped onto the couch near the woodstove, turning to "The Men That Don't Fit In," by poet Robert W. Service.

"If it keeps snowing like this we'll never be able to haul him to the cabin."

"It'll quit soon," I said, making the worst weather prediction of my life.

My nephew, Russell Winslow, a civil engineer in his early thirties, planned to fly to Alaska from the Lower 48, land in Anchorage, and then transfer to the Moose Gooser, the train that ran north to Fairbanks once a week in winter. Eight-foot snowbanks, piled high by the snowplow attached to the engine, channel wandering moose down the railroad tracks ahead of the train. The moose, unable to climb the banks to escape from the frozen chute, nearly always lose the race. The engine slams into their rumps, which accounts for the train's nickname. Hundreds of moose die annually in collisions with the rumbling engine.

The train conductor would let Russ off at the Colorado siding, which was a holdover from the days when gold miners hauled ore from a mine twelve miles back in the Alaska Range and loaded it onto railroad cars. Joan and I intended to meet Russ at the railroad siding, about a mile from our cabin.

"Honey," Joan said, "the sled will be hard to tow in this fresh snow with Russ and his luggage on board. I'm betting your snowmachine can't pull it."

"We'll make it." I turned my attention back to Service's poems. I would have to break a trail from the cabin to the siding once the storm moved on, but I had plenty of time.

Wrong again.

It snowed, and it snowed, and it snowed some more. After five more days with no letup, we had a problem; Russ would arrive the next day.

Before the storm began, six feet of snow lay on the ground. Now, nearly a week later, accumulated snow blocked several windows. The interior of the cabin resembled a dimly lit wine cellar. We climbed the stairs to look from our bedroom window to check the storm's progress. A veil of tumbling flakes obscured even the nearby trees.

"Can you dig down to the first-floor windows so we can see better?" Joan said. "I'll help."

"OK," I said, "but first I've got to repack the trail to the outhouse and dig new snow steps down to it. Then I've got to break trail to the railroad tracks. I'll take care of the windows after that." We descended to the dim living room.

I tried to check the outside thermometer that was screwed to the window frame, but snow packed against the window hid the thermometer. I guessed the temperature to be about five degrees above zero, balmy by Alaska standards.

I tucked my wool shirt into dark green woolen pants and slipped into my down vest. I pulled a green anorak on over my shirt and vest and slid my feet into my white bunny boots—those wonderful military arctic boots that kept my feet warm no matter how low the temperature dropped. I didn't need my parka; I'd be plenty warm while shoveling snow. I pulled on my insulated gloves and wool watch cap and opened the back door.

I hesitated for a second, then dove back into the cabin and slammed the door shut. I had heard the subtle shift of snow as the cabin's steep roof shrugged off its share of the mantle that smothered the land. I barely had time to close the door before another load of snow released its grip and schussed to the ground with a *crump*, adding to the pile that now reached the eaves. Joan laughed and I cussed. "Isn't this damned storm ever going to end?"

When I figured the cloud of snow dust had settled, I peeked out the back door. Although the roof overhang had kept the snow just far enough from the door to allow space for me to step outside, I faced a solid wall of snow. I would have to carve steps into that white wall so I could climb up out of the cabin and rejoin the world. With each shovelful that I tossed toward the surface far above me, half that amount of snow trickled back down over the snow steps to snuggle against the cabin door. I mumbled unkind words about snow and winter. Joan waved and smiled through the glass panes in the door.

My snowshoes leaned against the wall beside the door, buried. I dug them out, carried them up the snow steps, stepped into the harnesses, buckled the straps around my boots, and trudged to the outhouse, stomping back and forth to pack down the snow between the cabin and the privy. I removed the snowshoes and shoveled steps down to the outhouse and, since the door opened out, began clearing an area in front of the door so I could open it. I struggled to heave the snow up onto the surface several feet above me, glaring at the falling flakes that landed on the steps behind me while I shoveled.

Joan shuffled along the trail on her snowshoes and peered down at me as I attacked the snow in front of the outhouse. The tips of her snowshoes, well above my head, jutted over the edge of the hole I worked in.

"Whatcha doing down there, mister?" she said.

"Mining for snow. I think I found the mother lode."

Joan chuckled. "Here, catch." She tossed a cold can of Pepsi down to me. "Take a break."

"Thanks." I popped the top and drank half of it nonstop.

Joan tromped back to the cabin along the narrow pathway. By walking on snowshoes between cabin and outhouse, we used our weight to compress the snow, breaking trail. We had to showshoe on the new-fallen snow several times a day to keep the trail—a knee-deep trench—packed.

I finished digging out in front of the outhouse door and snowshoed around to the front of the cabin, planning to dig down to the deck.

"I found the bird feeder." Joan's muffled words rose from a snow pit, where she stood pouring sunflower and millet seeds onto the feeder tray. Snow deeper than her five-foot four-inch height enclosed her, except for the narrow shaft that she had dug across the deck to the feeding station. The balcony overhead had kept the snow from piling up and sealing in the front door, but the deck was buried.

"The redpolls and chickadees better eat fast before their food disappears," I said.

"When did you say this snow would stop?" Her sly smile and look of false innocence did little to brighten my outlook toward breaking a trail to the railroad tracks. Snowflakes whitened her eyebrows and spotted her glasses as she looked up at me. I ignored her remark. Snowstorms were now a taboo topic.

"I'm off to the railroad tracks," I told her, shuffling away from the cabin and angling toward Colorado Lake.

Rather than follow the longer summer trail around the lake, I chose the more direct winter route. Aiming my snowshoes down the bank of the lake and across the frozen body of water, now buried under several feet of flaky whiteness, I was a solitary speck of green in a world turned white. I stared into the flakes that eclipsed my sense of direction. Adrift in a featureless landscape, I probed the storm, searching for clues that would lead me to the far shore. The world ended a few feet in front of me, with everything else hidden behind a gauze curtain of falling snow. Snowflakes and my condensed breath froze to my beard, forming icicles that hung like walrus tusks from my mustache and chin whiskers.

One step, two steps, pause, repeat ...

My snowshoes sank deep into the fluffy snow. Then snow from both sides of the snowshoe track fell on top of the snowshoes, weighting them down. I struggled to lift each foot, shake it from side to side to knock off the snow, and then take another step. Could I break trail all the way to the railroad tracks in one day? I pictured Russ standing in city clothes beside the empty railroad tracks tomorrow, wondering where we lived as the train trundled north without him. One step, two steps . . .

A trip that required five minutes by snowmachine on a packed surface took me more than two hours as I broke trail through the worst snowstorm I had ever seen. The snow-filtered gray light interfered with depth perception, creating a condition known as whiteout. Only when I found myself leaning farther forward to keep my balance did I realize I had reached the far shoreline and started up the hill that led to the railroad tracks.

In spite of the cold, steam rose from my wool cap, sweat drenched my body, and twinges stabbed my thighs and calves. Only my ragged breathing, the crunch of my snowshoes on the snow, and the swish of falling snowflakes broke the silence. I loved it—both the solitude and the satisfaction of tussling with nature and winning. I forced the fallen snow to submit to my snowshoes, but the storm overhead continued to dump on me.

I panted up to the railroad tracks at last, tromped a large circle so I could turn a snowmachine around without getting stuck, and followed my tracks back home. Trail breaking, phase one, was complete.

Most Alaskans refer to snowmobiles as snowmachines, although Alaska Natives call them sno-gos. I dug deep into one of the snow-covered bumps in the yard, searching for my snowmachine, a black Arctic Cat Cheetah. By now this storm had dumped five and a half feet on top of the six feet of snow already on the ground. If I, at five feet ten inches, stood on bare ground with Joan standing on my shoulders, her head would not reach the surface of this incredible depth of snow.

When I tossed the last shovelful of snow from a two-foot-wide trench that I dug around the snowmachine, I stood at the bottom of a pit. To escape from it, I shoveled and tromped a fifteen-foot-long snow ramp that led from the machine to the surface. I would drive the snowmachine up the ramp and onto the snowshoe trail.

"You down in a hole again?" Joan said, peering over the lip of the hole.

"Get down here and help me push," I said, smiling. "And then maybe we'll change places and I'll supervise while you dig out your machine." My wife slid into the pit.

I yanked on the starter rope, started and warmed up the 385-pound machine, then, with Joan and me both pushing while I thumbed the throttle, we drove and pushed the snowmachine up onto the trail. We dug down and repeated the process with Joan's snowmachine, a green-and-black Arctic Cat Jag.

"Now I'm hungry," I said.

We took a break for a late lunch, but first I stood with my face above the woodstove. Water dripped from my thawing beard like snowmelt dripping from the eaves on a spring day. I melted my icicle tusks so I could towel my beard dry and comb it. Running a comb through a frozen beard is like pulling hair from your head with pliers, except yanking out icy facial hair hurts worse.

"You forgot a few frosty whiskers," my wife said after I dried my face, reminding me that gray and white hairs now peppered my black beard.

"Maybe I should borrow some of your hair coloring." Silence.

We munched on roast moose meat covered with a thin layer of horseradish and tucked between slices of Joan's homemade whole wheat bread. Moose, rich-flavored, fine-textured meat, replaced beef in our diet. We preferred moose to any other meat.

"Mmm, that's good," I said. "Makes all the work of getting that meat worthwhile."

The previous fall I had shot the moose, field dressed and quartered it alone, and carried the meat home on my pack frame. It's easier to carry fresh meat on a stiff pack frame attached to shoulder straps than to pack it out in a soft backpack. Besides, a 150-pound moose hindquarter won't fit into a pack. I toted all of the meat the three-quarters of a mile from the kill site to the cabin, taking eight trips to do so. Both of us cut and packaged the moose meat and then stored it in our propane freezer.

For our luncheon bread, Joan and I had ground the wheat with our hand grinder. She then made the bread, kneading it by hand. This lunch was the result of our joint efforts.

After lunch, dressed in dry clothes, we again faced the storm. I strapped my snowshoes to my snowmachine's rear bumper to use in case the machine broke down, and drove along the meandering snowshoe-packed trail. Because of the lack of visual references in the whiteout conditions, I had made a trail that wandered like a browsing caribou.

I drove my snowmachine across the lake and up the hill to the railroad tracks. Joan followed on her machine. We drove over the trail several times to pack it properly. Then, exhausted, we stumbled into the cabin, escaping the storm for a little while. By repeating the trip every six hours or so, we packed the new snow before it got deep enough to immobilize our machines.

I set an alarm clock before I crawled into bed, so tired I could barely kiss Joan goodnight. She was mumbling something about her tired muscles as I turned off the propane lamp and nodded off to sleep before the glow of the gaslight mantle faded.

At 2:00 A.M. I cussed at the alarm, dressed, and drove my snowmachine to the railroad tracks. I had to stop several times to clear snow from the headlight so I could see my meandering trail. I thawed and dried my beard and crawled back into bed about 3:00 A.M., shivering.

"Any problems?" Joan mumbled.

"Nope. Still snowing, though." And the snow continued to fall. The next day a faint muttering of the rails announced the approaching train. At the siding, Joan and I stood under a deluge of falling flakes that filtered the glow of the engine's headlight as the train rounded the bend and tooted its whistle twice. The snowflakes muffled the sound, as if the train were in a tunnel. The actual moose-gooser—called a cowcatcher on engines in the Lower 48— pushed a waist-high pile of snow ahead of the yellow-and-blue engine as it slowed to a stop just past us.

The entire train consisted of the engine, a baggage car, one passenger car, and a caboose. Finding a seat on the train in winter is easy. It's finding another passenger to talk with that's sometimes difficult, but there's always the conductor. He'll chat with travelers and stop the train almost anywhere to take on or discharge passengers.

Russ stood in the open door of the baggage car, waved at us through the snowstorm, grinned, then jumped from the train and sank to his armpits in the soft new snow. The grin disappeared. If we hadn't already packed the snow that he landed in, Russ might have disappeared along with his smile.

"Welcome to Alaska, Russ," I said, laughing and winking at Joan.

"Thanks a lot," he said, spitting snow and brushing flakes from his glasses.

The conductor tossed Russ's bags after him, chuckled, waved, and closed the baggage car door. The engineer blew the whistle once, and the train, trailing a swirl of flakes that muffled its departure, vanished into the storm.

We lashed Russ's luggage to the sled with bungee cords, added him to the load, and headed for the cabin on our packed trail. Few tourists experience this kind of an Alaska welcome. The Alaska State

Chamber of Commerce doesn't tout six-foot snowstorms as an indispensable part of a Last Frontier adventure.

It snowed the entire next day, too, finally quitting after eight days of nonstop snowfall.

"Sure is dark in here," Russ said as he stared at his reflection in the windowpanes. I hadn't had the time or energy the day before to dig a tunnel through the snow piled against the windows.

"Yeah, Russ, let's do something about that," I said.

Russ and I shoveled our way outside and up onto the surface, which was more than head-high above the threshold. We strapped on snowshoes and repacked the trail to the outhouse, then cut new snow steps down to the outhouse door. "I don't believe this," he said. I didn't either.

We shuffled back to the cabin, where only the roof poked up out of the snow, and we shoveled down to where I thought the windows were. We then dug a trench to the windows to let light into the cabin. Because the cabin rested on pilings, the eaves were twelve feet from the ground—nearly twice the distance from floor to ceiling in an average house. From the snow piled around the cabin, I snowshoed onto the roof. Looking down at him I said, "Russ, have you ever mined for clothes?"

My nephew squinted up at me, wondering what new form of torture I was about to inflict on him. "Uh, I guess not. Is that like panning for gold?"

"Not exactly," I said. "You're about to participate in a rare experience, one most tourists have never heard of." I stepped back off the roof.

Joan had hung laundry out the day before the storm arrived, and now Russ and I shoveled down several feet to find the clothesline. The buried line stretched between two tall spruce trees, so we knew where to dig.

The shirts resembled skinny Halloween scarecrows, arms frozen at their sides. Trousers, frozen to metal pant stretchers that Joan had inserted inside each pant leg, hung from the line with their legs apart like a dog musher standing on his sled runners.

"This is mining for clothes, Russ," I said.

I took one of my flannel shirts from the clothesline and handed it to him. Stiff as a credit card, the shirt looked as if Joan had dumped an entire box of starch into the rinse water. I passed several more shirts to Russ and he stood them in the snow, a line of winter-weary, emaciated Alaskans awaiting spring breakup.

We carried an armful of frozen clothes, stacked like a deck of cards, to the cabin and sidled through the door so the arms and legs would fit through the opening. Joan propped them against wooden clothes-drying bars next to the hearth. The clothes sagged slowly toward the floor as the heat from the stove softened them into a soggy heap. My wife then hung them on the bars to dry.

"My automatic dryer takes five days to dry clothes, Russ," she said.

"What do you mean?"

"I wash them in my wringer washing machine, then hang them outdoors on the line where they drip, then freeze. Then I bring in an armful at a time and let them thaw and dry by the stove. Takes about five days to dry them all each time I do the laundry," Joan said.

"Yeah," I said, "and where do you think all that moisture goes?"

"From the looks of the windows, I'd say that's where it ends up," he said.

The moisture migrated to the windows, condensed on the cold glass, and then froze into a sheet of ice that gradually thickened to a half inch or more. But at least light penetrated the ice and we could turn off the propane lamps at midday.

We went back outside to dig for wood. I had exhausted the wood supply in one woodshed two days earlier, but now that March had arrived, we knew we had managed our firewood consumption well and sufficient firewood remained. The other woodshed had disappeared under a mushroom cap of snow. We dug down through the mushroom and found the roof, and I sculpted new snow steps down to the upper tiers of wood stacked inside the open shed. Russ carried firewood into the cabin, one armful at a time, and piled it in the large wood box next to the stove. I popped open two beers and declared it quitting time.

The next day Russ and I, on snowshoes, broke trail four miles to the highway, taking turns leading. Later in the day I got stuck several times while attempting to ride my snowmachine uphill over the trail. Balancing a moving snowmachine on a narrow trail is difficult, sort of like walking a balance beam in a gymnasium, and I plunged off the packed trail and into soft snow several times. Standing in snow up to our armpits, Russ and I struggled to muscle the machine back onto the trail. Each time we lifted the snowmachine we sank deeper into the snow, sometimes neck-deep. Russ didn't say so, but I bet he wished he'd never left New Hampshire.

Four days after the storm ended, the snow had settled enough so we could ride our snowmachines without breaking a snowshoe trail first. We led Russ up a river valley flanked by massive mountains, then up a side valley that led to high country above the tree line. The beauty impressed him, but the snow depth shocked him.

"Lee," he said, "does it always snow this much?"

"I sure hope not," I said. "If it does, I'm moving to Hawaii."

Alaska didn't treat Russ kindly during his 1982 visit. As far as I know, he's never returned to the state.

☾

Bush life could be frustrating, but we loved it. We were happier breaking trail than driving through Anchorage commuter traffic to work in an office five days a week. And we didn't have to scrape ice from our car windshield before going to work, either. Digging out a snowmachine wasn't our idea of entertainment, but it kept our muscles toned. I preferred splitting wood to pumping iron in a gym.

Joan and I answered to each other, the weather, and an occasional wandering bear. Self-sufficient, we adjusted to each situation. We seldom faced problems we couldn't solve. If something broke, one of us figured out a way to fix it. If we couldn't repair it, we bought a new one on our next trip to town. Or we did without.

We quickly forgot minor inconveniences. Major struggles, such as six-foot-plus snowstorms, became part of our growing collection of Alaska bush stories.

Occasionally, while breaking trail alone and surrounded by Alaska's beauty, I thought about the winding trail that led me from a boyhood fantasy to the reality of a life in the Alaska bush. I recalled Henry David Thoreau's words: "Go confidently in the direction of your dreams. Live the life you have imagined."

This was the life we had dreamed of, and if the vision sometimes dimmed under twelve feet of snow that was OK. The snow would melt, eventually.

Alaska Dreaming

I shivered through the first ten winters of my life in East Burke, a tiny, hardscrabble village tucked into a narrow valley at the foot of Burke Mountain in northeast Vermont. Back then, in the 1930s and 1940s, Alaska was still a United States territory.

To this Vermont lad born in 1938, just hearing the word "Alaska" brought to mind dog teams, mushers in fur parkas, and herds of migrating animals. Stories about Alaska beguiled me, creating a fascination with the northland that would eventually lure me to the Last Frontier.

Gray granite underlies Vermont's Green Mountains. Some folks say granite accounts for Vermonters' toughness. Others claim it's the main ingredient in their heads. Both allegations may explain why I would want to live for years in a cabin in the Alaska wilderness. My

15

trail from Vermont to that Alaska cabin meandered nearly around the world. I followed that elusive path for more than thirty years before I found its terminus, but the journey began in East Burke.

☾

Because of the ten-year age difference between my older sister, Pauline, and me, after the age of seven I grew up as an only child. She and I had one thing in common in my early years—my dog, Cheeta. However, I loved the little black-and-white mutt; Pauline had no use for her.

One of my friends owned a pair of dogs of uncertain heritage, and the female had given birth. My friend offered to give me one of the pups.

"Can I have a puppy, Mom? Please, can I?" I begged. I was so thrilled at the prospect of owning a dog that my mother, probably to shut me up, gave in.

"OK," she said, "but you have to feed and take care of her. Promise?"

"I promise." I galloped back and forth between our kitchen and living room, so eager to hold my puppy I couldn't just sit or stand still. Pauline drew a deep breath and muttered something about worthless dogs.

Our mother made my sister hike the mile or so to the farm where the pups squirmed in their hay-lined washtub. Pauline had to carry the new puppy home. Neither the tiny pup, nor I at age five, could walk that far through snow and subzero temperatures. Disgusted and grumbling, Pauline carried the blanket-wrapped puppy in her arms and, along with our cousin, Eleanor, trudged through the snow toward home.

Pauline disliked dogs, cats, and pets of any kind. Having to tote a dog into her life was, to her, the ultimate insult. "Here she is,"

Pauline said when I raced to meet her on our front porch. "Darned dog." I named the pup Cheeta, after the chimp in Tarzan movies.

Pauline ignored my dog. High school girls in their junior year had more important things to do, like staring moony-eyed at movie stars' photos, painting their toenails bright crimson, or daubing tan makeup on their legs to make boys think they were wearing nylon stockings. World War II raged, and factories made parachutes and other war materials from silk and nylon. Stockings wouldn't be available until after the war.

Pauline earned a dollar or two a week at part-time jobs, such as ironing clothes and cleaning in the home next door. She followed the European and Pacific war news; former schoolmates fought in both theaters. Big Sister didn't have time to bother with Little Brother's activities.

❨

An older brother, Cecil, whom I never knew, died from pneumonia when he was three. My parents reacted to his death by becoming extremely protective when I was born, which turned me into a bit of a maverick. I was determined to lead my own life rather than one they chose for me. That conflict would continue throughout my childhood and beyond.

Although I had lots of friends, I often crept to quiet places in the woods and fields, places where I could watch crows dive-bombing a fox, or beavers hauling sticks to repair a dam rent by floodwaters. I enjoyed learning, in or out of the classroom, but nature's lessons were fun; lessons taught in the classroom left little time for daydreaming.

I learned to read in a two-room, two-story, slate-gray schoolhouse in East Burke. With four grades in each room, the children who weren't actively being taught by the teacher were expected to practice their lessons. While the black potbellied woodstove huffed and chuffed to heat the chilly classroom, I read tales about mountain men in the American West; tales of Jim Bridger, Daniel Boone, and Davy Crockett.

The school's vertical and horizontal windowpane dividers were like jail bars, and the school a prison that kept me from the fields and woods beyond the schoolyard. The jailer, or teacher, carried a ruler that cracked knuckles if we let our attention stray outside the room. I sometimes gazed through the windows, imagining a life on the remote frontier, but was brought abruptly back inside the classroom by the approaching teacher and the threat of a stinging smack.

Because our nation's westward sprawl had driven out the mountain men, I decided I'd have to move to Alaska if I wanted to live in authentic wilderness. I loved to read Robert W. Service's poems; his "The Spell of the Yukon" remains one of my favorites. Alaska became my goal.

I longed to meet fur-wrapped Eskimos, ride the frigid skies with bush pilots, and stake out a homestead where wolf howls echoed from surrounding hills. I wanted to hike through the remote Brooks Range, drift down the Yukon River and, surrounded by steep-sided silence, trap furbearers in frozen valleys.

Cold Vermont winters prepared me for Alaska's longest season. Alaskans say our forty-ninth state has four seasons: last winter, this winter, next winter, and July 4. Last year summer was on a Thursday.

Vermont winters aren't quite so long or cold as those in Alaska, but Vermonters still have a close relationship with snow and can recognize cold. Identifying a thaw is more difficult. Vermonters say that "three feet of snow and a hell of a blow" is a Canadian thaw.

Each Vermont winter morning I shivered, huddled atop the floor register that radiated heat and the smell of maple wood smoke into the dining room of our rented house. Our wood-burning furnace in the dirt-floored cellar failed to drive the cold from my bedroom, so I dressed in the dining room. That bedroom, added as an afterthought, exposed three uninsulated walls to the chilling blasts of Vermont blizzards. I sometimes scraped frost from the bedroom walls and threw it at my sister, who trembled beneath several blankets and a comforter in her bed pushed against the far wall of the tiny room.

"Lee, you cut that out!"

"Cheeta, go get Pauline," I said. With me throwing little frost balls, and with my dog tugging at her comforter, Pauline gave up and fled to the dining room floor register, muttering, "Darned dog. Little brat." I considered my day a success if I could irritate my sister.

☾

When the pale sun rose higher each day in its escape from southern exile, I belly-flopped onto my sled and plunged down steep Belden Hill. The sled runners rattled over the icy surface, throwing sparks from glancing blows on half-buried pebbles. I skied and snowshoed in the surrounding hills, puzzling over animal and bird tracks that pocked the snow. Only the squeak of snowshoe harnesses or the swish of my skis, or perhaps the distant rumble of a snowplow, interrupted the silence on weekends. During the week, huge saws in Crawford Davis's sawmill screeched their way through birch, maple, and spruce logs, turning trees into lumber and filling the village with the sound and scent of lumbering.

On winter nights we kids soaked cattails in kerosene, ignited them, and used the blazing torches to light our way while, in a rotating mass, we skated round and round on the millpond. We pretended our torchlight shadows that wavered on the snow and ice were monsters pursuing us. No matter how fast we skated, we couldn't outdistance the monsters.

I spent as much time outdoors as possible, summer and winter, poking about in the hills and meandering through meadows. But my life was about to change.

When I was ten, my father, who was a carpenter, built a new house for us in Lyndonville, six miles away. I begged to remain in East Burke. "Lee," my mother said," pack your clothes in those boxes by your bed." She pointed to a steamer trunk. "Put your toys into that trunk." Fighting back tears, I obeyed.

On my last day in East Burke, I slipped out and skied alone to a clearing in the nearby forest to take a final look at one of my favorite hideaways. Tears froze on my cheeks while I shivered in the wind that moaned through the spruce trees. Would I ever return to that hidden clearing? What would my life be like in new surroundings? If I had to leave this village, I thought, why couldn't I move to Alaska?

☾

In Lyndonville, on the first night in my new home, I looked through my bedroom window to see in the distance a ski area ablaze with light. I adjusted to my new surroundings by skiing on those slopes day and night.

Although no one lived on the land between my home and the ski slope, I had to skirt a cemetery along the way. The distant, twinkling lights of the ski tow lured me, but I had to overcome my dread of passing that ghostly burial ground on moonless winter nights. Six feet of frozen ground and three feet of snow sealed off the graveyard's occupants, but if ghosts could pass through walls, I doubted that winter would slow them down. I stepped into my ski bindings and glided alone across a half mile of rolling meadow, raced past the cemetery, then plunged through a dense, dark patch of evergreens to arrive at the slope.

The lights from the slope didn't penetrate that thick grove of trees, and my arms and legs pumped furiously in an attempt to shorten the time I had to spend in the fuzzy darkness. I burst into the open, glancing over my shoulder to make sure I was still alone.

I mastered cross-country skiing by poling and gliding so fast that ghosts couldn't catch me.

❰

When the snow surrendered to the spring sun and rushed to fill the creeks as it turned to water, I roamed the nearby fields and woods. I studied animal tracks and learned to identify various birds. I memorized the names of the wildflowers that scented the spring air. I sneaked up on woodchuck burrows, and watched the short-eared brown creatures nibble clover near the dirt mounds that disclosed their dens. On rare occasions, I saw a red fox, or, more frequently, startled into flight a ruffed grouse, which we called a pa'tridge. Each grouse encounter left undecided which participant was the more startled. The explosion of wings frantically slapping the air made my heart thump against my rib cage like drumsticks on a kettle-drum. I decided I needed a gun.

After months of arguments, my parents relented. They gave me a Stevens .22-caliber rifle for my birthday, and, teaching myself, I soon picked off squirrels that peeked through pine needles while hiding on high branches. My collection of squirrel tails increased sporadically until the day my mother, cleaning my room, felt something drop onto her head. I arrived home from hunting just then. My timing was terrible.

"Lee, come up here this instant." I didn't know what I'd done wrong, but I recognized that tone of voice: I was in trouble. I climbed the stairs to my bedroom.

"Look at that." She pointed to a maggot squirming on the floor. It had bounced off her head when it fell from the squirrel tail I had tacked to the wall. "And look up there." She pointed up to another white worm wriggling its way out of the hair on another tail.

"You get those nasty things out of here right now," my mother said. "And take that fresh squirrel tail I see in your hip pocket with you. No more squirrel tails in this house, ever."

I hadn't learned yet that I had to remove the bone and tan the hides to preserve the tail and to keep flies from laying eggs in the rotting meat. I had noticed an odor, but figured that was the way squirrel tails smelled. I dragged a chair over to my trophy wall and took down my squirrel tails. I checked out a book at the library and learned a little about skinning and tanning hides, but my squirrel tails were beyond salvage.

Later, I bought a larger rifle and a shotgun. I trapped beaver and hunted deer, rabbits, and pa'tridges. In the summer, I caught speckled brook trout in the streams that rushed clear and cold from the surrounding hills. Those outdoor skills would prove to be invaluable in the Alaska bush.

☾

I enjoyed those outdoor lessons more than the ones I learned in a classroom, although I was a good student. I graduated from grade school and entered Lyndon Institute (LI), the private high school that educated kids from the farms and small villages in the northern Passumpsic River Valley. Lyndon Institute also accepted boarding students from around the world. The freshman class chose me as their president, and the following year I served on the student council. I was admitted to the National Honor Society in my senior year. The academic discipline and leadership skills learned at LI would pay off in my future military career.

In the fall of my junior year a cute, petite girl named Joan Chandler arrived at LI. On the first day of school, she wore light-blue loafers, a pale-blue sweater, and a red-and-black-plaid kilt. Friendly and vivacious, Joan turned heads as she hurried along the hallway between classes.

Two days later, while I pushed a lawnmower across our lawn, four girls strolled along the narrow street in front of our Cape Cod style home. The neighbor girl, a friend, called to me to come meet some of the new dormitory girls. I spoke with them all, but kept my eyes on Joan. Her ready smile sparkled, and she seemed truly interested in me. Her blue eyes stayed on mine as I talked. My heartbeat quickened. The next day I asked other dorm girls about her.

Joan lived in a log cabin in Ocean Park, on the coast of Maine. Her local Maine high school wasn't accredited, so she spent her freshman year at a school in Portsmouth, New Hampshire, where her mother worked. Joan spent her second high school year at Northfield, a school for girls in northern Massachusetts. The following year, her parents enrolled her and her younger sister, Martha, in LI for the excellent education the school offered. The sisters transferred to LI at the beginning of Joan's junior year, and she completed her high school education as one of my classmates.

Joan and I dated off and on during that junior year and, because I was falling in love, I visited her in Maine once during the summer and met her parents. Her father, a carpenter and avid hunter and fisherman, seemed to think that if I knew how to hunt and fish I might have more to offer than the other teenaged boys who chased after his oldest daughter. The fact that my father was also a carpenter bolstered my meager, undistinguished credentials.

Joan accompanied her father to his duck hunting blinds and caught brook trout in the stream behind her house. She grew up on a diet supplemented by venison, waterfowl, and trout. As a young child, she played in the surrounding woods and floated stick boats in the stream that trickled across their property. She loved New England's woods and streams, and so did I.

I roughhoused with my friends on the lawn in front of the girls' dormitory, awaiting Joan's arrival in September of our senior year.

Along with the other local boys, I checked out the new crop of dorm girls, an annual ritual.

"Hi," I said, as Joan stepped from her parents' car.

"Hi yourself," she said. "Had a good summer?"

"Thought it would never end."

Within a week or so we were dating frequently, picking up where we left off the previous spring. I asked her to "go steady" on November 11, 1955, called Armistice Day back then. We dated only each other for the rest of our senior year. Nat "King" Cole sang "Our Love Is Here to Stay" on the jukebox in Willey's—a local restaurant that was our favorite teen hangout—and Perez Prado slurred his trumpet on his hit, "Cherry Pink and Apple Blossom White," which my sweetheart and I claimed as our song. Our class selected "Moments to Remember" as our class song, and we all danced to "Graduation Day" as our graduation day neared.

Because I couldn't bear the thought of our being separated for the four years of college that our parents had planned for us, I decided to ask Joan to marry me.

One warm May night, in my father's gray Chevrolet pickup truck with "C. H. Basnar, Contractor" lettered across each door, I proposed. We were in our favorite place to park after a movie or dance date—a dark graveyard. By this time, cemetery ghosts no longer concerned me.

Joan said yes.

Three weeks prior to our graduation day, I asked my father to join me in my bedroom, upstairs and away from my mother. "Dad," I said, trembling, "after Joan and I graduate we're going to get married, probably in July."

Gray-faced, he turned without a word and left the room. He stumbled down the stairs and called, in a shaky voice, for my mother. I had just shattered his dream of watching me graduate from college.

My father had never completed high school, nor had my mother. They married when she was seventeen and Dad was twenty-one.

My mother, more understanding, accepted what she couldn't change. She and Dad must have discussed my future several times, because within a few days he gradually came to accept my impending marriage and the fact that I wasn't going to college. Even when I earned a college degree many years later by taking classes at night and on weekends, in his mind it didn't count because I hadn't attended college full time right after high school. Nevertheless, my parents loved Joan and welcomed her into the family.

☾

As newlyweds, Joan and I rented a second-floor apartment in a brown, shingle-clad two-story house in Lyndonville. Joan worked as a clerk in a local variety store, and then in the accounting department of the Lyndonville Savings Bank until she gave birth to our only child, Lorraine, in 1959. I went to work as a carpenter for my father the day after my high school graduation. I had worked for him on Saturdays and in the summers during my last two high school years, more to earn money to spend on dates with Joan than to learn the trade. Marriage at the age of eighteen changed my outlook. Dad gave me a raise to a dollar an hour.

My father taught me how to build houses, beginning with erecting the forms for concrete foundations. By the time I quit five years later, I had supervised several jobs and was a journeyman carpenter. I could read construction plans, lay out a foundation using a transit, pour and finish concrete floors, do every bit of framing on a house, and install shingles on roofs. I laid hardwood floors and tile floors, and could cut and fit linoleum. I applied wall tile in bathrooms, installed windows, and hung doors. I installed the trim around doors and windows, the baseboards along the floors, and the molding between the walls and ceilings. I built stairs and the fancy banisters that served as hand railings. I even built cabinets. Working nine hours a day, six days a week, with no vacations, I learned the trade. After taxes, I took home about $43 a week. Rent was $35 a month.

I gradually acquired skills that would give me the ability and confidence to cope with a wilderness lifestyle. Although I didn't realize it at the time, I had learned how to build a cabin in the Alaska bush.

☾

The severe Vermont winters eventually pointed me in a new direction. The deep, prolonged cold drove carpenters indoors. Unless my father had a house or two well under construction when the gray clouds lowered, the temperature dropped, and snow descended upon Vermont from late fall until early spring, I found myself unemployed.

My parents vacationed in the Florida sunshine during the coldest parts of Vermont's winters, while I supplemented my meager unemployment check by shoveling snow from roofs and performing minor repair jobs. I struggled to find ways to support my wife and baby daughter.

I stood droop-shouldered in unemployment lines for three winters in a row, staring at the floor or making dispirited small talk with other out-of-work locals. We signed up for unemployment pay in a dingy room above the old railroad station, a relic of the glory days of the Canadian Pacific Railroad that connected Montreal to Boston by way of Vermont. The railroad tracks passed through the abandoned railroad yards where my paternal grandfather, long dead from the Influenza Pandemic of 1918, had worked when he emigrated from Canada.

A state unemployment agent drove to our village on Thursdays. Glum-faced men and women waited, slouched against grimy walls, forming a line that wound around inside a former railroad official's office. Pipe and cigarette smoke blended with the odors of age and neglect. Desultory talk ceased when the agent strolled into the room and scanned the waiting line. He edged behind a beat-up desk whose top bore the scars of neglected cigarettes, and plopped into a decrepit swivel chair that squeaked when he leaned forward to talk to an applicant. It was the only chair in the room.

"Did you work last week?" he asked.

"No."

"Did you look for work?"

"Yes."

"Did you turn down any job offers?"

"No."

"Sign here," he said. "Next."

I had qualified for my $32 benefit for another week, but the demeaning process drove me down a different trail—one that eventually led me to Alaska.

I decided I would prefer an army chow line to the unemployment line. The military offered a career with a steady paycheck. Perhaps I could see the world, maybe even Alaska.

"Dad," I said, after I walked to his house upon his return from Florida that year, "I won't be working for you anymore."

His face turned to a lump of white putty. He sat down. "Why?" he said.

"I'm going to join the Army. I'm sick of unemployment lines."

He thought that over but couldn't seem to grasp it. "What about your family?"

"Joan agrees with me. She and Lorraine will join me after I reach my permanent assignment."

He had nothing else to say. I had just shattered another of his expectations. I dawdled as I walked home to my family, aware that I had made a decision that might prove to be wrong, but one that set me free to pursue my own life with Joan and Lorraine.

A few days later Dad said, "If you stick with me, Lee, I'll sell you the business for one dollar when I retire." He was at least fifteen years from retirement.

Ignoring my parents' severe disapproval, I joined the infantry. The Army would teach me to withstand hardships and test me under the toughest conditions. I might stand in lines, but they wouldn't be unemployment lines.

Joan, who would be left temporarily at home with our two-year-old daughter, supported my decision in spite of the unknowns we faced. Where would I be assigned? Could she cope with raising Lorraine until she could join me? With tear-stained faces, the three of us hugged each other. I said goodbye and turned away, embarking on a military career.

☾

Ordered to Germany without my family, I served in the Third Armored Division. My battalion went on full alert on August 13, 1961, when the East Germans and Russians sealed the border with West Germany and began to construct the Berlin Wall. The communist regimes were desperate to stop the flow of immigrants who poured across the border from east to west, seeking a better life. Maybe they didn't like unemployment lines either.

For several days, perched in the hatch of an armored personnel carrier, I stared down the valley at the enemy across the border. They aimed their main tank guns at us, and we registered our guns on their positions. I expected World War III to roll over us at any moment. However, tensions soon eased, and we stood down from the alert.

I transferred to France shortly thereafter, where Joan and Lorraine joined me for the remainder of my extended European tour. I hadn't forgotten about Alaska, but my career kept those thoughts in the background.

❨

Midway through my Army career, Vietnam burst into our lives. I spent many months in combat in Vietnam's rice paddies and dense jungles. Combat may have bolstered my survival skills and my self-confidence, but I paid an emotional price to acquire that experience. I served as an advisor in a South Vietnamese infantry division during my first one-year tour in Vietnam in 1967–1968. I commanded an American infantry company when I returned to the war zone for my second tour in 1970–1971. Seeing my men blown apart by mines and booby traps, or riddled by machine guns, or blasted to bits by mortar fire, piled layers of survivor guilt on me.

My company operated as a single unit, miles from our battalion firebase. At the end of one two-week patrol in the rain-soaked jungle, where we encountered deadly cobras, green bamboo vipers, blood-sucking leeches, and a well-camouflaged, elusive enemy, I led my company out of that green mass of misery and into an abandoned agricultural area. I ordered a platoon leader to establish security on a nearby hill that rose twenty meters above a small clearing where I set up my command post.

Ten minutes later, an explosion rocked me. I whirled to look at the hilltop in time to see one of my men tumbling back to earth after being blown high into the air by the booby trap he had detonated.

A second soldier rushed to help him, and triggered another booby trap. I watched his shredded body cartwheel into the air above his buddy, then descend to join him in the matted jungle grass. Smoke from the explosions drifted away, disappearing into the monsoon rain.

I ordered my company medic to check the casualties for any signs of life. I doubted that anyone could survive a blast from those explosives, which were likely 105 mm artillery rounds attached to trip wires. I radioed for a dust-off, or medical evacuation helicopter.

Within minutes, several platoon members, slipping on rain-soaked grass and mud, descended from the hill. One soldier carried his dead buddy over his shoulder. Tears streamed down his face as he staggered under the burden. His friend was going home the hard way.

Four other soldiers had turned a poncho into a makeshift stretcher. In the sagging poncho, awash in his own blood, the second victim looked up at me as I peered at his mangled body. His eyes met mine.

"Hold my hand, sir," he mumbled. I couldn't. He didn't have a hand; all four limbs had been blasted from his body. The dust-off chopper arrived, and we loaded the still-conscious man aboard. The pilot looked from his helicopter at the dead soldier lying in the mud. Rain spattered onto the lifeless body.

"Is he dead?" he radioed to me.

"Affirmative," I replied.

"Can't take KIAs. They go to Graves Registration. I only haul the living." KIA means killed in action. The dead man was of no further concern to the pilot.

I stood in the rain and stared at the broken body sprawled before me in the mud. I removed my helmet and prayed. Rain streamed down my face and mixed with the moisture leaking from my eyes. A few of my soldiers quietly gathered beside me.

The job of a combat commander is the loneliest job in the world. A commander strives to keep his feelings bottled inside. He can't show fear, can't reveal his frustration, can't turn to someone for help over the rough spots. An infantry commander must distance himself from his men. That way, watching his men die destroys a smaller portion of a commander's very soul. The loss of my men hurt like hell, and nightmares would haunt me for years to come.

One of my former commanders, Colonel Bernie Jones, wrote to me while I fought in Vietnam and asked if I'd like to be assigned to Alaska upon completion of my second combat tour. Would I! I read that letter several times, sitting on a rice paddy dike in the tropical humidity—tired, filthy, drenched in sweat. My Alaska dream hovered in that sweltering heat, and then the enemy brought me back to reality.

A sniper's bullets snapped past my head as I reread the letter. I dove for cover, then sent a patrol to find and kill the enemy. A few minutes later, the concussion from a loud explosion blasted my ears. That exploding booby trap wounded three of my soldiers. Chasing the sniper, they had run into a trip wire attached to an 81mm mortar round. How many more men would I send to be maimed or killed?

My dream of Alaska faded. I had to survive the several months remaining on this tour before I could allow myself to think much about my next assignment. Only during the endless nights when there was no enemy activity did I allow myself to think about Alaska. What would Joan and Lorraine, living in Green Cove Springs, Florida, in an apartment complex occupied primarily by other waiting military families, think about a move to The Last Frontier? I wrote and asked.

Joan responded as she always did when I sought her opinion and advice. If an assignment would further my career or take me to a place I wanted to see, she invariably said, "If that's what you want, let's go."

My wife wanted to see Alaska. She hadn't forgotten my desire to live in the far north. Her love and support carried me through many sleepless nights in the jungles and rice paddies. Her frequent letters, and the notes from Lorraine, age eleven, took me away from the horrors of combat. When their letters arrived, the longing to be with my family was difficult to conceal. I waited until I had an opportunity to move a little distance away from my radio operators before I opened Joan's letters.

My second combat tour finally ended. I had survived, but survivor guilt burdened me like it did many combat veterans. I had the good fortune to return to a loving family. Not all Vietnam veterans were so lucky.

Shortly after I embraced my family upon my final return from Vietnam, I promised Joan and Lorraine that I'd resign my commission rather than return to a war we weren't allowed to win. The waste of lives sickened me, and no more would I participate in the slaughter. The war ended before I had to make the decision to face a third combat tour or resign.

The Army packed our household goods and moved us to Alaska in October 1971. Finally, my dream of living in Alaska would come true.

North to Alaska

We descended from the Alaska Airlines plane into the bright sunshine of an October afternoon. The Chugach Mountains, coated with the season's first snowfall, dazzled in the distance, rising above Anchorage as if to protect one side of the city. I wondered if I'd have to climb those mountains while I trained with the Army at nearby Fort Richardson. I hoped so.

An irrepressible smile split my face as I saluted Colonel Jones, who had met the plane, and I felt for the first time in many years that I had come home. I had survived Vietnam and finally made it to Alaska. The future looked full of flawless promise.

During my first three-year tour of duty in Alaska, which turned out to be a fun, family-oriented affair, I taught Lorraine to ski, I spent many days in the wilderness hunting and fishing, and the three of us explored Southcentral Alaska on skis and snowmachines. I attended Alaska Methodist University at night and on Saturdays, graduating with a bachelor's degree. When I sent my father a photo of me in cap and gown receiving my diploma, he was amazed that I could get a real diploma without going to college full time.

❨

From Alaska, I was assigned to Fort Benning, Georgia, in 1974, followed by an assignment to the San Francisco Bay area from 1975 to 1977. There, I commanded a team of recruiters whose job was to try to convince young Californians to join the Army. I couldn't believe the incredible pressure put on me to make recruiters meet their quotas in the new volunteer Army. My recruiters and I had to compete with the famed California surf, sand, and sun. It was the worst peacetime job I ever had.

For several months prior to the end of my two-year recruiting assignment, I called Infantry Branch once a week. That office, in Washington, D.C., managed the careers of infantry officers.

"This is Captain Basnar," I said each time I called. "I want to go back to Alaska at the end of this assignment."

At each call, the answer was the same: "Captain Basnar, we don't have a vacancy in Alaska for your specialty." My assignment officer would then suggest other assignments such as Fort Hood, Texas, or Fort Polk, Louisiana. Korea was available too. I turned them all down and continued to call Infantry Branch.

One day my assignment officer answered the phone and said, "Captain Basnar, I have some good news. I found a vacancy for you in Alaska."

My recruiting office in Dublin, California, shared a common wall with the office of insurance agent Bill Foster. My joyous yell on hearing that news brought Bill running to see what the trouble was.

"Bill," I said, "I'm going back to Alaska!"

"I'm glad for you," he said, "even though I hate to see you leave."
We had become close friends, and he knew how much I loved Alaska.

☾

My second Alaska tour spanned my final years in the Army. I received a promotion to major and had the good fortune to be the first officer assigned to the position of senior advisor to the 207th Infantry Group, Alaska National Guard, even though the slot called for a lieutenant colonel, one rank above mine.

One of the Guard's missions was to defend the western periphery of Alaska, and they used three Eskimo scout battalions to assist with that assignment. A mechanized infantry battalion and a boat battalion, plus the normal administrative and support units, made up the rest of the group. As the group senior advisor, I journeyed throughout Alaska, traveling by airplane, helicopter, boat, dogsled, and snowmachine. I spent considerable time with the three scout battalions, which were headquartered in the remote Alaska Native villages of Kotzebue, Bethel, and Nome. I traveled from those transportation hubs to remote communities that tourists seldom visit.

I visited Eskimo scouts on the island of Little Diomede, which looks beyond the International Date Line to Big Diomede, two and a half miles away across the Bering Strait. Big Diomede belonged to the Soviet Union. I could stand in Tuesday, looking at Wednesday across the date line; the date change, though, was minor compared to the cultural differences between the United States and the Soviet Union. While going about their subsistence activities, the Eskimo scouts kept their eyes on the Russian soldiers over on Big Diomede. The scouts reported their observations to their battalion headquarters in Nome, which forwarded the intelligence information to the 207th Group headquarters in Anchorage.

The village of Little Diomede clings to the side of a mountain thrust upward by tectonic forces from the Bering Sea. There are no trees on the tiny island, and not much vegetation—mostly just rocks, pebbles, and cliffs assaulted by the arctic winds. Small prefab houses perch helter-skelter, like scattered seabird nests. The modest homes crawl up the mountainside above the sea, which is frozen for more than half the year.

In summer, the sea rambles and rumbles at the base of the island, grasping vainly for the weather-tortured houses beyond its reach. This forbidding environment is a Native hunter's utopia. During winter, polar bears roam the ice pack, feasting on fat seals. Eskimos hunt the bears and the seals. In the summer, the Natives shoot and harpoon whales when tons of that blubber-rich biomass migrate between today and tomorrow, en route to feeding grounds where the summer sun never sets. Thousands of sea birds lay tasty eggs in nests on cliff ledges, and king crabs scuttle on the floor of the Bering Sea. Walruses drift by the island during the endless daylight, diving for shellfish from the edge of the floating pack ice. Eskimo men take to their umiaks, or large skin boats, to hunt the whiskery, tusked mammals for their meat and ivory.

Many Eskimos in Little Diomede carve ivory walrus tusks into trinkets and pieces of art, which they sell. Theirs is a subsistence economy, and they welcome a little cash in exchange for their carvings.

☾

To reach Little Diomede, the battalion commander and I flew by helicopter from the mainland across twenty-seven miles of untidy drifts that wrinkled the frozen ice cap, passing over several seals resting on the ice next to their escape holes. A wandering polar bear, spooked by the chopper, raced across the ice in front of us. His rocking gait jarred his white fur each time his feet pounded on the frozen surface. Puffs of frosty bear breath ballooned into the air, condensing in the subzero cold.

Our helicopter landed on a smooth patch of wind-scoured ice, one of the few level spots among the frozen pressure ridges, and we trudged to the village a quarter mile away.

An Eskimo wrapped in a dirty sealskin parka sidled up to us. He wore army fatigue pants that were stained with some sort of grease, probably seal oil from skinning fur seals. Well-worn sealskin mukluks, or boots, protected his feet. Ragged sealskin mittens covered his hands. He wore a black military wool hat, or balaclava. Long black hair emerged from beneath the hat, and a sparse and straggly, soot-black beard wandered across his chin. His black mustache drooped beyond the corners of his mouth. He stood about five feet, two inches tall.

"Wanna buy some ivory?" he lisped. His grin revealed a gap where his front teeth used to be.

"What have you got?" I said. "I'd like to take a look at it." When I visited Eskimo or Athabascan Indian villages I often bought hand-crafted gifts to take to my family.

"Come," he said, and turned to lead me along a narrow, icy path that wound through the tiny village anchored to the mountainside. While the pilot and battalion commander entered the general store, I followed the Eskimo while I withdrew my head into my parka hood to avoid frostbite from the frigid blasts. The windchill factor was about fifty degrees below zero.

We passed weatherworn, metal-roofed, prefab wooden houses. Drifted snow leaned against most of the houses, which had the odd effect of allowing a person to walk onto the roof of nearly any house in the village. Ruddy-cheeked Eskimo children hauled their hand-made sleds onto the roofs and then slid down, coasting onto the drifts on the uphill sides of the houses. If they had aimed their sleds down the steep mountain, their speed would quickly have gotten out of control. Only near the base of the village did the kids point their sleds downhill and scoot out onto the scrambled drifts that angled across the frozen sea.

After shuffling along for perhaps half the length of a football field, the man stopped and turned around and said, "I live in an igloo."

Right, I thought. *This Eskimo is going to have a little fun with this cheechako.* Cheechako means tenderfoot, or newcomer.

"That's OK," I said. "I've never been in an igloo before."

He turned, took a few steps, dropped to his knees, and disappeared into a snow tunnel. I followed. Two frozen eider ducks hung from the roof just inside the tunnel entrance. A pair of metal, military snowshoes leaned against one wall, and the remnants of several walrus tusks lay next to the snowshoes. Although the ambient temperature outside was minus twenty degrees, a quarter of an inch of water lay atop the frozen ground at the igloo end of the entrance tunnel.

The Eskimo swept aside the dirty army blanket that hung across the entrance to his house, and we crawled into the igloo and stood up. An electric cord hung from the roof that curved about six inches above my head. Powered by the village generator, a one-hundred-watt light bulb glowed, hanging upside down from a socket on the end of the cord. The single bulb heated his home. The small amount of heat that escaped melted the ice on the floor of the tunnel just outside the hanging-blanket door. I doubted if the temperature inside the igloo was much above freezing, but in contrast to the outside temperature, it seemed downright balmy. I wondered at the safety of a flimsy electrical cord that ran under the snow and ice that covered the island.

Overhead, tacked to the driftwood that supported the ice block roof, several army ponchos kept meltwater from dripping onto his bed. He slept in a rumpled army sleeping bag on an air mattress atop three driftwood-gray planks pushed together on the dirt floor. A gas Coleman stove and an army mess kit and eating utensils lay on the floor against the back wall. A chipped blue enamel pot contained a congealed substance that looked like stew. A hand drill, a few carving knives, some carvings, and a few ivory scraps were clustered near his bed. A pile of nondescript clothing lay near the entrance to the tunnel. There was nothing else in his house, not even a chair. The igloo smelled of dampness and rancid fat and unwashed clothing.

He picked up a carving and held it out for me to examine. The quality was good, not excellent. He squinted at me in silence as I looked around his home. I glanced at him quizzically.

"My house burnt," he said. *OK, I thought, that explains why he lives this way.*

"When did it burn?" I said, expecting him to tell me it had burned down within the past few weeks.

"Three years ago. I hope this summer I can get a new one. BIA promised me one." BIA is the Bureau of Indian Affairs, the federal agency that provides support to Alaska Natives and other Native Americans.

I bought a small carved salmon and crawled back through the tunnel. After taking a few steps, I looked back at the igloo, but other than the dark hole in the snow that was the entrance to the Eskimo's shelter, there was no other indication of a dwelling at that spot on the mountainside.

Although the igloo wasn't an exact copy of the traditional snow-block houses of cartoon fame, living in it still presented hardships that few non-Natives would endure. Eskimos are tough and adaptable. Otherwise, they wouldn't have survived in the Arctic for thousands of years.

During my flight back to Anchorage, I thought about that Eskimo and his home. I wondered whether Joan and I could live in a bush cabin, which would be a palace compared to a Diomede igloo. However, we wouldn't have the benefit of a village generator or neighbors to help us over the rough spots. It was time to talk seriously about our future.

The Search

In our house in Eagle River, near Anchorage, my wife and I looked beyond my impending retirement and discussed our plans. Joan worked in the Central Accounting Office at Fort Richardson, but she had no plans to work there for the rest of her life. We had talked for several years about moving to the bush.

"Joan," I said, "I don't want to become a bureaucrat when I retire. I can get a job at Fort Rich or in Anchorage, but I don't want to." I wanted to escape the ruts of habit and break a new trail of my own choosing, away from the stress and turmoil of urban madness.

"That's OK with me," she said. "Still want to move to the bush?"

"Yes. I need elbow room. I can't forget Vietnam, and I need time to deal with that."

"I understand. Can we afford to live out there?" she said.

"I think so. We've saved enough money to buy land and build a cabin. My Army retirement pay should more than cover our monthly living expenses." I glanced toward my gun cabinet, which stood against the wall of our family room. My fishing poles hung on a rack next to the gun cabinet. "I doubt if we'll have to buy meat."

"If that's what you want, let's do it," she said. We embraced. I loved that woman as much as ever—my childhood sweetheart, already turned world-traveler, and about to turn into a bush rat. I was a lucky man to have been mowing the lawn when Joan walked by so many years ago.

Joan agreed to take on the hardships of a life without electricity, running water, telephones, and television. The possibility of injury or illness 200 miles from a hospital and no way to request medical help didn't intimidate her. The thought of bears roaming the forest didn't bother her. She was fond of the outdoors and loved to study wildflowers and learn their names. She enjoyed cross-country skiing, roaming through the woods on snowshoes, and examining and identifying animal tracks.

When she said, "Let's do it," I knew that she would support me as I tested myself against the challenges of bush living.

Lorraine, a student at the Anchorage campus of the University of Alaska, accepted our decision with her usual humor. "Wait a minute," she said. "You've got it backwards. It's the children, not the parents, who are supposed to leave home."

By this time, Lorraine lived in an Anchorage apartment and worked part time in a printing shop. She had acquired some of my self-determination as she grew up, and at twenty-one no longer needed our guidance. She didn't mind if we moved to a remote cabin 200 miles from Anchorage.

"Can I come visit you?" she said, knowing the answer to that question. She knew we'd welcome her visits anytime. Lorraine loved the outdoors as much as we did. She climbed mountains in the Chugach Range, went fishing and canoeing with friends, and joined us on snowmachine jaunts. Skiing, both downhill and cross-country, was another of her favorite pastimes.

Joan and I began planning, starting with the search for property. We turned to the classified sections of the Anchorage newspapers, and, following those leads, we hitched our snowmachine trailer to our four-wheel-drive pickup and spent weekends exploring. Lorraine joined us occasionally. She had become an accomplished photographer, and she loved the opportunity to photograph winter scenes. We parked our truck and trailer at roadside turnouts, unloaded the snowmachines, and roamed the countryside.

Snowmachines were still new technology back in the 1970s, and they allowed us to venture into locales that we would never have seen without them. They were replacing sled dogs in Alaska, and they became an essential means of transportation for bush dwellers. However, we were uneasy about the impact the noisy, foul-smelling machines had on the animals and their habitat, and eventually we would disparage snowmachines as assault vehicles driven by largely irresponsible hooligans. Still, the machines offered a convenient means of transportation, and we used them responsibly. We explored valleys, ridges, hillsides, and river drainages. We looked at lots of property and ate lots of frozen sandwiches in the winter wilderness, but none of the properties suited us

❨

One day I read a classified ad that mentioned "hunting, trapping, and fishing in the shadow of Mount McKinley." I said, "Joan, here's a real come·on, but we might as well check it out."

"OK," she said

The advertised property was located ten miles south of the lowest pass in the Rocky Mountains, which led to Alaska's great Interior. A tundra plain undulated across Broad Pass, altitude 2,345 feet, separating the Alaska and Talkeetna mountain ranges. Bull Lakes, Squaw Lake, Summit Lake and several unnamed ponds were scattered across the pass, filling depressions gouged by glaciers and left behind when the melting ice retreated thousands of years ago.

Twenty-five miles north of the property, the small village of Cantwell—a scattered collection of small frame or log houses, tended or neglected, but shelter nonetheless—straddled the Jack River at the northern limit of Broad Pass, hard against the Alaska Range. The metal post office, which resembled a converted mobile home, anchored the tiny town. Several Athabascan Indian families lived in that village, along with a slightly larger number of non-natives.

North of Cantwell, craggy, snow-clad peaks thrust into the sky, defeating the Matanuska-Susitna Valley's attempt to join the Interior.

The Denali Highway, a 135-mile stretch of pot-holed gravel road, unplowed in winter, wandered east from Cantwell, skirting the southern bases of the broad-shouldered mountains that formed the headwaters of the mighty Susitna River. The road ended where it intersected with the Richardson Highway at Paxson, which consisted of a roadhouse and little else. We had stayed in the roadhouse—Paxson Lodge—several times when I hunted moose or ptarmigan in that area.

☾

On a windy, subzero day in February, Joan and I in our pickup, followed by two friends, Mike and Kathy Barth, in theirs, drove north on the Parks Highway. The road climbs a vast plain that rises from Cook Inlet to the arc of the Alaska Range, which includes Mount McKinley.

Leaving our pickups at a roadside turnout, we unloaded our snowmachines from the trailers. A fresh two-foot snowfall, on top of the four feet already on the ground, bogged down our snowmachines several times, and we struggled to dig them out.

After a heavy, fresh snowfall of a foot or more, those early snowmachines couldn't break a trail. Unpacked snow couldn't support the 400-pound weight of the machine plus the rider. The endless track propelling the snowmachine spun and dug a trench under the machine, which then settled onto its foot rests and sat there, suspended over the ditch it had dug for itself.

We learned, after we moved to the bush, that if we waited for four days after a big storm, the snow compacted and we could break a trail on snowmachines; if we attempted to travel on the machines within three days of the snowfall, we got stuck. If travel became absolutely necessary during that three-day period, we broke trail first on snowshoes. The snowmachines would perform quite well on the snowshoe trail, provided we didn't swerve from the packed surface.

We dug out our snowmachines several times on this trip. I packed a trail by tramping on snowshoes. I then returned to the snowmachine, started the engine, and gained as much speed as possible on the trail I had just made. Momentum carried me several yards before fluffy snow again captured the machine. I repeated the routine, following directions on a hand-drawn map until we found the advertised property.

Mike and Kathy were far behind us, kept busy digging out their single snowmachine. Riding double, they had a tough time staying on the trail I made. It's difficult for two people to make the subtle body shifts that balancing a moving snowmachine requires. They ran off the trail several times.

Spectacular landscape surrounded Joan and me while we stood, shivering, on a frozen lake in February's chill. To the west, towering peaks of the Alaska Range flanked North America's highest mountain—Mount McKinley, also called Denali, the High One. Sprawling in a massive, semicircular sweep from southwest to northeast, those mountains fed glaciers that crept into the silence of remote valleys. I longed to hike into those valleys in summer and learn their secrets.

I thought of the ancient native hunters who had stalked this valley for hundreds, perhaps thousands, of years. Did their spirits still roam the land on frosty nights in search of the perfect moose to take to the village for a potlatch that would honor the dead of centuries? Native Alaskans gather at potlatches to exchange gifts and feast on moose, caribou, salmon, and other subsistence foods. The celebrants remember departed ancestors and honor those who recently died.

I turned toward the east. The Talkeetna Mountains soared almost overhead. Some peaks were as sharp as tips of ski poles; they pierced the sky, daring us to live in their shadow. My hopes rose nearly as high as the jagged peaks. Maybe, just maybe . . .

I turned to my wife. "Joan, just look at those mountains."

"Yes." There was little else to say. We kept looking at each other and back at the lofty mountains.

Spruces and willows straggled to the top of a ridge a half mile away, slumping under their snow burdens. We watched a husky-voiced raven glide above the snowscape, a hungry, black survivor in a frost-white, frozen world.

Beyond, only the tops of dwarf spruces and willows speckled the sparkling snow as the Talkeetnas rose in cold glory to dominate the valley. The pale sun, low on the horizon and far to the south, cast long shadows onto the drift-covered lake, shadows that rippled with the wind through the trees.

Within minutes, the sun disappeared below the horizon, dragging the temperature with it. Now alpenglow kissed the tips of the Talkeetna Mountains, an alluring and seductive phenomenon.

We looked at each other again. Joan reached for my mittened hand. Could this be the end of our search?

❰

The lake adjacent to the property was called Colorado Lake. I made one more trip to the area that winter and snowshoed alone for hours through the surrounding forest. Memories of my Vermont childhood accompanied me, reassuring me that all of the years and all of my experiences had led me to this spot. I remembered my final boyhood day in East Burke, Vermont, alone and forlorn in my favorite clearing. I was alone now, but this time a sense of fulfillment warmed me against the chilly day.

Animal tracks marked the snow in all directions. Squirrel tracks, their front paw prints inside the bigger prints of their hind feet, left a series of closely grouped tiny holes spaced two feet apart. Widely spaced marten prints told me that a marten had leaped across the open spaces in the spruce forest, chasing the squirrel. The back feet of marten usually land in the prints made by their front feet, creating a track that looks as if it were made by a two-footed animal.

Fox tracks, a line of evenly spaced two-inch holes, one behind the other, wove in and out along passageways formed by stooped, snow-laden bushes. A moose, leaving huge prints that resembled those of a giant dairy cow, had nibbled the tips of willows, leaving bits of shredded bark on the snow below. Rabbit and weasel tracks intermingled, but the weasel had hopped across the snow first. The rabbit had peeled bark from a willow trunk, leaving bark crumbs scattered about under the bushes. Wildlife wrote its stories in the snow, and I read each line with care.

Grouse had walked over snow-covered blowdowns—dead trees uprooted by winds. Ptarmigan left their three-toed footprints under willow bushes. Tiny chickadee tracks left a mere trace of a brief journey, barely whispering the story of their maker's search for food. A gray jay chortled on a spruce branch as if eager to welcome me into this frozen land. I struggled to repress my excitement; I had to see the area without its winter coat.

☾

Joan and I hiked the four miles to the Colorado Lake property in June, strolling in tree-dappled sunshine along a ridgetop that led obliquely to the land offered for sale. White dwarf dogwood blossoms had replaced the winter snows, softening the surface of this rugged land. The land invited us to touch it, feel it, respect it. Joan picked a dogwood blossom and put it in her jacket's top buttonhole. I whistled, not only because I was happy, but to warn bears of our approach.

The spring-green of alder and willow leaves contrasted with the darker green of moss and the near-black spruce trees. Birds warbled, and a small stream murmured and chuckled its way down the ridge. We hopped across the trickle, slid in the mud, and scrambled to regain our balance. We laughed. What a great day to be hiking with each other through the Alaska wilderness.

I glanced at the ground. "Joan," I said, "come look at this."

She walked over and stared at grizzly bear tracks that crossed the little stream. The three-inch claws left puncture marks just in front of muddy prints that measured nearly as wide as the length of my boot. I eased my slung rifle from my shoulder.

"How old is that track?" she said.

"Hard to tell. Probably a day or two. The water in the track's clear, so the prints aren't fresh." We walked on, peering more intently into thickets. Bear tracks have a way of focusing your attention on your surroundings when you're meandering through the woods.

The waters of Colorado Lake, glimpsed through the spruces, twinkled and glinted. We stepped into a clearing. The lake below now dazzled us with the reflected summer sun. We raised our eyes to Denali and the Alaska Range. The snow-capped mountains dominated the horizon.

Awestruck by the beauty, we looked at each other. "Lee," Joan whispered, "that's magnificent."

"Wow," I said. "Sure looks different in the summer."

"The pond is bigger than I thought," Joan said, referring to a small body of water between Colorado Lake and the ridge where we stood. "Last winter, I couldn't tell where it started and the land began. And just look at that lake sparkle."

"I wonder why nobody has bought this property," I said. "Must be something wrong with it." I didn't dare hope that we might eventually own this piece of Alaska.

Afraid we'd be disappointed, we forced ourselves to leave that magnificent view and descended from the ridge to the lakeshore.

Ducks—Barrow's goldeneyes, surf scoters, wigeons, pintails, and mallards—bobbed on the surface of Colorado Lake. Arctic grayling rose through clear water, sipped mosquitoes from the surface, and left doughnut-shaped ripples when they submerged. I could almost taste fried grayling as I watched them finning near the shore.

Black-and-white tree swallows swooped and darted, straining the air as they gorged on the multitudes of mosquitoes. They didn't get them all; we swatted constantly at the clouds of swarming insects. We smeared insect repellent on our exposed skin to keep them at bay. They still hovered a foot or two from our heads, patient winged predators that could drive an unprotected person insane.

I waved my hand through a gray, humming cloud. "Looks like we'll need head nets this time of year."

"Darned things get behind my glasses," Joan said, wiping her eyes and spitting out a mosquito.

A belted kingfisher, its large head and oversized bill out of proportion to its chunky body, sat on a dead spruce limb, eyeing the grayling below. Down the lake, a pair of red-throated loons made extended dives, surfacing many yards from their submersion point. If they saw us, they gave no indication.

A beaver dam—a tangle of mud-daubed sticks, chunks of sod, and grass—had blocked the lake's outlet, backing up water and drowning several spruce trees, although they remained standing. Peeled willow limbs floated among the sedges, evidence that unseen beavers were present and active.

We stood on an isthmus—a strip of land between the lake and the pond—that averaged perhaps 200 feet in width. A half-dozen unoccupied cabins were scattered on the far shore of the lake. We turned our back on them and gazed at the shallow pond that lay in the low area between the isthmus and the spruce-covered ridge beyond. Northern phalaropes skittered about on the pond, looking like wind-up-toy birds as they picked insects from the surface. Their rust, white, and brown plumage blended with the colors of the land. Their *tic tic* call reminded us of the crucial timing of their brief breeding season. The short Alaska summer governed their lives, as it would mine when I built our cabin.

Here, too, ducks dotted the water, quietly quacking while feeding in the tall grasses around the irregular shoreline. We spoke in hushed tones, not wanting to disturb the wildlife.

We peered at the bottom of the eight-acre pond, which I guessed to be two to three feet deep. A tiny stickleback—a spiny, minnowlike fish—darted about, just above the peat-covered bottom, feeding on aquatic insects. Water beetle larvae and fairy shrimp were abundant.

"I don't see any grayling in the pond," I whispered.

"Maybe it's too shallow," Joan said. "If it freezes nearly to the bottom, there won't be enough water left to support larger fish."

"I bet you're right," I said.

Several tiny islands poked above the surface, providing resting places for ducks and other birds. A pair of arctic terns nested on the largest island, their white feathers, black heads, and salmon-colored beaks contrasting with the green and brown moss that cushioned their eggs. We marveled that these small birds could migrate annually from the southern tip of South America to the arctic and subarctic regions of Alaska.

Forest odors scented the air—pungent spruce pitch, sweet wildflowers, musty mud at water's edge, the dry smell of old grass. At our feet, a profusion of pink blueberry blossoms colored the ground.

"Joan," I said, "I can almost taste fresh blueberry muffins and pies right now."

She smiled. "Maybe we ought to build a cabin before I roll out the piecrust."

I tramped along the shore of Colorado Lake and found two property markers, then located the other two corners on the low ridge across the pond. The property within the markers included most of the pond. White-crowned sparrows hopped about in the tundra, flying to nearby willow bushes when I approached them. A lesser yellowlegs, a member of the sandpiper family, yodeled near the pond's edge, exhibiting the strange bobbing behavior common to the species.

Joan explored the sedges that softened the edge of the lake. The eight acres included the majority of the pond plus nearly a quarter of a mile of lake frontage, with plenty of land for a cabin and outbuildings. When we met at what would be the obvious building site, we knew.

"Honey," I said, "what do you think?"

"This is just beautiful," she said. "Did you find anything wrong with it?"

"The land is low between the lake and the pond. That may present a problem for a septic system, but an outhouse will work just fine. How does using an outhouse at forty below strike you?"

"I can think of things I'd rather do, but I guess if you can stand it, so can I. Let's do it." Her eyes sparkled, just like the blue waters of Colorado Lake.

We hugged, standing amid blueberry blossoms. This was it, the setting for our future bush home. I felt at peace; I had finally arrived at the end of my long journey that had started in East Burke, Vermont, many years ago.

One Stick at a Time

Woo, woo, wooo, woooo. A strange noise penetrated the green canvas
of my tent. I struggled awake, exhausted after a tough day. What
made that racket? *Woo, woo, wooo, wooooo.* Each rapid repetition
began softly, grew louder, then abruptly ceased. In my half-awake
state, the noise seemed to come from above. Was it an owl?

Gentle rain pattered on the tent roof, scribbled its way down
the canvas sides, and dribbled onto the soggy moss below. I unzipped the door, peeked out at the raindrops, and withdrew to pull
on my boots. I had to know, at 2:00 A.M., what made that noise.
Wearing ankle-high L. L. Bean boots, boxer shorts, and a rain
jacket, I stepped out into the drizzle. A few yards behind the tent,
raindrops gave Colorado Lake goose bumps.

Woo, wooo, woooo. I looked overhead, for there was no longer any question about the general location of the noise. Above dripping spruces, a small, long-billed bird gained altitude against the rain. I ignored the bird and searched the treetops, seeing nothing that would make noise. Then I heard the sound again and looked up through the rain at the bird, startled to see it in a wing-beating power dive, rushing toward the water headfirst. As the bird plummeted, it beat its wings more frantically and the sound, spilling from its wingtips, grew louder. Pulling out of its plunge, the speckled, striped bird again gained altitude in preparation for another energetic dive toward the lake. I had just seen and heard the mating flight of a common snipe. Satisfied, I returned to my tent and went back to sleep.

Building a cabin is hard work, and I had just finished my first day alone in the bush, staking out the cabin perimeter and digging postholes. My duties as an active Army advisor to the Alaska National Guard required me to work four ten-hour days in the summer, with a three-day weekend. The situation was ideal for a soon-to-be-retired major. Joan's five-day-a-week job at the Central Accounting Office on Fort Richardson prevented her from joining me as I traveled 185 miles north on the Parks Highway each Thursday evening.

I worked mostly alone every weekend all summer, building our cabin. Because of the long hours of daylight, I didn't crawl into my tent until I grew so tired that I could no longer swing a hammer or saw a board. My muscles usually rebelled by 11:00 P.M., and I grabbed a few hours of sleep, only to repeat the process for another sixteen hours or so the next day. Because the property sloped gently toward the pond that our cabin would overlook, I decided to use pilings as a foundation for my cabin rather than trying to level the land with a hand shovel. The thought of mixing and pouring a concrete foundation by hand, alone, was too discouraging to seriously consider. Besides, the space under the piling-supported cabin would be useful as a winter storage area for my rowboat and salmon smokers.

During the first two days of that first weekend working in the bush, in early June 1979, I dug holes in the gravel that lay under the moss at our cabin site. Digging piling holes in that rock-choked ground while suffering the never-ending rain started to make me wonder why I wanted to live in the bush. I wore out a pair of leather gloves and damned near wore out my determination. I didn't know it at the time, but I had chosen to build a cabin in the bush during the second-rainiest summer on record in Southcentral Alaska. In hindsight, rain was actually good fortune. The water helped loosen the soil, which made rock removal somewhat easier.

When I had excavated twelve holes to a depth of three feet, I wrestled a heavy creosote-treated railroad tie into each hole. I plumbed and braced each one with two-by-fours and then tamped gravel around the ties. I cut the ties off at a uniform height, using my chain saw.

At the end of that first weekend, the upright railroad ties looked like alert sentinels amid the spruce trees that guarded our homesite on three sides.

Polishing my rusty carpenter skills, I continued to work alone that summer, using only hand tools, except for the chain saw. My thoughts often wandered back to early days in Vermont, to my father and his crew of carpenters and laborers. We relied more on hand tools than power tools back then, and I was glad we did, for I learned skills that now paid off.

I chose to build a frame cabin instead of a log cabin because few of the spruce trees on the property measured more than eight inches in diameter. A log cabin built from such small logs would not be warm enough for Alaska's long, harsh winters. Unless the logs are large, say about twelve inches in diameter, and exceptionally well fitted together, log cabins can be drafty and cold. My frame cabin, constructed of 2" x 6" studs and insulated with Fiberglass, would be warm and draft-free. And building a frame house is easier than building with logs, especially when working alone.

I contracted with a building supply company in Fairbanks to load all of the building materials for the cabin onto a single railroad flatcar. The Alaska Railroad engineer backed the flatcar onto a railroad siding that paralleled the main line. The siding was across the lake, over a mile away. The brakeman unhooked the flatcar, which was piled high with lumber, windows, insulation, plywood, and all the other parts and pieces that would become our new cabin. He said, "Well, there it is. You've got three days to unload it." If I took more than three days, extra charges would apply.

Joan and I had managed to drive and winch an old beat-up four-wheel drive pickup in over the ridge, to the railroad siding. Even with chains on all four tires, I had to use a hand winch, or come-along, to pull the old truck through swampy areas. I pumped the winch handle while Joan applied engine power, and we inched along until we found solid ground again. That ancient truck paid for itself when Mike Barth, Bob Huddleston, and Steve Larson helped me haul the cabin—stick by stick, board by board, pane by pane—around the lake to the edge of our property.

A swampy area about 200 yards from the building site prevented us from driving the loaded pickup any closer to the construction area. We unloaded the truck at the edge of the boggy spot and sorted the materials into piles of lumber, windows, roofing, and insulation, among others. Consequently, every piece that became part of that cabin traveled the remaining distance on someone's back. My friends helped for that one weekend, and then the rest was up to me.

I had never carried an entire house for 200 yards, one stick at a time, on my back before. I have no idea how many miles I walked between the pile of building supplies and the cabin site, but I wore a lot of tread off my boots while I toted each board, box and bag. Given the choice between doing it again and having a root canal, I'd opt for the root canal. The pain doesn't last nearly as long.

I built our cabin mostly by myself, with occasional help from Joan. Fort Richardson was joining the computer age, and Joan had to work overtime throughout the summer, helping with the conversion to computers. On the occasional Saturday when she didn't have to work, she drove alone 185 miles up the highway and hiked in to help me with cabin building. Our small green tent, too small to stand erect in, served as kitchen, bedroom, and living room.

I built the cabin floor, which gave me a level, smooth platform to work from, and then assembled the walls on the flat floor. With a little help one weekend, I raised the walls into place, braced them, and installed the floor joists for the second story.

The following weekend I nailed the exterior siding to the walls. The interior knee walls on the second story were only four feet high, stretching from the floor to the rafters, so, after the rafters were in place, I built the knee walls without help.

The sixty-degree pitched roof was designed to shed the several feet of snow that fell each winter. The peak rose thirty feet in the air, and I struggled to keep from slipping on the rain-soaked lumber and crashing to the ground. Adding to my misery, mosquitoes swarmed and buzzed around my head in gray, stinging clouds. Bug repellent worked only briefly before the never-ending drizzle washed it away. Then the vicious hordes returned to the attack.

The temperature remained in the fifties for most of the summer, a good temperature to work in, but when I quit for the day, a cold, damp tent awaited. Usually a few dozen mosquitoes that had worked their way in around the zippered door greeted me when I crawled into the canvas shelter.

I shivered in the rain and wallowed in the mud each weekend all summer long. Joan never complained, and she usually brought a pie or cake to lift my soggy spirits. But most of the time I labored alone, harassed by mosquitoes and surrounded by wildlife. Bird songs cheered me, red squirrels fussed at me. Garrulous gray jays, called camp robbers, ate food scraps from my hands. They perched on the spruce branches above my head and chortled while I worked. Common and red-throated loons voiced mournful cries that spoke of solitude and wilderness. I loved solitude and I rejoiced in building our future home in spite of the endless rain.

I heated water on a Coleman camp stove inside my tent and poured the hot water into my freeze-dried meals, a reminder of my Army days in Southeast Asia. I often thought about the unappetizing army-issued rations that I ate in Vietnam. But gentle, not monsoon, rains fell here at my cabin site, and although an occasional combat nightmare interfered with my sleep, whizzing bullets never interrupted my meals. Washed down by a beer or soft drink, which I cooled in the lake, the meals became brief, welcome interruptions in my busy day.

I worked and lived in a water-filled world and crawled exhausted into my sleeping bag each night. I wondered if I should construct an ark instead of a cabin. I figured Noah's job was easier; he built the ark before it began raining.

Cabin construction monopolized my spare time for about a year and a half. I started building in June, completed the roof by snowfall in September, and worked on the interior as time and weather permitted throughout that first winter. However, my work schedule in winter didn't permit three-day weekends, and the long drive over the icy Parks Highway, always in the dark, slowed progress on the cabin to a crawl.

Winter was a busy time for the Alaska National Guard and us advisors. Instead of summer camp, the Alaska Guard went to winter camp. Training to fight in arctic conditions was one reason, but perhaps the primary reason to train in winter was that in summer the Alaska Natives go to fish camp. Moving to riverside camps for a few weeks each summer, Eskimos and Indians catch and preserve the salmon and other fish that will sustain them and their sled dogs during the winter. They can't afford to give up two weeks of their brief summer to attend military training. During the second summer, I spent every three-day weekend at the cabin. In September I took a thirty-day leave from the Army and, although Joan visited me twice during that time and Lorraine joined us once, I didn't leave the bush for the entire month. But I did steal brief breaks from the drudgery of cabin building.

One sunny day I took off my nail apron, laid aside my hammer, picked up my 12-gauge shotgun, and hunted for grouse on a nearby ridge. The pleasure of easing through the sunlight-and-shadow-quilted woods, not caring whether I shot grouse or not, gave me a taste of what life would be like after I retired and moved into the cabin. I thought of freedom and peace and contentment. A flock of twittering redpolls passed overhead. Most migratory birds had left for the winter, and silence stretched into the distance.

I leaned against a fallen spruce, content to just look and listen. Alder leaves rattled slightly in the infrequent breeze, as if eager to drop from the branches and hide their ugliness under the winter snows. Alder leaves don't turn color in the chill of Alaska autumn. Instead, they darken somewhat to a deep, lusterless green. Dark splotches form on the leaves, a measly end to a brief but glorious summer existence. The heavy winter snows and short growing season limit alders' growth, so they languish as mere bushes, unlike their cousins in the Lower 48, which attain tree stature.

Golden willow leaves, still attached to the branches, fluttered alongside a small stream as if boasting to the alders. See, the willows seemed to say, this is what autumn is supposed to look like. Death doesn't have to be drab and colorless. Go out in a blaze of color! Let the world know you have gladly lived and now proudly die.

My thoughts strayed to Vietnam, which happened often when I glided quietly through wooded areas. I thought of the men who had died in the spring and summer of their lives, and sadness hovered around me. I recognized it, acknowledged it, and drove it away. Time to get on with my life. I picked up my shotgun and stepped slowly toward the willows.

From beneath the yellow bushes, three spruce grouse exploded into the air and darted between the spruce trees. I shot twice, killing two. I field dressed them, stuffed them into my game bag, and shoved the thoughts of death out of my mind. Grouse that have fed on blueberries are one of the tastiest game birds. If we were going to subsist on wild game and fish, I couldn't allow my conflicting emotions to prevent me from hunting and fishing. I returned to the cabin, thoughtful but content.

Joan cooked the spruce hens, as we called them, when she arrived the next day. "Tastes better than pa'tridges," I said, using that Vermont word for the first time in years.

"Ayuh," Joan said, reverting to her Maine accent and agreeing with me.

We finished the meal with several handfuls of fresh blueberries sprinkled with sugar. It was the last time we would enjoy fresh berries that season. The early mornings were frosty now, and the rains had stopped. Snow sprinkled the mountains like powdered sugar on cupcakes, and each new snowfall frosted the slopes a little lower.

Just prior to freeze-up, I stapled fiberglass insulation between the studs in the six-inch-thick walls, and stuffed ten inches of insulation between the rafters. Joan helped with that itchy job. I had placed ten inches of insulation between the floor joists and sealed it in with plastic sheeting before I laid the plywood floor. Our cabin would be snug against the subarctic winters.

☾

I had installed our new woodstove earlier in the summer. That Earth Stove, which was the brand name, burned wood so efficiently that little ash remained. It was simply a square black steel box with the edges rounded. It sat upright on four stubby legs, and had a draft that could be tightly controlled. The door, which was on the front, was easily removed. A screen that came with it fit over the door opening so we could watch the flames—sort of a substitute for a fireplace. We soon learned that the screen option introduced so much air into the firebox that the stove gobbled wood faster than a marten ate a squirrel. We never used the screen again.

The stove was rated to heat 1,000 square feet. Our cabin measured about 890 square feet inside. The fit was perfect, and that little stove kept us warm for sixteen long winters.

I lighted the stove after installing it, to begin to dry our damp cabin. I then positioned our new propane cooking range and, with a length of copper tubing, connected it to a one-hundred-pound propane cylinder that stood on a pallet outside. Without electricity, we relied on propane for cooking, lights, and refrigeration.

I bought an old gas refrigerator—a Servel that was probably manufactured back in the 1940s. It rode in on the back of the old pickup. I walked it along planks that stretched to the cabin door, then grunted and huffed while I rocked it, moving one side at a time, across the floor to its place in the kitchen. It must have weighed more than 300 pounds. The gas range was a lightweight compared to that old refrigerator.

❦

Joan joined me for my final weekend of leave. She hadn't been to the cabin for three weeks, and she marveled at the progress I had made. I led her on a tour of our future home.

Downstairs, the kitchen opened into the living room. Both rooms had large windows facing the Talkeetna Range. Those mountains, often reflected in the pond, dominated the scene.

"Lee, I'll never tire of that view," she said, looking from the kitchen window. "Say," she continued, "that section of tundra that juts into the pond in front of the cabin looks like a raven's head. See, the beak is open, just like a squawking raven."

And that's how Ravenhead Pond got its name.

"The loons are still here. Do you hear them often?" Joan asked.

"Yeah, they call back and forth to each other. Sometimes they wake me up. I guess they don't sleep much. I haven't seen any chicks this year. Maybe a mink or an eagle got them." I turned away from the window. "Here, come see the bathroom."

We had no running water, aside from running down to the lake and hauling water to the cabin in a bucket. I had dug an outhouse out back, which replaced the usual commode. I built a bathroom inside the cabin, but installed only a sink and bathtub, draining the gray water into a dry well I dug a hundred feet from the cabin.

Digging that ditch and well was about as much fun as digging the foundation holes. I wore out another pair of gloves on that project.

"How do we take a shower?" Joan asked.

"See that pulley hanging from a hook on the ceiling above the tub? I heat water on the woodstove, pour it into that five-gallon plastic jug, and pull the jug up to the ceiling with that cord and pulley." Joan looked skeptical. "That showerhead at the end of the plastic hose that hangs from the jug works great," I said. "I need a shower curtain, though. When I open the valve and let the water spray onto me, some of it splashes onto the floor. But it works. Sure beats taking a bath in that cold lake." Joan made a note to buy a shower curtain.

I led her to a small room just off the living room. "This is our all-purpose room," I said. "I think I'll put my desk against that wall, under the window, so I can see to write my articles and poems. OK? Your treadle sewing machine can go over there, if you like, and I think my gun cabinet might fit against the wall by the closet. What do you think?"

"Sounds good. When the wringer washing machine is not in use, will it fit in that closet?" she asked, nodding toward the open closet.

"Probably. Hadn't thought about that. Not a bad idea, now that you mention it. Working in these grubby clothes day after day, I guess I forgot about the need to change clothes occasionally." Joan wrinkled her nose, gave an exaggerated sniff, and turned away.

The room occupied the southwest corner, looking onto Colorado Lake. Our living room, in the opposite end of the cabin, faced the pond out front.

An arctic entry, a tiny room that enabled us to seal the main cabin from winter blasts before we opened the outer door, led to the back entrance. "Can you build some shelves along the back wall of the arctic entry so I can use this space as a pantry?" Joan asked.

"Good idea. I hadn't thought of that, either," I said. "You mean we have to plan ahead and stock food on the shelves instead of just catching a fish or shooting a grouse when we're hungry?" She ignored my feeble attempt to cover up my oversight with humor and added shelving material to her list.

To save floor space, I planned to install a circular staircase that would spiral to the two bedrooms upstairs. But to see our master and guest bedrooms right then, Joan had to climb a ladder that led through the stairwell hole in the living room ceiling.

"When will you order the circular stairs?" she asked, climbing up the ladder. Joan doesn't like heights, and the circular stairs had been her idea.

"Soon. But I've got lots of interior work to do before I get to that project."

I followed my wife up the ladder. She walked to the door that led from our bedroom to a narrow balcony that provided an uninterrupted vista of the pond and the mountains beyond.

"Oh, Lee, look at that termination dust," she said, gazing from the open door. Alaskans call the first snow at summer's end "termination dust." It signifies the termination of the short summer season.

The Talkeetna Mountains gleamed in the sunlight. Snow clung to the peaks and partway down the sides. Their reflection in the pond in front of the cabin shivered slightly in the breeze, as if dreading the oncoming winter.

A few surf scoters quacked in the pond below, but not many ducks remained. The fall colors of red and gold framed the pond, showing off before disappearing under the coming snows.

Joan turned away from the scene out front, closed the balcony door, and walked across our bedroom to the open landing at the top of the stairwell. I opened the door to the guest bedroom. We strolled across the small bedroom and stood with our arms around each other as we gazed out that window onto Colorado Lake.

"Quite a view for our guests," she said.

"Hope they don't stay too long," I said, grinning. "Just think, we won't have to attend any more military social functions or entertain "the brass" at dinner. I won't miss that a bit." Joan laughed and agreed.

The short knee walls in the two upstairs bedrooms gave us a vertical place to hang paintings, photos, and other wall decorations. The slant of the rafters caused by the steep pitch of the roof would have left slanting walls from the ridge to the floor that would be of little use other than to keep the insulation from falling on us. I lost floor space because of the knee walls, but gained hidden storage space under the eaves.

Joan inspected the storage space, sticking her head through the access door and peering into the dark cavity. "We can't put stuff out here that will be damaged if it freezes," she said, her voice muffled. "But it's a great place to store off-season clothes."

"And just what is the off season up here?" I asked. "If summer ever comes to this country, that'll be the off season." Although the rains had ended, I was rain-weary. I helped Joan to her feet.

We descended the ladder, and Joan began preparing the first of the many meals she would cook on our new propane range.

Although I had hauled one propane cylinder to the cabin, later I would buy four more tanks, giving us a five-month supply of propane with which to cook, run our refrigerator, and power our lights. For now, a Coleman lantern and candles lighted the cabin.

With 560 square feet of floor space on the ground floor and 330 feet upstairs, we would enjoy the luxury of an 890-square-foot cabin. But despite having an indoor sink and shower, we had no indoor toilet.

A short trail led from the cabin's back door to the outhouse. Joan inspected it and proclaimed it "the finest outhouse I've ever seen." We christened the outhouse "the little house out back."

She later hung a small sheer curtain over the screened window hole that I had cut into the outhouse door to let in light. In curtained privacy, the occupant could gaze at the Talkeetnas while contemplating the joys of bush life. I constructed a steep roof so the snow would slide off, and made a small cabinet that hung on the inside wall. We stored extra toilet tissue in it.

Joan and I spent several weekends at the cabin during the early winter as my Army career neared its end. The trip in from the road on snowmachines in winter took a lot less time than traveling on foot in summer, provided we didn't have to break a trail on snowshoes following a two-foot snowstorm.

I bought a twelve-foot-long dogsled that came with a steel tow bar designed to attach to a snowmachine hitch. That sled, made by an Eskimo in Kivalina, an Alaska Native village up on the Arctic

Coast, turned out to be one of my wisest purchases. I hauled many tons of supplies on that sled over the years that followed, and I can't imagine living out there without it.

I retired from the Army in 1981, and Joan resigned from her job. By the middle of February we were ready to move. Our new home was unfinished but livable, and we planned to move in on the first of March. I still hadn't installed the circular stairs. Joan, at that point, raised one of her few objections. "Lee, if I need to go to the outhouse at night, I'm not going to crawl down that darned ladder while holding a flashlight. I want those stairs installed," she said.

"Yes, Ma'am."

I bought the stairs, hauled them to the cabin on the dogsled, and stored them in the all-purpose room until I had time to install them. Joan's comments left no doubt what my first priority would be after we moved in.

A couple of weeks before I retired, Colonel Dave Pinney, my boss, called me. "Lee, do you need help moving your household goods to the cabin?"

"Yes, Sir," I said. "I sure could use some help."

"I've got to take some leave or lose it," he said. "I'd like to use up some leave time helping you move." Not only was Dave a great leader, he was a true friend.

On my last day in the Army, Joan and Lorraine stood behind me, just as they had for my entire career. I stood at attention in front of the reviewing stand as the troops stood in formation facing me, honoring me at my retirement ceremony. I saw the ranks of those young soldiers in front of me and flashed back to the ranks of my Vietnam comrades who had not lived to see their retirement parade. It was a poignant moment at the end of my career.

That evening, after my retirement ceremony and subsequent farewell activities at the officers' club, I removed my uniform for the last time. It was time to look forward, not back.

I rented a truck so Dave and I could move some household items while Joan finished packing odds and ends and prepared our house in Eagle River for rental.

Nature took one final shot at trying to discourage me from living in the bush. A heavy snowstorm blew into the region on the day Dave and I chose as moving day. In a blinding blizzard, we spent all day and evening hauling boxes and furniture on the dogsled attached to my snowmachine. We struggled to see ahead of our snowmachines and remain on the trail. But on that snowy, blowy February day, my boyhood fantasy came true at last. I was moving to the Alaska bush.

☾

Joan and I turned our backs on the comforts of urban living that first week in March and, with the skeptical comments of friends echoing in our minds, we drove north, past bullet-riddled signs that warned of moose crossings.

"Well, Honey, here we go," I said, looking at Joan across the seat of our pickup.

"Are we really ready for this?" she said. "I'm nervous."

"We'll make it. And if we don't like it out there, we can always move back into our house in Eagle River. But then we'd have to go back to work. Now there's an incentive for you."

We were determined to stick it out for a year, at a minimum, in order to experience all seasons. With the exception of Dave, few people expected us to live out there for more than six months. Some friends didn't give us that long.

However, when we went to town every three months or so for supplies, friends were always eager to hear about our latest adventures. We entertained them with stories of our experiences—tales of bear and moose encounters, bush flying, hunting, trapping, and living a subsistence lifestyle.

At the age of forty-two, we began our life's greatest adventure. We knew that life in the bush required a total commitment. Halfway measures would surely result in failure. For example, we couldn't run to the store each time we needed something. If a piece of equipment broke, I'd either fix it or do without. We knew we would have to rely on ourselves, rather than someone else, to solve our problems.

And proving all of our skeptical friends wrong, we did just that for the next sixteen years.

To Catch a Train

"There's another meteorite," I shouted into the darkness, trying to make myself heard above the shrieking, numbing wind. Joan mumbled something about too many meteorites and not enough trains. She huddled against her windbreak, a small, unoccupied former stationmaster's cabin a few feet from the railroad tracks. As if cowering from the howling north wind, the old cabin leaned toward the south. I resumed my foot-stomping, arm-slapping, train-waiting winter dance, glancing up the track every minute or so, hoping to see the "southbound."

❨

A couple of months before moving into our cabin, Joan and I had driven there for the New Year's holiday weekend. Because of the severe cold, we drove a few miles beyond our usual parking spot beside the highway and left our pickup near the Broad Pass section house, a flag stop on the Alaska Railroad. The two-man section crew lived there, in separate dwellings, and I figured if we had serious problems because of the cold, they'd welcome us into one of their homes to warm up.

At the section house, we transferred to our snowmachines. The chilly seven-mile run to our cabin site at Colorado Lake took about thirty minutes, longer than from our usual parking place. Thawing the cabin out took much longer. Our breath frosted the air inside, condensing on the windows to form a latticework of ice crystals. I had laid a fire in the woodstove before I left the cabin the last time I worked on it and merely had to touch a match to the paper and dry kindling, but we didn't remove our heavy outer clothing for an hour or so.

Joan and I spent the New Year's holiday working inside the cabin. Installing wall cabinets and shelves took most of the brief holiday weekend. With the insulation and wall paneling in place, the cabin began to exhibit a little character.

The temperature outside dropped to thirty below zero and stayed there. The wind picked up on our last day, causing windchill factors of minus eighty degrees and colder. We had little hope of starting our truck, but we bundled up and drove our snowmachines back to Broad Pass to make the attempt. Wearing goose-down facemasks, hooded parkas, and bunny boots, we resembled a pair of space walkers as we perched on our machines, bundled against the sledgehammer cold.

The frozen pickup battery was useless, and after an hour of attempting to thaw and start the truck I said, "To hell with it. I'm nearly frozen. Let's go back to the cabin." The relentless wind made working on a vehicle impossible.

"OK," Joan said. She, too, trembled from the heat-robbing wind.

We mounted our dependable snowmachines and traveled the seven miles back to the cabin. I built a fire in the woodstove and we settled in to wait for the train, scheduled to rumble south at 3:30 A.M. the following morning.

The Alaska Railroad operated a rather casual passenger service. If we stood beside the tracks, we could flag down the train and climb aboard or, reversing the maneuver, debark at nearly any location by informing the conductor of our destination. However, certain days are express days, and on those days the train makes fewer stops. Wise travelers check the train schedule before trying to flag the train. Otherwise, they might futilely wave at the engineer, who always waves back, as the train roars past.

Before we left the bush many years later, the winter service was reduced to one northbound passenger train on Saturdays and one southbound train on Sundays, but in 1981 a midweek southbound rolled through the early morning darkness, and it was this train that Joan and I intended to flag. At 2:30 A.M. we leaned into the wind and snowshoed the mile to the railroad tracks, leaving our snowmachines at our cabin.

☾

Wearing a facemask, bunny boots, and lots of wool and down clothing, I could stand the wind for about fifteen minutes at a time. Then the windchill drove me to shelter behind the old cabin while Joan stumbled out to where she could watch for the train. The train was due two hours ago and should be rolling around the curve at any minute.

The moonless night was perfect for stargazing, and the meteorite display helped keep our minds from dwelling on the incessant north wind. Time passes slowly in such situations.

As we waited, I realized just how insignificant and fragile humans really are when they stray from their contrived environments, in which they take comfort for granted. Out there on the tracks, exposed flesh would freeze in a couple of minutes. A fire might have been possible, if I'd had an ax to chop wood. However, the wind-driven flames would be of little use, and my ax rested on a chopping block in the woodshed back at our cabin.

The erratic sweep of the train's headlight finally parted the darkness. We waved our flashlights in an arc to signal the engineer to stop for passengers. Two toots on the train whistle let us know we'd been spotted, and the yellow-and-blue engine squealed to a stop just past us. The train had arrived two and one-half hours late, a common occurrence.

No shelter ever felt better than the heated passenger car. We couldn't stop smiling for several minutes as we peeled layer after layer of clothing from our slowly warming bodies.

"Where are you folks headed, Anchorage?" the conductor asked.

"Right. Sure hope it's warmer there than up here," I said. He smiled and collected our money. He'd seen half-frozen passengers many times, I'm sure. Six hours later, we arrived in Anchorage and stepped from the train into a warm minus ten degrees.

Bush Fireworks

One December morning, I padded down the circular stairs in my terry cloth bathrobe and sheepskin slippers, traded the slippers for boots, donned a headlamp, and made the essential morning trip to our outhouse. After a brief contemplation of the drawbacks of life in the Alaska bush, I hurried through the darkness to the relative warmth of the cabin.

I opened the stove's mouth and fed it a few tender kindling hors d'oeuvres, followed by an entrée of tough spruce chunks. I adjusted the damper to a fully open position so the hungry stove would draw well, and then pulled on my shirt and pants. I often went to the outhouse in just my bathrobe and boots, preferring to eat breakfast before putting on my wool clothing in preparation for a day outdoors. Because the cabin was quite chilly, I changed the routine on this morning and dressed before I ate. Joan remained in bed until the cabin warmed to a more comfortable temperature.

The slumbering woodstove awakened, inhaled air through its draft, and exhaled sparks up the chimney into the blackness. Looking out the window, I watched an occasional spark drift downward, winking out as it hit the four-foot snow pile beneath the window. The stove radiated heat; I warmed as I sat near it and sipped my hot chocolate. Life was good.

Then, as if suffering an asthma attack, the stove began to gasp, tremble, and rattle. It demanded more oxygen. The stove door fluttered and clattered. Little streamers of smoke escaped around the clanging door, fled the stove's odd behavior, and puffed across the room. A strange outside glow flickered through the windows, casting a reddish hue on the floor and walls. The snow turned rosy, and sparks like those from a welder's torch arced downward, creating a glittering curtain outside the window.

I ran out the back door, eyeballed four feet of flame erupting from the metal stove pipe like a blazing gusher in an oil field, and darted back inside shouting, "Joan, get up and get dressed! The chimney's on fire!"

Joan struggled into her clothes as she scurried, hopped, and stumbled down the stairs. She grabbed her jacket, slipped into her bunny boots, and joined me to rush outside.

"What are we going to do?" she said.

"There's nothing we can do," I said. "Chimney fires burn till they run out of fuel."

It's impossible to stand around and casually observe the huffing and shaking of a chimney fire that threatens to ignite your house. So, we ran around in small circles.

Inside the now-glowing metal chimney, large chunks of soot ignited. Some dropped into the stove below. Others, smaller and lighter, exploded from the top like shells launched from a mortar.

The fireworks display rivaled any we had seen on Independence Day, and created much greater excitement.

The cabin snuggled against a forty-foot-tall spruce tree. Sparks and burning debris filtered through its branches, transforming it into a living, glowing Christmas tree. Occasionally an ember pulsated on the bare tip of a branch, reminiscent of the old bubble lights. The cold temperatures and the elongated snow marshmallows piled on the branches protected the ancient spruce.

"Will the tree catch on fire?" Joan asked.

"I doubt it, but if it does we'll lose the cabin." I grabbed a snow shovel, prepared to throw snow onto the tree if it did ignite. I wondered how high I could toss snow with a shovel.

More embers shot into the sky, turned over, and sped to earth like miniature meteorites, hissing as they plunged into the snow.

"Look!" I said, pointing to another fiery eruption. I clapped my mittened hands and cheered. Roman candles, sparklers, tracers, flares, little cherry bombs—we had them all.

"That's nothing to cheer about, wise guy," my frantic wife said. "Look at that chimney now!"

The metal chimney trembled and shook. Like a cherry-red NASA rocket, it strained to leave earth's gravity, but it was unable to rise, tethered by the braces that clamped it to the roof.

The rocket engine eventually ran out of fuel and the shaking subsided to a clatter, then an occasional twitch. The chimney faded from cherry to pink, then to maroon, and finally to black. Smoke poured from the top, obscuring the stars. We entered the cabin.

Smoke and creosote, squirting from around the pulsating stove door, had fouled our home.

"Phew," Joan said. "Chimney fires smell bad."

We opened the doors and windows, but the smoke and sharp odor of creosote drove us back outside. We moved upwind in the subzero temperature, letting the stink by-pass us on its way to somewhere else.

"I think I'll clean the chimney," I said.

"Fine time to be thinking about that," Joan said, with a wry glance in my direction.

While we waited outside for the worst of the odor to clear, I found my wire chimney brush, attached it to a long fiberglass pole made especially for that purpose, and set a ladder against the eaves. My intent was to clean the remaining debris from the chimney so I could restart the fire and thaw out the cabin. At minus ten degrees a cabin with its orifices open cools off remarkably fast.

I climbed the ladder and thrust the brush down the chimney, surprised at the ease of its passage. That fire had cleaned the chimney better than I ever did, and in less time.

"Chimney's clean," I said. Joan, watching from below while aiming her flashlight upward, just shook her head.

I descended the ladder, stomped through the soot-blackened snow, leaving white footprints as I went, and tracked more soot into the cabin. Scooping the ashes, soot, and partially burned, still-smoking firewood from the firebox, I dumped the hot debris into my coalscuttle and chucked the mess outside. I laid a new fire and lit it. The chimney drew as well as when new, and white smoke rose gently into the darkness, trailing toward the lake.

We ate breakfast while wearing parkas and bunny boots. If I didn't inhale too deeply the creosote odor was acceptable, especially if I kept my nose over my fresh cup of hot chocolate.

Joan said dryly, "You might consider cleaning the chimney more frequently."

"You know," I said, "that idea occurred to me while I was watching the fireworks. Strange you should think of it too."

"You're hopeless," she said, and began cleaning up the sooty mess around the stove.

The chimney fire taught me that woodstoves require a fair amount of attention when burning spruce twenty-four hours a day. I figured cleaning the chimney would be a better option than living in a tent in subzero cold while we built a new cabin. For the duration of our life in the bush, I climbed the ladder once a month during the winter and shoved a wire brush down the chimney. Now and then, when we toted the heavy wooden ladder through deep snow prior to one of my chimney-sweep stints, I lamented aloud that life seemed somehow less exciting without occasional bush fireworks.

Joan just shook her head.

Chinooks and Outhouses

Outhouses are small structures, normally designed like miniature cabins, depending on the whims and skills of the owner. They're functional, require little maintenance, and provide protection from mosquitoes, snowstorms, and—most of the time—from raindrops.

In summer, our outhouse never failed us. It sat there—silent, prepared to fulfill its purpose efficiently, a study in the conservation of energy. The screen door strained mosquitoes from the gentle breezes and sifted the sun's rays. Happiness is a warm outhouse seat.

Although an outhouse generally performs its mission without help from its owner, a judicious application of limestone at appropriate times, sifted just so into the dark void below, enhances visits to the facility, making the breezes pleasant. Breezes containing unlimed "essence of outhouse" tend to interfere with concentration on the scenery or other activities. Consequently, I regularly applied lime.

I located our outhouse so it faced a most impressive scene. Ravenhead Pond out front reflected craggy, towering peaks, and the outhouse, tucked among shaggy spruces, offered a visitor an unimpeded panorama of the reflection and the rugged mountains that lounged against the skyline.

A bit of birdseed in a container attached to the outside wall often attracted avian entertainment during a visit to the little house out back.

Then the sun began its retreat toward the southern horizon, dragging summer with it. The trip over the outhouse trail became a dash; the stay inside the shack abbreviated. Darkness required the use of a flashlight, and thoughts of prowling grizzlies added urgency to an already urgent mission. The wooden seat, as cold as the ambient temperature, was retired for the winter. A seat carved from a piece of Styrofoam, which instantly returned body heat, took its place.

The days shortened, the snows deepened, and I sculpted snow steps that led down from the deep, hard-packed snow surface to the level of the outhouse door. The outdoor facility protected us against the north winds and swirling snow during our essential visits.

Frost, that by-product of moisture and cold, began to build on the inside walls and underneath the roof as the winter progressed and temperatures dropped. One inch, a couple of inches, and soon a hoary wonderland surrounded visitors to the little house out back. Thousands of frost-crystal mirrors reflected the flashlight's beam, but the inadvertent brush of a parka sleeve against a wall triggered minor avalanches of frigid whiteness. Visitors easily brushed the fallen flake-like frost aside. All seemed well to the uninitiated.

Once or twice each winter the weather pattern changed. A chinook, or warm wind, blew up out of the Gulf of Alaska and flowed into the state's interior. Temperatures rose from subzero to above the freezing point. Most people welcomed the break from the severe cold. Outhouse users did not.

The frost that had glorified the outhouse interior now melted. Slowly, a drop at a time, each frost flake seemed to zero in on the current visitor at the most inappropriate moments. A rain suit would protect the guest, but it was inconvenient to add attire prior to an activity that often involves at least partially removing attire. Umbrellas in outhouses are impractical. So are ice skates. The floor, in contact with the frozen ground, instantly froze the drops, creating a skating rink, and fancy footwork was required at the "brink." Chopping at the ice with a shovel vibrated the structure, bringing down fresh torrents.

The paper, on a holder on the wall, became a useless, soggy mess. The solution was to place the roll under an inverted coffee can, and then listen to the erratic drips tunking onto the can like the offbeat offerings of a novice drummer in a bongo band. Our outhouse began to lose its appeal at that point.

When the chinook winds retreated, allowing the north winds to again pour arctic cold through passes in the Alaska Range, the frost returned, growing on the inner walls until arrival of the next chinook or spring breakup, whichever came first.

Perhaps our outhouse wasn't the perfect structure after all. Still, we paid no monthly sewer fee, unlike those who dwelt in cities and towns. A delightful view enhanced our daily rituals. And perhaps best of all, visitors were not apt to remain with us too long when chinook winds and melting frost dampened their, ah, spirits during their stay at our cabin.

Wheels, Skis, and Floats

I didn't know how to fly airplanes when we first moved to the bush. Before long I realized that, to see remote Alaska and enjoy all it had to offer, I needed an airplane and the skills to fly it. I bought a plane, a 1946 Taylorcraft, and hired a flight instructor. I drove to Anchorage, staying there for a week at a time while I took flight lessons. I flew twice a day for the week, an hour each time, then went home and hit the books for a week. I studied meteorology, principles of flight, flight rules and regulations, communications, and the multitude of things a pilot has to know to fly a plane safely and legally. After a week of intense study, I returned to Anchorage for another flying session.

I learned to fly in six weeks. Proud and happy after passing my private pilot's exam, I piloted my plane north from Anchorage. I expect Joan could see the smile on my face when I banked over the cabin prior to landing on the primitive dirt strip where I would tie down my plane. I only bounced twice on landing.

I roamed Alaska's skies, honing my flying skills and learning the many valleys, river drainages and mountain passes that became important checkpoints during my Alaska flying career. After I accumulated 200 hours in the air, I returned to Anchorage and learned, in a rented Cessna 172, to fly on instruments. I added that rating to my license and then passed the commercial pilot's exam. Although the Taylorcraft wasn't equipped with the proper instruments to fly in instrument weather conditions, I wanted to learn as much about flying as possible.

I practiced short-field landings and takeoffs at every opportunity. My skill increased rapidly as I landed on gravel bars, on frozen ponds little bigger than a puddle, and on tundra ridges far from any habitation. I reveled in the freedom that flying offered, and my spirits soared as high as the plane while I piloted the tiny T-Craft above the magnificent Alaska wilderness. Not even the time and cost of attending to the plane back on the ground could dampen my enthusiasm for bush flying.

Maintaining an airplane in the bush requires hard work and not a little ingenuity. Larry Draveling, an outstanding and ingenious mechanic who lived in Trapper Creek, fifty miles south of our cabin, performed the required annual inspections and other routine maintenance. However, other demands tested my patience and ate up a lot of my time.

At first I flew on wheels in the summer and on skis in the winter, but because we lived on a lake, I also wanted to fly on floats. Mechanics use a hoist to lift the plane from the ground while they remove the skis and install the floats. Alone and without a hoist, I couldn't change my plane from skis to floats, so I bought a second airplane, a 1941 Taylorcraft on floats.

Alaska pilots call Taylorcrafts, also known as T-Crafts or T-Crates, a "poor man's Super Cub." I bought the wheel plane for $5,000. I paid $11,000 for the floatplane. For a total of $16,000—the price, at that time, of a new, bare-bones pickup truck—I gained access to all of Alaska. Bargains like that don't appear often.

Close friends owned some vacant land about a mile from the cabin. Their property included a dirt airstrip, and I leased the primitive strip for all the years I flew in the bush. No words can express the gratitude I have for Charles and Pamela Towill, who owned the property. I built an eight-by-eight-foot fuel shed beside the airstrip, stained it a deep redwood, and installed an orange windsock on its roof. That small shack added a patch of color to the dirt-brown airstrip in summer, and bright relief from the solid white surface during the winter.

I hauled fuel to the site in fifty-five-gallon drums lashed to the sled towed behind my snowmachine. I used a hand-operated pump to slowly transfer the fuel to the plane's gas tanks, carefully straining the fuel through a chamois to remove any moisture or dirt that might contaminate the gasoline. At any temperature, moisture in fuel is dangerous. At subzero temperatures, frozen moisture in a carburetor or fuel line can be deadly.

In late September, when snow covered the dirt strip, I removed the T-Craft's wheels and installed skis. Unlike floats, skis and wheels could be swapped without a hoist. Once the ice had thickened to a foot or so, usually no later than early October, I moved the ski plane from the dirt landing strip to a tie-down on Colorado Lake behind the cabin. I flew from the lake's snow-packed surface all winter. In May, I reversed the process.

The floatplane floated beside our boat dock in summer, just a few steps from our cabin door. When freeze-up arrived, usually about mid-September, Joan and I used a come-along to winch the plane from the water. I tied the floatplane down on the shore, where the ice wouldn't crush the floats. We floated the airplane again when breakup ended, usually about the last week in May.

I cared for and flew my planes with little difficulty in the summer, but winter flying was a tough business. Before each flight, I had to remove the nylon wing covers that prevented frost and snow from sticking to the wings when my ski plane wasn't flying. Smaller covers protected its tail feathers, and a windscreen cover shielded the Plexiglas in the cockpit, and I removed those too. An insulated cowling cover prevented snow from sifting into the engine compartment, and I removed that cover after preheating the engine prior to starting it. Although the floatplane remained grounded in winter, the fabric was susceptible to snow and ice damage, so a similar arrangement protected that plane.

An hour or two of winter flying consumed most of a day. First, I had to shovel a ramp from the skis up onto the snow's surface so I could taxi out of the hole the plane sat in. Annual snowfall exceeded 200 inches, and I added to the already deep snow around the plane whenever I swept the wings and fuselage during and after each storm. Thus the need for a ramp.

Then, using my snowmachine, I packed a strip of snow on the lake to allow a shorter takeoff. Unpacked snow created so much drag on the skis that the takeoff run would require more than the available space. I had to lift off about halfway down the lake in order to clear the trees at the end. If we had had strong winds, which created frozen, hard-packed drifts, I had to shovel the highest drifts flat and fill in the hollows so I wouldn't damage the plane while bouncing along trying to get airborne.

I poured warm oil into a small generator, started it, and plugged a heater into the generator; the heater warmed the plane's engine. Then I poured warm engine oil into the plane's oil tank. The cowling cover retained the heat until I was ready to start the engine.

After I started the eighty-five-horsepower engine, a long warm-up prevented damage that could result if I applied full power to a cold engine. My breath would condense on the inside of the windscreen if I climbed aboard before the slightly warm engine air had defrosted the cold Plexiglas. Fifteen or twenty minutes after I started the engine I could finally crawl into the plane.

When flying in winter, I wore a RefrigiWear one-piece insulated suit over a goose-down vest on top of a wool shirt, which I donned after I put on my long johns. I tucked the wool shirt into my green wool Johnson pants, and shoved my wool-sock-covered feet into my bunny boots. My insulated hat, made of elk skin and trimmed with beaver fur, kept my head warm. I wore insulated gloves inside army surplus arctic mittens. If the weather wasn't too cold, say only zero or so, I kept the mittens on the seat beside me and wore only the gloves. Sunglasses protected my eyes from the weak winter sun's rays that reflected from wind-polished drifts and frozen waterfalls.

The plane's heater worked, but just barely. The doors fit loosely, and the wind whistled through the cracks around them—nature's air conditioning at subzero temperatures.

I carried a survival pack that consisted of, among other things, a goose down sleeping bag, freeze-dried food packets, a gas-operated backpacker stove, first-aid kit, bright orange signal panel, hatchet, shotgun, revolver, ammunition, fish line and hooks, flashlights and batteries, an extra down vest, wool shirt and socks, a tiny tent, a space blanket, a signal mirror, some candles and waterproof matches, and a cooking kit. Other odds and ends changed from summer to winter, but that basic load flew with me across Alaska no matter the season. I usually carried a granola bar or two in my pockets, along with some peanuts and a candy bar. If forced to land, I could survive until the search and rescue folks from Elmendorf Air Force Base found me. My battery-operated emergency locator beacon would lead them to my location. The signal activates automatically in a crash, or I could turn it on manually if I managed to make a good emergency landing in an open area. I was equipped to survive, summer or winter, although a winter emergency would have been a greater challenge.

Pallid daylight seeped through the cabin windows about 9:30 A.M. in December, but the reluctant sun didn't actually rise until 1:00 P.M. Its feeble rays then daubed the cabin wall for about twenty minutes before the sun surrendered to the cold and slunk back below the horizon. Twilight lasted longer, of course, giving me a flying window of perhaps four hours. Having spent a couple of hours getting the plane ready to fly, and allowing an hour on the end of the day to wrap things up again, I worked hard to fly for an hour or two. My midwinter flying became less frequent as the years passed.

After I landed from a winter flight, I drained the engine oil into a gallon plastic milk jug and carried it into my cabin where the oil remained warm until the next flight. I tied the plane down and reinstalled all the covers. While I flew, Joan, who hated to fly and called herself the ground crew, shoveled snow into the hole the plane had occupied, making a new, higher level to depart from next time. Otherwise, the hole would have been ten or more feet deep by spring. Some years I had to add extensions to my tie-down ropes so they would reach from the ground, up through the deep snow to the wing struts.

❰

Neither of my T-Crafts had electrical systems, and therefore lacked interior and exterior lights. Consequently, I made it a practice to land before darkness swallowed the last of the winter afternoon twilight. Usually.

I left Anchorage on a December afternoon, flying north on the return trip to our cabin, which normally took about two hours. I planned to arrive at the lake with perhaps a half hour of twilight remaining. Somewhere south of the village of Talkeetna my progress over the ground slowed to a creep. The engine ran fine, but I chugged along into an increasing headwind, chagrined to see cars below on the Parks Highway passing me and slowly widening their lead. A Volkswagen bug outdistancing my airplane was embarrassing. Furthermore, they had lights and I didn't.

At a bend in the Chulitna River that I dubbed Windy Corner, just north of Mary Carey's old McKinley View Lodge, violent winds slammed into my plane. The T-Crate shuddered and slowed to a ground speed slightly faster than that of a glacier. My left elbow banged against the door and I cinched my seatbelt tighter while I squinted at the ground in the gathering dusk to see if the plane was flying backward. Wind-lashed snow whipped along the frozen river. Landing on a wind-rumpled surface in darkness might not be a great idea.

My survival pack, stuffed with my sleeping bag and other emergency gear, rode in the space behind my seat. But the howling wind and the minus-twenty-degree temperature convinced me that a rough flight was preferable to landing and camping out. Adding to the shakes caused by the tossing plane, I shuddered at the thought of spending the night on the banks of the frozen river. The windchill factor was about seventy degrees below zero—a lousy night to sleep in a tent.

Soon I could no longer see the gauges on my instrument panel. Snow on the ground below reflected what little light existed, and the drifting, wind-driven ice crystals that raced south just above the frozen river gave me a rough idea of my altitude. I flew the plane low along the winding river, staying between the banks and below the treetops, attempting to avoid the worst of the wind that made my plane shake and quiver. Blood circulating through the veins of a hibernating bear probably moves faster than my Taylorcraft did against that headwind. Maintaining altitude and directional control was tough; I hauled and shoved on the yoke, rolled it left and right, walked on the rudders as if I were riding a bicycle, and pressed on.

Somewhere ahead, the river took a dogleg to the left. I would have to leave the river at that point, or else fly into a steep-sided, twisting chasm on the West Fork of the Chulitna River. A cliff rose from the river bottom at the dogleg.

I pulled a small flashlight from my plane's glove box while I bounced along in the turbulence, and then decided not to turn it on. I didn't want to lose my night vision. As long as the engine sounded OK and I could see the ground blizzard below, I didn't need to see the gauges. I knew that old plane so well that I could judge revolutions-per-minute by the sound of the reliable Continental eighty-five-horsepower engine.

I peered through the darkness, made out the cliff straight ahead, pulled back on the yoke and staggered upward and over the cliff against the north wind. Now I learned what it was like to ride a bull in a rodeo as I bucked and rambled through that frigid, dark sky. Below me, spruce trees bent and thrashed and strained to head south, their dark branches contrasting with the white, wind-driven snow. My old airplane quivered and trembled. Aside from combat, life doesn't get much more adrenaline-inducing.

Off to my right somewhere, the railroad tracks could lead me northward. I bounced sideways in that direction, spotted the straight white slash through the trees that indicated I had found the tracks, and felt a little more confident that I might even find our cabin.

Flying low enough to keep the tracks in sight, I rattled along in the arctic night, wondering if I could land the plane on drift-ragged Colorado Lake in the dark. That is, if I could find the lake.

When I arrived at a point that I figured was about five miles from our property, I left the railroad tracks, flew across the trees at low level, and spotted a pinprick of light no bigger than a distant star, winking through the wind-whipped trees off to my right. The propane lamps in our cabin cast a dim glow onto the snow, giving me an aiming point. I flew toward it.

On the lake, near the beaver dam, stood a beaver lodge, a prominently visible mound summer and winter. In the dark, it blended into the faint whiteness below and I couldn't see it. I needed to land just to the left of the lodge, on the main part of the lake. If I landed too far past it, I was in danger of flying into trees at the far end of the lake, or else getting stuck in unpacked snow and facing the tough chore of digging out the next day. Slamming into the lodge itself was another concern.

I buzzed the cabin, and my savvy wife knew exactly what to do. While I circled, fighting the wind and wondering if I could land the plane under such conditions, dim light splashed onto the snow at the back of our cabin. The pale glow disappeared as the door closed, and then light from a bobbing headlamp wandered across the snow, stopped, and jerked back and forth a few times. Joan was pulling on the snowmachine starter rope. The snowmachine headlight shot a light beam across the backyard, and then the light began bouncing through the trees and onto the lake. I circled, watching.

Joan drove her machine down the lake, circled around below the beaver lodge, and stopped. She had aimed the machine so its headlight illuminated the lodge and the beginning of my snowmachine-packed runway. Now I had a spot of light to aim for, although the light dimmed and flared as the wind-driven snow crystals swept through the light beam.

I flew downwind beyond the lake and turned into the wind, straining to see the airspeed indicator on the instrument panel. No other instrument was critical at this stage of the landing process, but I had to verify that my airspeed was higher than the stalling speed of the plane. For a safety margin, I had to maintain a little higher speed than normal as a cushion against a sudden drop in wind velocity.

I held my tiny flashlight in my mouth, controlled the yoke with my mitten-covered left hand, and adjusted the throttle with my right. The plane descended over the trees, bounced down through the gusts, skimmed over the beaver dam, and touched down beyond the beaver lodge, just past the spot of light Joan had provided. She realized that I couldn't see to taxi, so she gunned the snow-machine after I landed and pulled up on my right side, just off the wingtip, lighting the way to my parking place. I taxied to my tie-down ropes and shut down the engine. My T-Crate had brought me home, and my wife had brought me down safely.

Joan ran over and held the upwind wing while I attached a rope to it, then she tied the tail while I ran around and tied the other wing to the ground anchor on that side. I shouted into that shrieking wind: "Forget the wing covers! I'll put them on tomorrow."

"OK!" She handed me an empty plastic one-gallon jug.

I drained the engine oil into the container and, half frozen, we leaned into the screaming wind as Joan's headlamp lighted the way to the cabin. Even after I thawed out next to the woodstove, my legs still shook. With a cup of hot chocolate in one hand and my other arm around my ground crew, I began to relax.

"You're late. How was the flight?" Joan said, looking at me with a skeptical half grin.

"Not boring," I said. "Not boring at all."

☾

I killed a large bull moose early one September afternoon on a lake about twelve miles from our cabin. I butchered it, put the quarters and other parts into game bags, and began ferrying the meat home, a process that required five trips in my little float-equipped Taylorcraft.

On the final trip, I loaded the last of the moose into the airplane and swung the prop to start the engine. Enough twilight remained so I could easily fly home with that load and land before full dark. However, my trusty T-Craft chose that moment to balk.

When the airplane engine cooled to a temperature about halfway between normal operating temperature and a cold engine, a condition known as vapor lock could develop. It seldom happened, but now, when I was in a hurry, vapor lock blocked my attempts to start the engine. With a plane full of meat and a grizzly family that I'd spotted earlier still in the area, I wanted out of there as fast as possible.

Sweat dripped from my nose and chin while I hand-propped the engine, and gas dripped from the carburetor, splashing into the lake. Frustrated, tired, worried about the gathering darkness and the grizzlies, I had to force myself to wait and let the flooded carburetor drain. I spun the prop backward, a standard procedure when vapor lock occurs, and then sat, nervously listening and watching for bears while I waited for the gas vapor to dissipate. The nearby gut pile from the moose filled the air with the scent of blood and meat.

An hour later, after several failed tries to start the engine and long after dark had consumed the twilight, the engine sputtered to life and I scrambled aboard, looking ahead down the lake at a glassy water condition. I circled to make waves, which would help break the suction that occurs when floats skim across ripple-free water. I had a heavy load aboard and wanted to get off the water quickly since I couldn't see the end of the lake in the darkness.

I took off without difficulty, gained enough altitude to avoid any hills en route, and soon spotted Colorado Lake glinting slightly in the distance. My landing direction was optional in the no-wind condition, and I circled once to see which way favored a glassy-water landing in the dark without a landing light.

Landing on smooth water in daylight is tricky; night landings without lights can be a nightmare. In daylight, a pilot looks down at the lake and sees the sky reflected in the water, a condition that makes it difficult to determine the plane's altitude above the surface. I always approached glassy water in the daytime by landing close to the shore and using my peripheral vision to see the shoreline, which gave me an idea of how high I was above the water's surface. At night, that option disappeared along with the daylight.

As I circled, Joan realized my problem and rushed to the dock. She grabbed an oar from our rowboat and began to slap the water, creating ripples that broke up the mirror image of the night sky. I decided to approach from the north, descended over the trees, and landed on the ripples.

Once again, my favorite ground crew had assisted me to a safe landing. We had never discussed night glassy-water landings, but my occasional comments about the difficulty of no-wind landings on water stuck with her, and she responded perfectly.

"Where've you been?" she asked as I stepped from the plane onto the dock. "You really had me worried this time."

"Vapor lock. Couldn't start the damned engine." I explained the situation while we tied the plane to the dock. "Thanks for the ripples, Ground Crew," I said.

Joan stuck her tongue out at me as she handed me a cold Pepsi.

☾

A fist of wind clobbered my airplane like a punch from a heavyweight boxer. My tiny Taylorcraft staggered sideways and then dropped in a sickening plunge that left my stomach floating somewhere above me. In the sudden weightlessness, my feet vaulted from the rudder pedals and my knees smashed against the underside of the instrument panel. The plane shuddered, bounced, then shot upward, jamming me into the seat. I shoved the yoke forward to stop my ascent, but the vertical speed indicator slid off the upper end of the scale. Within seconds, the plane reversed itself again, plunging like a meteorite. I yanked my seat belt even tighter, grateful for an empty bladder.

Before the wind slapped me, I had been navigating across the sprawling Susitna River basin in calm conditions, en route to Susitna Lake after setting up a remote hunting camp on a small lake in the heart of caribou country. My hunting partner, Scott Coonce, was waiting for me to pick him up at Susitna Lake, just off the Denali Highway. That dusty gravel road wriggled across the tundra a few miles ahead of me. I would soon land on the lake and then fly my friend to our remote campsite.

Without warning, this violent windstorm had roared out of some remote mountain pass, pummeling my two-seater plane and shocking me out of my daydreams. Called williwaws, these sudden, intense winds swoop out of nowhere. The unwelcome blasts are more common along the mountainous coast of Alaska, but interior mountains spawn williwaws too.

The williwaw now tossed my plane around the way rumbling rapids hurl a raft from wave to wave. Ahead, whitecaps roiled the surface of Susitna Lake. Scott hunched beside his vehicle, facing away from the stinging, wind-driven spray. I had no way to communicate with him and tell him to move to Swampbuggy Lake, about five miles away. The rugged shoulders of the mountains sheltered that small lake from the williwaw.

The wind screamed down the length of Susitna Lake, piling waves against the western shore. Since the wind wasn't whipping across the narrow lake, I decided I could land without too much difficulty. However, directional control would be dicey after I landed. Controlling a light airplane on the water in a fierce wind is akin to convincing a salmon to swim downstream to spawn. If Scott hadn't been waiting there I'd have returned to my campsite, but, like the salmon, my mind was made up.

I yo-yoed past the lake, banked sharply into the wind and set up for a landing. My plane flopped like a Slinky unwinding down a staircase as it bounced ever lower on final approach. When it plopped onto the waves, I stomped the right rudder pedal to the floor in an effort to turn downwind and taxi toward Scott. The plane nearly capsized when, broadside to the wind, one wing lifted. I regained control when the gust eased, but I couldn't turn the plane downwind. It nosed into the wind and stubbornly remained in that posture.

I gave up, allowing the plane to drift backward, rolling with the waves like a seagull on the ocean. Because of the galloping wind gusts, I couldn't beach the plane where I intended. Instead, I drifted farther to the right, into a cluster of alder bushes and a collection of beaver cuttings. These cuttings, the sharp, pointed ends of stumps that beavers leave when they cut down small trees, become rigid spears that can stab a plane's thin aluminum floats.

As I approached the shore, I leaped onto the left float and then jumped into the knee-deep water, grabbing the wing strut to keep the aircraft from being blown over backwards. The gusts must have been fifty miles an hour—more than ten miles an hour above minimum flying speed for my plane. Another gust roared through, lifting the front of the floats completely out of the water. The soles of my boots were a foot above the surface by the time the gust passed. The plane plopped back onto the water.

"Scott!" I yelled. "Come grab the other wing strut quick, or we're going to lose her."

He sloshed to the opposite side of the T-Craft and clamped his arms around the strut just as another violent gust hit us. This time the wind lifted the plane and both of us before letting us all splash back onto the lake. "Damn!" Scott shouted, a surprised look on his face.

"Throw your hunting gear into the plane while I hang on," I yelled against the shrieking wind. "Then drive your truck down the road about five miles to Swampbuggy Lake. It's relatively calm. I'll fly your gear to our camp and then pick you up at that lake."

"OK," Scott yelled, and began stuffing his hunting gear into the back of the wildly tossing plane.

I couldn't swing the propeller and hold onto the strut at the same time, so I clambered aboard. "Scott, prop her for me," I said. He swung the prop, the engine caught, and, as soon as Scott stumbled sideways out of the plane's path, I applied takeoff power. I wanted to get out of those alders and beaver cuttings as soon as possible.

In that ferocious wind the plane came up onto the step—planed across the water—almost instantly. I applied left aileron to roll the plane onto the left float, which was my normal takeoff routine. That maneuver reduces the drag on one float, and the plane flies more quickly. This time it didn't work.

The right float refused to come out of the water, and the wind propelled me toward the tree-lined southern shore. I had applied maximum power, but the plane wouldn't fly. I stomped fully on the left rudder pedal, worked the ailerons and pulled back on the yoke, hoping I could get off the water and clear the trees. The plane would smash into the trees if it remained on the water. It might crash into them even if it flew. Either result would wreck the plane, but at least I had a chance to save the plane if I could make it fly.

By now I knew I my right float contained water, which is why I couldn't roll the plane onto the left float. I gave up on that maneuver, applied full left rudder to maintain direction against the wind, and hauled back on the yoke one final time. If the plane didn't fly now it would collide with the trees.

The plane popped off the water at the last possible second and rocketed upward against the williwaw winds. My right wingtip barely cleared the trees. Because I wanted to climb quickly as an altitude cushion against the sudden downdrafts, I applied more back-pressure to the yoke than normal, forcing the plane into a maximum rate of climb. Right then the wind died.

There I was, about 250 feet above the ground, nose pointed skyward, and just hanging there on the prop. I needed all the wind over the wings I could get, but the wind decided to take a break. The plane did what planes do when asked to fly and there isn't enough airspeed over the wings. It stalled.

When a plane stalls under full power, the stall turns violent. That's what happened to me.

The plane whipped to the left and dropped like an avalanche roaring down a mountain, leaving every loose item in the cockpit and baggage compartment floating in the air. Gravity took over again, and everything behind my seat rushed to join me up front. Scott's duffel bag crashed against the back of my head, driving me forward against my shoulder harness. My rifle slid under the panel and tangled with my feet on the rudder pedals. A waterproof bag landed in my lap between the yoke and my chest, interfering with my ability to operate that control. In a steep dive, staring at the rushing ground and fighting with wayward baggage, I wondered how to get out of this predicament alive. If my life passed before me, it was in a hell of a hurry and I missed it.

Gravity yanked the plane toward the tundra, but I felt some response when I pulled back ever so lightly on the yoke. I had chopped power when the plane slammed into the stall, and now I had to be sure I had enough flying speed to regain control of the plane. If I pulled the yoke back too quickly, the plane would stall again, and that would be fatal at this low altitude. A gust hit the plane. This one I welcomed.

I eased the yoke back and the plane recovered from its dive about ten feet above the ground. I jammed the throttle fully forward while I increased backpressure on the controls, and the plane climbed. The wind-lashed willows below me shook only slightly more than my knees did.

A small hill rose above the east end of the lake. When the plane stalled and dove toward the ground, it disappeared behind the hill, out of Scott's line of vision. He told me later he thought I had gone straight in, crashing and killing myself. Suddenly he saw the plane rise above the hill and keep on climbing, turning away from him and disappearing to the west. He drove down the road to Swampbuggy Lake.

I sorted out the mess in the cockpit and began breathing somewhat normally again, still fighting the turbulence but feeling more confident as I increased my distance from the heart of that williwaw. Soon I flew in calm conditions, landed a half hour later, and taxied to shore near our campsite.

I carried Scott's equipment to my tent and then conducted a careful airplane inspection, saving the floats for last. The wings, tail, and fuselage passed inspection. I opened the hatch covers and checked each float compartment. Water completely filled one compartment in the right float. A beaver-chewed willow stub had poked a pencil-sized hole in the bottom. I pumped the water out with my hand pump, shrugged at the small fountain bubbling in from the bottom of the float, closed the hatch cover, started the engine, and took off.

Scott waited at Swampbuggy Lake. I landed, coasted to the shore near Scott, and shut down the engine. "Here," I said as I handed him my hand-operated pump. "How about pumping out the second compartment on the right float?"

"OK," he said, and pumped water from the leaky float compartment, propped the engine, and scrambled aboard. I had to get airborne fast before the float filled with water again. The takeoff was uneventful.

At our campsite, we made two patches, using the leather from my hatchet sheath. Scott poked a hole through the leather patches, placed one on the outside of the hole in the float, and put the other over the hole on the inside of the compartment.

"Lee, how about running that small bolt through the leather washers and through the hole in the float? I'll put a nut on the threads from the inside." I complied, and Scott tightened the nut with a wrench.

Scott, a pilot who had been wounded while flying helicopters in Vietnam, said while we worked, "I thought you'd crashed for sure on that takeoff at Susitna Lake. Good job recovering from that stall."

"Yeah, thanks. If I'd crashed, you'd have had no way to get out here. So I pulled out of the dive just for you."

"I appreciate that. Now let's hunt caribou."

The patch held perfectly two days later while I made the five trips necessary to fly our camping gear and the meat from two caribou out to Swampbuggy Lake.

☾

As time went by, I found myself flying more on floats and skis, until one day I realized I hadn't landed on wheels in more than three years. The scores of lakes and rivers within my plane's range made floats my choice in summer. If I went lake fishing, I simply landed, taxied to the upwind end of the lake, and shut off the engine. I stood on the floats while casting for fish, letting the breeze drift me to the opposite end of the lake while my thoughts drifted to bygone years.

Vietnam intruded less frequently as the years accumulated. I learned, with time, that none of my anguish could bring back the men killed alongside me in combat. The demands of bush living shoved Vietnam aside, leaving room for healing. The nightmares, less frequent now, retreated to a hidden place, emerging rarely. Drifting and pondering gave me time to realize that I had truly survived and shouldn't feel guilty because of it.

After drifting with the breeze to the downwind end of the lake, I started the engine and taxied back to the distant shore and drifted again. Depending on which lake I fished, lake trout, grayling, rainbow trout, and red salmon chased after my flies and lures. If the fish weren't biting at one lake, I took off and flew to another one. If I spotted people fishing on a lake, I took care not to fly directly over them. I enjoyed the solitude of fishing Alaska's lakes and figured others did too. I never landed on a lake where others were fishing.

Lake landings were routine, but river landings required a different technique. I preferred landing pointed upstream, against the current, but the prevailing wind didn't always allow that. I didn't need as much room when landing upstream because the current slowed me quickly after I touched down. Downstream landings took up lots of river.

Taking off was even more difficult. Hand propping the engine while standing on the floats, then scrambling aboard as the plane started downriver with the current, kept me agile. Once inside the plane, I had to grab the yoke, place my feet on the rudders, shove the throttle forward, and control the plane against the rambling current while I buckled my seat belt and shoulder harness. I preferred to take off pointed downriver, using the added force of the current to accelerate quickly to flying speed. Takeoffs against the current took longer.

If I flew my wheel plane, I landed on gravel bars beside fish-laden pools. I usually buzzed the adjacent forest before I landed, hoping to shoo away any fishermen who wore black or tan fur coats. I shared a gravel bar with a bear only once, and he came out of the woods after I had fished there for half an hour. The black bear grumbled some when he saw me at his favorite fishing hole. I understood his complaint; we both preferred solitude. I shouted at him, and he trotted off into the brush. I gathered my five silver salmon and left. The fishing hole belonged to him, not to me.

I caught some mighty fine fish in the rivers, primarily grayling, silver salmon, char, and chum salmon, so flying onto and off rivers provided us with most of our fish for canning and smoking. For immediate eating, I fished the local river and lake, a simple matter of walking to the bank and casting a fly or spinner. But I never passed up the chance to fly and fish, which combined two of my favorite pastimes.

Northwinds

When we moved to the bush, we couldn't communicate with the rest of the world. That didn't bother us at first, but one incident convinced us we needed a way to listen to radio newscasts. We drove to nearby Cantwell on one of our infrequent trips for mail, and the postmaster said, "Isn't it a shame about President Reagan being shot?"

We knew nothing about the assassination attempt. We owned a battery-operated AM radio, so I tried to devise an antenna that would receive the Anchorage and Fairbanks stations; my effort failed.

During our next trip to Anchorage, I walked into a Radio Shack. I explained my problem and described our geographical location to the manager, who promptly handed me a two-inch-thick plastic disk, about the size of a dinner plate, which he said was an antenna. A knob as big around as the bottom of a Pepsi can protruded from the center of the device, surrounded by a dial with numbers that corresponded to radio frequencies.

He said, "Try this. I sold it to a man who lives in Glennallen, but he returned it because it didn't work there. It may or may not work at your location. If it doesn't, throw it away. If it does, and if you happen to think of it, drop a check in the mail when it's convenient."

I wondered how many merchants in other states would be as trusting to a stranger who lived 200 miles away and lacked a telephone or street address.

I took it home, tried it, and it worked. I sat down right then and wrote a check and a thank-you note, and we were back in touch with the outside world. Now we could receive messages, even if we couldn't send them.

Although some remote cabin dwellers owned generators and used powerful single side band radios to call a telephone operator to request a "phone patch," many cabins, such as ours, had neither two-way radios nor electricity. The battery-operated AM radio became the only communication link with so-called civilization. It enabled us to receive messages from friends and loved ones, such as this one:

"To Lee and Joan at Colorado Lake: Please bring your income tax statement on your next trip to town. I need it for my student loan application. From Lorraine."

That message from our daughter, sent without charge over a commercial Anchorage AM radio station, typified the messages city residents sent to their relatives and friends who lived in the bush.

Our favorite Anchorage radio station, KHAR, broadcast messages to the bush on its *Northwinds* program at 7:05 P.M. daily, and repeated the messages two hours later. Because of the flexibility of our bush lifestyle, Joan and I didn't follow any schedule; *Northwinds* was the only exception. Joan timed our evening meal to coincide with the news, followed by the messages. If we happened to have guests, all conversation ceased while we listened to the *Northwinds* program. Even when the northern lights created static, we listened to *Northwinds*.

The daily messages featured drama, comedy, tragedy, birth announcements, and more. We never met most of the participants, but we anxiously followed each episode to its conclusion. We heard frustrated wives, in town shopping, query husbands at home in the bush about chain saw model numbers, snowmachine repair parts, and valves for propane tanks. Other messages asked for help from neighbors: "Please feed the dogs; we're weathered in and can't fly home" or "I forgot your wolverine pelt; please send it in on the next mail plane."

Bush residents received warnings, such as, "I hit overflow on the way out and recommend that you use the north trail." When bush rats reached town safely on a resupply trip, they informed family members and friends who remained in the bush. On Mondays, "Thanks for a wonderful weekend; we made it home safely" was a common message.

One year we followed the plight of a bush dweller who had stabbed himself in the eye while skinning an animal. Another time, we thought a boatload of plywood never would reach its destination. It finally arrived, but we followed every agonizing delay caused by bad weather and repeated equipment failure.

Promise of a job, prices received for furs, medical reports on sick relatives in the Lower 48, birthday wishes, and death notifications all reached remote locations via the radio.

Other radio stations in Anchorage offered a similar service—*Bush Pipeline* on KYAK was one. And radio stations in other Alaska locations broadcast messages in their listening areas. *Caribou Clatters* and *Trapline Chatter* were the names of two of the message programs.

Even inhabitants of bush villages depended on radio messages. Government agencies sometimes informed villagers of impending visits by staff members. "To the residents of Tyonek: The Fish and Game representative will be there from 10:00 until 2:00 on Thursday."

Although official agencies occasionally used the service, the guidelines for sending messages prohibited commercial messages. The rules required the text to be brief, reasonably important, not slanderous, and subject to editing by the radio station staff. Most stations accepted either phoned-in or mailed messages. Deadlines varied, but submitting your message an hour or two prior to the scheduled program usually ensured that the message would be broadcast that day.

Satellites now make access to telephones more commonplace. And the ubiquitous cell phone has changed communications in the bush forever. Still, where cell phones don't work, some bush residents rely on the few remaining stations that broadcast messages to bush locations.

We sent and received free messages for several years, and we're grateful to the radio stations that provided such an outstanding service. Here's our final message to those stations: "From Joan and Lee, formerly of Colorado Lake: A heartfelt thank-you for your services."

☾

When I began flying from Colorado Lake I could see the local weather, but I couldn't find out what the weather was like where I was going. An FAA remote repeating transmitter, located ten miles north of us, at the Broad Pass dirt airstrip, broadcast a weather summary, but to hear it I had to start the plane, take off, and fly up that way. The small, battery-operated radio in my plane had only a five-mile transmitting and receiving range. I decided I needed a telephone at the cabin so I could get weather reports.

An old, bare copper telegraph wire, which the Alaska Railroad used for years before dispatchers began communicating with trains by radio, still stretched between telegraph poles along the railroad tracks about a mile from our cabin. I contacted the Matanuska Telephone Association to inquire about getting phone service to our property. The phone technicians were not sure if there was sufficient power to communicate over the twenty-five miles of bare wire between the central office in Cantwell and our property, but they were willing to try. They installed a device called a CM-8 on one of the telegraph poles, connecting it by telephone cable to the overhead bare wire. Running the cable from the pole through the woods to our property was my responsibility.

On a minus-eighteen-degree December day, with the north wind hurling ice crystals in stinging clouds and lowering the windchill factor to sixty below, I started stringing the cable. Wind-driven snow ghosts slithered across the lake and swirled around me.

I hauled the cable from the cabin, trudging through the trees along the isthmus between the lake and pond. By mounting the huge telephone cable reel on a pair of sawhorses next to my cabin, using a steel pipe as an axle, I could drag the cable behind me while I plodded through the woods on snowshoes. The reel turned freely on its axle, but I retraced my steps many times to untangle the cable from branches and brush. I tugged it across the beaver dam, then wove through more trees until I reached the railroad tracks and the telegraph pole. Then I retraced my steps and hung the wire high enough in the trees so animals and snowmachiners wouldn't become entangled in it. I fought my way up through tangles of spruce branches, climbing numerous trees while the bitter wind poured into my parka hood and down my collar. The entire process took two days.

I installed a telephone in the cabin and connected it to the cable. Then I contacted the phone company from a phone in Cantwell, and the dispatcher sent a lineman to connect my cable to their equipment on the pole. I met him at the highway and, using my snowmachine, transported him and his equipment to the work site. In short order we talked with our daughter in Anchorage via our new telephone.

We experienced lots of problems with the phone, but the phone company always responded quickly, summer or winter, and never complained about the challenge of maintaining my line. The phone company's responsibility ended at the pole; consequently, I learned a lot about tracing and repairing telephone cable along the mile between the telegraph pole and our cabin. I owned a portable telephone test set, which was actually a special phone with alligator clips on the ends of its wires, and used it to trace problems in my cable. I usually was able to repair problems without contacting the phone company.

One day, while clinging to the telegraph pole several feet above the ground next to the railroad tracks, the test set rang. I had just completed another repair, and my test set was still alligator-clipped to the cable. I answered and found myself talking to Joan's sister, calling from California. She wanted to visit us, we agreed on a date, and I hiked back to the cabin.

"Joan," I said, "I told Martha that July 9 would be a good time to come for a visit." She looked at me strangely, as if she couldn't believe what she thought she heard, and said, "What are you talking about?" I had a hard time convincing her that I had talked to her sister while I clung to a pole a mile from the cabin.

One winter the line failed, and the repairman convinced himself the problem was in my stretch of wire. It wasn't, but we didn't learn that until after breakup. Nevertheless, I climbed all of those trees again and lowered every inch of that mile-long cable, searching for a possible break. I couldn't find any indication of a break, so the repairman gave me a mile of extremely light wire as a substitute. I ran that wire on top of the snow, thus restoring my phone service until summer, when he would repair the regular cable. Although passing animals broke the wire several times, I spliced the breaks, reconnecting us with the outside world.

In the spring, the lineman made a permanent repair to the regular cable where it attached to the pole—that is, as permanent as repairs ever got out there—but I left my stretch of cable on the ground instead of attaching it high in the trees like before.

A couple of days later, the phone again went out of service. I traced the wire and soon found the problem. A beaver, either annoyed that I'd run a wire across his dam, or perhaps thinking a new type of stick had fallen on top of the structure, chomped through the insulation in several places. I repaired it, only to have him bite through it again several days later. After making a few unkind remarks about the beaver's ancestry, I again made the necessary splices.

I mentioned the beaver the next time I saw the repairman. He said he'd heard about some strange causes of phone line failure, but this was the first time he'd heard of a beaver biting through one. He enjoyed telling that story to his fellow workers.

The consideration the Matanuska Telephone Association gave us deserves special mention. I doubt if any phone company in the Lower 48 would have even attempted to provide us phone service under such remote, difficult conditions. The engineers, the repairmen, and the dispatchers who received my requests for repair service were cheerful and responsive, willing to do whatever it took to support their customers. Without their concern and assistance, our communicating from the bush would have been much more difficult.

Alaska Morning

I guided my plane toward home, swooping low over Curry Ridge, a mosaic of rounded peaks and narrow tablelands that rise above the Susitna River north of the small town of Talkeetna. Although spring had arrived, snowdrifts rimmed some of the ponds below me like windrows of sheep's wool. Mount McKinley, ghost-like in the morning twilight, filled my left window with its massive bulk.

Thirty miles to the north a tiny silver boomerang sliced through black spruces. The boomerang—Colorado Lake—reflected the expanding dawn of an Alaska morning. I would soon land on its surface and join Joan in our cabin for breakfast.

After a week in Anchorage attending an Alaska Board of Game meeting, I looked forward to returning to the simpler life. As chairman of the Denali Fish and Game Advisory Committee, I presented the opinions of our region's residents to the board. A week of listening to public testimony and speaking on behalf of my committee had drained me. Facing crowds of contentious Alaskans, plus small crowds of Outsiders clamoring for local media attention—each group pursuing its special interest—was tiresome.

The coffee I had drunk before takeoff demanded release, so I decided to land, take a leak, and unwind before continuing the flight to my cabin. I swooped low around one of the ponds, looking for debris on or in the water. Beaver cuttings and other hazards in remote ponds and lakes await the unwary pilot. Damaged floats out here would mean a long walk.

I scanned the surrounding hills for bears. Alaskans say "meaner than a spring bear" for a reason. When a bear emerges from its den in spring, it hasn't eaten for many months. Until it kills a moose or digs up some roots to start replenishing its severe weight loss, a bear is apt to be cantankerous. I preferred to avoid spring bears.

Pleased at the lack of bears and floating debris, I banked my Taylorcraft into a tight turn to line up with the pond's long axis, leveled out, and prepared to land.

My plane touched the pond, skimmed across the surface like a skipping stone, slowed, and settled onto its floats. I shut off the engine and coasted to shore, rocking gently on waves my landing created. An easy jump from the left float landed me on the grassy bank.

Alder clusters crowded the shore on either side of the clearing and grew in jumbled clumps around the pond. The smell of damp, decaying leaves rose from the thickets. Diminishing ripples chuckled against the floats. Silence, having fled as I circled and landed, sneaked back into the scoop-shaped basin.

I looped my tie-down rope over the cleat on the right float, tied the other end to a nearby alder, and then reached into the plane's cargo compartment. I retrieved my shotgun from my survival pack in case any spring bears lurked in the bushes.

The rising sun splashed its salmon-colored rays onto Mount McKinley. Across the pond, most of the mountain's bulk was screened by the low hills, but the glowing, sunlit peak seemed to perch on the small hill that rose from the pond's edge.

I ran up the steep hillside as fast as possible, seeking a better look at the mountain before the glow faded in the morning's increasing brightness. Alders that grew helter-skelter clawed at me, their branches tangled and partly flattened by heavy winter snows.

I finally broke free of the tangled bushes and climbed from spongy tundra onto a wheelbarrow-sized boulder, crushing lichens under my boots. The spring smells of emerging growth, pungent yet subtle, enveloped me. I turned to look at the mountain, eager to see its profile in the rising sun.

Mount McKinley—Denali, the centerpiece of the Alaska Range—towered above me, piercing the cobalt-blue sky. The shoulders and peak of that mighty mountain looked sharp, the peak wind-honed to the keenness of a skinning knife. Now the color of a pink rose petal, the mountain was the center of a surrealistic scene. Denali radiated light as if a flood lamp deep within it had been switched on. Lesser snow-capped peaks lounged in the foreground, still untouched by the sunlight. Their darker silhouettes contrasted with the highest peak in North America, framing the mountain at its base and sides as if respectfully deferring to Denali—The High One. I stood there—alone, silent, insignificant.

The silence and solitude of that wilderness scene expelled the tensions of the past week, renewing my energy, restoring my inner balance. The mountains presented a timeless, humbling reminder of my brief presence on this earth. The issues I had argued during my week in Anchorage meeting rooms shrank to their appropriate size. I hardly dared to think for fear of disturbing the silence.

Splashing sounds interrupted my musings. I looked down at the pond to see an otter family hunting for breakfast. They battled through the alders on shore, first diving under partly submerged branches, then clambering ashore awkwardly to thread their way among the snarl of bushes. Their search for food reminded me that breakfast awaited at my cabin.

Looking up at Denali once more, I attempted to recapture the incredible serenity I felt when I had first seen the glowing mountain and its subdued guardians, but the fleeting moment was now a memory. Denali's rosy hue had faded to white and, although still impressive, the mountain now melded into the Alaska Range, prominent but not dominating. The subordinate peaks acquired their own blush from the rising sun's rays, but the higher sun angle subdued the color. The huge mountain had swiped most of the pink tones from the sun's palette, leaving little rouge for the rest of the range. I climbed down from the rock.

Slowly, I picked my way back through the alders to my airplane. The otters spotted me and porpoised across the pond to investigate. Unafraid, they paddled to within a few feet and chittered, discussing my presence. Their brown heads and whiskered faces reminded me of little old men having a chat to pass the time on a spring morning. Even when I spoke to them, wishing them luck in finding food, they remained unconcerned. The four of them soon tired of inspecting this intruder and resumed their hunt along the shoreline.

I untied the plane and climbed into the cockpit, relaxed and renewed. I waved to the otters as I lifted off into that deep blue sky, and nodded at Denali out my left window. All was well with the otters, the mountain, and me as I turned toward home.

Sliding Bears

"Aren't you afraid of the bears?" many people asked when inquiring about our bush lifestyle. We encountered bears occasionally during the warmer months, but we didn't fear them; we respected them. Nevertheless, when I observed a bear from my airplane I felt much more relaxed than when I faced one on the ground.

The power and stamina of bears, both blacks and grizzlies, is astonishing. One day, while flying in the vicinity of the Dunkle Hills area of Denali National Park and Preserve, I popped over the top of a 6,000-foot snow-capped peak at the head of Costello Creek. Movement on the steep mountainside across the deep valley that cleaved Easy Pass caught my attention. Curious, I pointed the plane's nose in that direction and soon identified a small band of caribou running up a ridge that led to the crest. I wondered why caribou would run up a mountain. Caribou are stupid, but they don't run straight up a mountainside without a reason.

A series of ridges descended from the mountain peak, like fingers extended from a hand pointed toward the ground. Deep draws, eaten into the mountain by melting snow and summer rains, separated the ridges. Clumps of brushy shrubs clung to the sides of the draws, but caribou moss and sparse grass were the primary vegetation. No trees grew on the rocky ridges.

I discovered why the caribou were headed uphill. A chocolate-brown grizzly loped up the spine of that ridge behind the band of twelve cows and calves. The hump at his shoulders rocked forward and back as his muscles propelled him. He didn't push himself; he just maintained a steady pace, probably confident that he would soon dine on caribou.

One of the cows darted away from the band and down into a draw. Perhaps an injury slowed her, although she didn't limp or stumble. Perhaps parasites or lung problems affected her breathing and she couldn't keep pace with the others. Perhaps she was old, had no calf to protect, and simply wanted to get away from that bear. Whatever her motivation, she made the wrong decision.

The grizzly didn't see her leave the group, but when he came abreast of her location he either heard or smelled her and instantly shifted gears. He charged down into the draw, and the cow bolted up onto the ridge. She reached the ridgetop in three or four seconds and dashed down the spine, directly away from the caribou above her. The bear bounded out of the draw. His powerful body rippled under his dark brown fur, which quivered each time his feet struck the ground. The grizzly caught up to the cow in less than one hundred yards, leaped onto her back, and she collapsed under him. Together they skidded several more yards downhill. With three massive bites to the neck, he killed her.

I circled above, watching the action. I figured the bear would now settle down for a meal of caribou steaks and chops. Instead, that big bear clamped onto the cow's neck and began carrying the carcass to the valley floor. The front two-thirds of the caribou dangled and bobbed above the ground, with only the hindquarters dragging. The bear's display of strength amazed me. I don't know why he didn't eat the caribou where he caught her. Maybe he wanted take-out food.

☾

I once saw a grizzly attack a moose. The broad valley between the peaks of the Alaska Range and the Talkeetna Mountains is good bear habitat. The wild, rugged mountains offer excellent denning sites, and the lower, brush-covered knees of the high peaks provide good cover for bears. The willows scattered along the river bottoms serve as fair moose habitat, and bears are attracted to that moose hangout.

One early spring, snow smothered the area. Many of the alders and willows had disappeared under the six or more feet of accumulated snow, and visibility was excellent, both on the ground and from the air. Willows poked above the surface among scattered spruce trees, providing enough cover for a grizzly to stalk a young moose.

I flew overhead just as a medium-sized grizzly charged a yearling moose. The moose never had a chance in the deep snow. The bear leaped onto his back, the moose collapsed, and the grizzly started eating, tearing chunks of hide and meat from the moose's back while the suffering animal tried to crawl out from under the bear. After several minutes, the bear bit deep into the moose's neck and killed it. I turned away from the gruesome scene and flew off to piece together the story by looking at the tracks.

The grizzly tracks told me that the bear had stalked the moose for several hundred yards, probably by scent. The meandering moose tracks indicated that the young moose and a larger moose had browsed among the willows, unaware of the bear until the final minutes of the youngster's life.

Having satisfied my curiosity, I flew up a river valley for five miles, enjoying the sunny day and unlimited visibility. I identified a wolverine by its distinctive rocking gait as it made its way upriver ahead of me and disappeared into thick willows on the riverbank. A mink darted across the snow and disappeared into a hole. Some days were like that—animals seemingly everywhere. On other days, I flew for long periods without sighting any animals in the vast wilderness.

I flew back to the site of the moose kill. A pile of brush and snow now marked the location. The bear had hastily covered the dead moose, a common practice, and followed a second set of moose tracks. I followed the trenchlike trail that the moose and bear had shoulder-plowed through the snow below me.

From my vantage point, I watched the moose, with the bear about a hundred yards behind, struggling to survive in this harsh land. But the winter-weakened moose had little chance of escaping. This animal, larger than the yearling killed earlier, was probably the dead moose's mother. The cow lunged through the deep snow, nostrils flaring, eyes bulging. I seldom interfered with nature, but that bear was bloodthirsty and already had one moose to feed on. I forced the plane into a dive and buzzed the bear. My low pass halted the grizzly temporarily, so I buzzed again and again, always diving the plane between the bear and the moose. My tactic worked, and the grizzly turned back toward the kill site.

☽

I spent lots of time observing wildlife from my airplanes. In general, the animals and birds behaved pretty much as expected, seeking food and water. However, some creatures seemed to delight in playing. Bears in particular enjoyed sliding down a snowdrift just for fun.

Northwest of our cabin, the white peaks of the Alaska Range rose to 6,000 feet and more on either side of my tiny, two-seat Taylorcraft. The plane's shadow raced me across the vertical cliffs and shale slides that scarred the mountainsides. Snow still covered the upper half of the treeless mountains where bears den, but the early-June sun had bared rocks and exposed boulders on the lower slopes. The peaks stretched toward the sun as if trying to escape the cold embrace of a lingering winter.

I was flying simply to enjoy the feeling of freedom that flight through Alaska's skies provides, to gaze at the gorgeous scenery, and to look for wildlife. I reversed course in a box canyon near the headwaters of the Bull River, a mountain stream filled with sediment and snowmelt. A broad valley contains the river, herding the water toward a gorge where the flow leaps from rock to boulder as it rushes to join the West Fork of the Chulitna River.

I flew away from the headwaters and came to a series of low hills just above the Bull River gorge. The winter winds had piled the snow into hard-packed drifts nearly as solid as the underlying rock-strewn terrain, and large patches of snow resisted the sun's efforts. I looked down from my T-Craft and saw a grizzly family working out the kinks of a long winter's sleep. The sow and twin one-year-old cubs were sliding down a large snowdrift that still clung to a steep slope. I circled, amused at the scene below.

Like children lining up for a ride down a slippery slide, first one, then another bear ran onto the snow at the top of the drift. The melting snow and steep slope sent the bears whizzing down the hill. Sometimes they remained standing for the entire ride, but usually they fell over and rode it out on side or back. One rolled over slowly several times during the descent, seemingly on purpose.

When they arrived at the bottom of the snow slide and reached bare ground they shook themselves, their long winter coats whipping back and forth the way a dust mop flops when shaken. The sun had yet to bleach their chocolate-colored hair to the blonde shade common in late July, and the fur looked rich, vibrant. The bears climbed back to the top of the one-hundred-yard slide, walking on the bare treeless tundra beside the snow, and launched themselves onto the drift again and again. They were still at it thirty minutes later when I left, leaving them to enjoy the spring day undisturbed.

☾

One year I happened to fly over a grizzly minutes after he emerged from his winter den. In the northern Alaska Range, the male bears, or boars, come out a month or more before the sows and their cubs appear. That schedule makes sense for several reasons. First, the boars are hungry and they immediately search for the first available food. Tender bear cub would make a tasty appetizer for a hungry boar. Boars eat cubs when they get the chance.

Secondly, even if no boars are on the prowl for a spring snack, the deep snow presents a formidable challenge to a tiny cub. By spending an extra month growing in the safety of the den, the cubs gain enough stature to navigate the remaining spring snow.

This particular boar grizzly had denned high on the treeless south side of a mountain. Six to eight feet of snow plastered the upper reaches of the mountains that formed the secluded valley. Even on the lower levels, snow still covered the ground, although in lesser amounts. When I arrived overhead, I spotted the boar's abandoned den—a simple black hole in an unbroken expanse of white mountain.

The grizzly was a very dirty bear, and he was cleaning himself by rolling over and over in the snow while sliding down the steep mountainside. When he came to a temporary stop he shook himself vigorously, then repeated his rolling, downhill slide. His passage stained the snow brown, and the furrow the sliding bear made resembled a bobsled run without the sharp curves. I circled, watching. When he reached a small plateau, I expected him to cross it and descend to a lower altitude where patches of bare ground allowed easier traveling. The bear had other plans.

He shook himself for the last time and started climbing up the mountain he had just descended. The grizzly passed his den and strode upward until he reached the summit. He had gained at least two thousand feet in elevation during his ascent and seldom stopped to catch his breath. He paused briefly at the 6,000-foot peak before rambling down the north side, slipping and sliding, until he reached the tree line. Perhaps he knew the odds of finding a moose were better in the Ohio Creek watershed. Two days later, I saw him on a moose kill near the river bottom.

☾

I flew a bear hunter into Ohio Creek valley on a sparkling spring day. A boar grizzly had killed a moose in scraggly brush on the riverbank, and Mike Goffena hoped to bag the bear. I landed my airplane in four-foot-deep snow two miles down the valley from the bear. A few hundred feet from the river, Mike pitched his tent at the base of a narrow plateau, or bench. Dense willows blotched the steep, snowbound slope from the river to the bench. Above the bench, the muscular mountain bulged into the sky.

Alaska game regulations prohibit hunting on the same day a hunter has been airborne. The regulation helps protect animals from hunters who would land beside a bear or moose and blast away. Therefore, after Mike stepped out of my ski plane he had to spend the night on the ground before he could hunt. I told Mike I'd return the following day to check on him, and then took off.

When I popped over a ridge the next day and flew into the valley where the bear and Mike had spent the night, I saw that bear ambling along the bench about a quarter mile from the hunter, moving in his direction. Neither was aware of the proximity of the other. I circled slowly above the developing drama, staying high so as not to interfere.

Mike, bent over while he strapped on his snowshoes, faced away from the bench and the bear. His rifle leaned against his pack next to him. His orange tent formed a garish inverted vee a few feet away.

The grizzly wallowed along the bench above the unsuspecting hunter, paused, sniffed, spun to his left, and charged down the steep slope toward Mike.

I shoved the yoke of the ski plane forward to force the T-Craft into a dive, hoping to spook the bear before he could maul Mike.

Thick willows and deep snow slowed the bear as he charged downhill. Mike heard the bear, whirled, looked upslope toward the charging grizzly, grabbed his rifle, and aimed. I couldn't hear the shot, but I saw Mike's shoulder jerk backward from the recoil. His shoulder jerked twice more, and the bear crashed headfirst into the snow and willow tangle just above the hunter. I pulled out of the dive, regained altitude, and circled some more. When I saw Mike just standing there, watching that bear lying motionless about fifty feet above him, I decided to land.

The young hunter was still edgy, glad to have some backup before he approached the dead grizzly. I had enjoyed watching the interaction between bear and hunter from above. On the ground, with the excitement over, I went to work and helped skin the bear.

I'll bet Mike never forgot his bear hunt. The bear was of average size, but to Mike that bear must have looked like a world record when it charged toward him through the willows.

In 1998, several years after he shot that charging grizzly bear in the Alaska Range, Mike Goffena—helicopter and fixed-wing pilot, Silver Star recipient in Somalia, flight instructor, bear hunter, and a personal friend—died in an Army helicopter crash.

Trapline Trails and Tales

Bush dwellers live with the land and on the land and as a part of the land, but the need for cash hovers above the homestead. I trapped, and trapping was an intense part of my bush experience for a few years. I would be dishonest if I omitted that phase of my life, but I'm not proud of it. Shooting an animal for food is one thing. Torturing an animal for its hair is another. Trapping is exciting. But the trapper who considers the pain and suffering that his occupation causes may well decide to choose another way to make money. I did.

☾

We seldom bought meat. We ate moose, caribou, game birds, and fish because we preferred those sources of protein to beef and other domestic meat. The cost of procuring game and fish was low, but we still had to buy flour, vegetables, fruit, freezer paper, toilet tissue, and hundreds of other items. We ate in restaurants when we traveled to Anchorage or Fairbanks every two or three months to buy supplies. Alaska restaurants were expensive. Even a simple hamburger cost $5.00 or more, and a pizza was over $20, an exorbitant expense in those days. Non-food items were also expensive. Materials for construction or repairs, such as lumber, sheet metal, nails, screws, and other necessities came with a high price tag. Our airplanes, three-wheelers, snowmachines, and pickup truck drank cash. We used three-wheelers for summer access to the cabin via the trail from the Parks Highway, hauling supplies in a small trailer that I towed behind my machine. We depended on our snowmachines and sleds in the winter.

We were fortunate to have as friends Dick and Eleanor Lochner, who repeatedly invited us to spend the night in their Eagle River home throughout the many years we lived in the bush. However, when we spent a night or two in Anchorage or Fairbanks, we stayed in guesthouses at Fort Richardson or Fort Wainwright, another expense.

Our expenses were small when compared with living in Anchorage and making mortgage payments, but our income shrank along with our cost of living. My retirement pay covered our expenses, but it left little for savings or extras. We had to save money for our old age, for replacements when our vehicles wore out, and for a cushion against injury or bad luck, such as a fire turning our cabin into a pile of coals. Thankfully, that never happened. Even in the bush and off the highway, money is an important family issue.

After I had completed the many tasks that turned our cabin from a mere shelter into a warm, attractive home, I decided to trap animals to earn cash. First, so I would have a place to skin the animals I expected to catch, I had to build a shop. The shop would also serve as a place to repair broken equipment; to hang, cut, and package moose meat each fall; and to pursue my woodworking hobby.

I built my shop from old timbers that a friend and I recovered from remnants of an abandoned bridge located ten miles up the West Fork of the Chulitna River. The 1964 earthquake collapsed the structure. I salvaged the beams that had supported the planking and constructed my shop from the beams. By stacking the timbers on edge, I built eight-foot-high walls, using thirty-two timbers in the process. The finished shop measured twenty feet by twenty-six feet, and even had an upstairs storage area.

I built a stove from an old steel barrel and ran the stovepipe up through the roof. The shop would now be a warm place to skin my catch and stretch the hides. And four years later, when I came to realize that I couldn't torture animals in traps anymore, Joan and I made souvenir items in the shop, selling the crafts to gift shops all over Alaska. We made extra money at Christmastime by selling our products at bazaars.

☾

Even before we moved to the bush, I had planned to run a trapline out there. Trappers never walk, stroll, or traverse traplines. I don't know why, but trappers *run* traplines. During a portion of my trapping career, I occasionally flew part of my trapline. But I didn't tell traditional, land-bound trappers. My reputation, such as it was, would have suffered. Even in the air, I *ran* a trapline.

The trapline would be not only a source of income, but also an excuse to spend my winter days outdoors, seeking furbearers in the glacier-plowed valleys that separated the mountains surrounding our cabin. But first I had to acquire a trapline.

In Alaska, traplines aren't registered. A trapper scouts a region to determine whether anyone is trapping there. If not, the trapper can establish a line, and other trappers generally respect that line and won't encroach on it. Untrapped land is rare, so most trappers acquire the rights to trap an area from a trapper who has grown old or tired of trapping and is willing to sell or give the line to the new-comer. Families transfer traplines from generation to generation. I acquired my trapline from a trapper who had moved away from the area that I moved into. That experienced trapper not only gave me his trapline, he loaned me his traps so I could start trapping without spending a lot of money. Kenny also loaned me a home-made ice chisel and a beat-up trapping sled that I pulled behind my snowmachine. I hauled traps, bait, wire, my ax, and the ice chisel in that old sled, which had been cobbled together from the skis and engine compartment of a defunct snowmachine.

Although I had trapped a little in Vermont, many years had passed since I pinched my fingers while setting a trap. I was eager to explore Alaska's remote valleys, improve my trapping skills, and make some money.

Fur prices fluctuated according to the demands of fashion. Some years, the time spent trapping a particular species simply wasn't worth the effort. Other years, the price skyrocketed, and novice trappers, out to make a quick buck, swarmed through the forests. Cheechakos seldom lasted long. They discovered that most animals, other than marten, aren't easy to outwit.

I decided to trap beavers first. I had trapped them in Vermont, and I knew, before I set my first trap in Alaska, that trapping beavers is harder work than trapping other critters. But I knew how to do it. Where we lived in Alaska, frigid temperatures locked the ponds and lakes under a depth of three feet or more of ice. And sometimes six feet of snow lay on top of the ice. I understood and accepted the hard work involved in trapping Alaska beavers.

To make a beaver set, I first removed some outer clothing to avoid becoming overheated. Perspiration could be dangerous on the trail, soaking my clothes and then freezing as I cooled off. Before I completed the set, sweat rolled down my face, even in subzero temperatures. With only quilted underwear, a wool shirt, and a down vest covering my upper body, I shoveled down to the ice, and then chipped at the ice with the ice chisel. The chisel, a wide-bladed piece of sharpened steel on the end of a peavey handle, weighed fifteen pounds or so. I lifted the five-foot-long tool above my head and thrust it downward as hard as I could. Chips of ice flew in all directions. I repeated the process time after time, sometimes for as long as a half hour, until I finally broke through the ice and water geysered from the hole.

I dodged the waterspout, snowshoed to nearby trees, and chopped down a small spruce. After I stripped the limbs from it, I toted the pole to the hole in the ice. Several small branches wired together made a crib, or platform, for the trap to rest on. I wired the crib to the pole about two feet above the butt end, and then wired a cluster of birch or willow twigs to the pole about six inches above the crib. The twigs served as bait. On the pole above the twigs, I slashed the bark with my ax, making a blaze, or white scar, that would attract the beavers' attention underwater. I gave a name to my efforts: Underwater Trail Blazing 101.

I wired the trap chain to the spruce pole, set the trap and loosely wired it to the crib, shoved the pole into the water, jammed it into the mud at an angle of perhaps ten degrees, and checked to see that the trap was on the topside of the slanting pole, not on the underside. Once the pole was secure, I shoveled snow back over the hole. Snow insulated the hole so I wouldn't have to chop through so much ice a second time to check the trap.

When a hungry beaver spots the blaze, swims over to investigate and sees the twigs, it steps onto the platform to brace itself while tugging at the wired branches that serve as bait. The beaver steps into the trap that rests on top of the platform, and the trap snaps around its foot or leg. The beaver lunges to escape the trap, but since the chain is wired to the pole, the animal soon drowns.

I didn't check my beaver sets as frequently as I did my traps for land animals. A trapped beaver drowns within minutes, and the cold water preserves the pelt. Shoveling snow and chopping ice to check the trap was hard work, and the activity disturbed the surviving beavers. I checked beaver sets once a week or so.

A super blanket, or extra large beaver pelt, sold for around $60.00. Most were smaller, and I received less money for them, averaging around $30.00 per pelt. I didn't figure out how much I made an hour, but trapping gave me an excuse to spend my days outdoors in the wilderness, and you can't place a price on that.

Unlike beaver sets, marten sets are easy to make, and the catlike marten, about two feet long, with a soft rich brown coat, is the easiest animal to catch. Large, dark males brought $60.00 or so in a good year, which highlights one of the problems with trapping. There's no way to keep small light-colored females out of a trap. They died, even though their pelts were worth only $6.00 or so— hardly worth the time it took to skin them. Killing such a magnificent animal for such a small amount of money makes no sense at all. That was only one of the reasons I quit trapping.

To make a marten set, I chopped down a small spruce, limbed it, and set one end on the ground. Placing the other end against a tree about shoulder high, I wired it there, creating an enticing pathway for a marten to follow to reach the trap. Marten climb trees with ease, but they'll run up almost any slanting pole, either out of curiosity or because they smell the bait.

Marten are not trap shy. Foxes won't go near an exposed trap, but marten don't seem to recognize the trap as an object to avoid. Each trap comes with a chain attached, normally about eighteen inches long. At the end of the chain, a steel ring provides a convenient way to secure the trap to a tree. I wired the ring to the tree, leaving plenty of slack in the chain between the tree and the ring, and set the trap.

Traps that are the right size for a marten are easy to set. I rested the trap on my knee, opened the jaws, and slipped the trigger over the tab on the back of the trap pan. When an animal steps on the trap pan, the trigger releases, and spring steel snaps the trap around the critter's leg. The marten lunges to escape the pain, falls off the slanted pole, and hangs there, struggling to escape. Often the trapped animal will climb up the chain and remain crouched on the pole until the trapper comes along and kills it. Other marten freeze or starve to death, tumble from the pole, and dangle, frozen, at the end of the chain. The dead animal's frozen expression tells a silent tale of misery and suffering.

Trapping is a cruel, insensitive business. Leghold traps are instruments of torture. I used them, but I hated them. I hardened my conscience, similar to the way I hardened it when killing enemy soldiers in Vietnam. Yet trapping is different from combat. The animal isn't attacking people, or setting booby traps. It merely tries to make a living, and the living is hard. The search for food is constant, and a whiff of bait entices a mammal to check out the source. The result is sudden, excruciating pain and a slow, agonizing death.

Trappers use euphemisms when they talk about trapping. They "nab a critter," or they "pinch his toes." They outwit animals that may be able to run faster, climb higher, have a better sense of smell, sharper eyesight and keener hearing, or that have stronger jaws and more efficient teeth than humans. But the contest is lopsided in the brainpower department. With our superior ability to think, and to make and use tools, the contest is seldom in doubt.

Nevertheless, I trapped and enjoyed the contest. I admired an animal that could outwit me. I loved traveling across the winter landscape, many miles from the nearest human. I thrived on the freedom to travel wherever I wanted to go, to stop and inhale the scent of wilderness at my leisure, to stand on snowshoes and gaze at mountains and valleys so beautiful that even skilled poets can't describe them.

Did I have to kill animals to enjoy the wilderness? No, but somehow the trapping and the solitude and the beauty came together and created an experience that seemed right at the time.

One day I came upon a wolverine track in the deep snow. Wolverines are large members of the weasel family, and they have acquired a reputation for strength and for being cantankerous and nasty. Tales of their exploits around cabins are legendary. A few of the stories may be true. I decided to follow this wolverine's track to see what he was up to.

On snowshoes, I tracked the critter for about a mile and came to a large beaver pond. The track in the snow meandered across the frozen pond. I followed. On the far side, near the shoreline, a beaver lodge rose above the flat surface. Actually, the lodge looked like nothing more than a mound of snow, about shoulder high and the circumference of a round, ten-person table. The wolverine had climbed up onto the lodge and dug down through three feet of snow, trying to reach the beavers that wintered safely inside. When the wolverine reached the tangle of sticks that was the roof of the beaver house, it gave up and loped off into the nearby trees.

I decided to make a wolverine set on top of the lodge. Wolverines often travel in a roughly circular route and will revisit an area within a few days or weeks.

I snowshoed into the trees, chopped down a small spruce tree, and cut the butt end of the tree off about three feet from the end. This would be my drag.

With no trees available out on the pond, I had no anchor to wire my trap to, so I used a drag. When an animal as strong as a wolverine steps into a trap that's securely wired or chained to a tree, the wolverine may "wring off," or twist, tug, and pull until its foot or leg breaks. At that point, the animal may tear its leg loose, leaving the foot and perhaps a piece of its leg in the trap. It's that foot in the trap that leads to the belief that trapped animals gnaw their leg off to escape. I don't believe that happens. An animal may break its teeth biting at a steel trap, but I doubt if it chews on its own foot or leg.

A drag moves, so the wolverine has nothing to brace against while trying to tear loose from the trap. Instead, when the trapped animal pulls, the drag follows. A trapper uses a heavy log; the wolverine can drag it, but tires and uses up its strength. The drag usually becomes entangled in a clump of bushes. The bushes, too, give a little when the animal tugs against the trap. Because the animal is weaker after hauling the trap and the drag for as much as a mile or so, it can't wring off and escape.

I normally carried skinned beaver meat in my trapping sled, so I snowshoed back to my snowmachine and shoved a fist-sized portion of meat into my backpack. Back at the trap site, I scraped snow into the hole the wolverine had dug on top of the beaver house. When the hole was nearly full, I placed a chunk of beaver meat into it. I covered the bait with more snow, and then placed my trap on top of the snow. I wired the trap chain to the chunk of spruce, and buried the drag near the trap.

To keep the trap jaws from freezing open, I smeared a piece of waxed paper with beaver meat to kill the man smell, and laid the paper over the set trap. I sprinkled snow over the paper, concealing it and the trap. A spruce bough made a good broom, and I used it to sweep the surface, removing most of the evidence that I'd been there. My snowshoe tracks remained, but wolverines and other animals don't spook at those tracks. In fact, they often travel along a packed snowshoe or snowmachine trail.

I checked my trapline every day or so, depending on weather. Two days after I made the wolverine set on top of the beaver lodge, I checked it. The wolverine had returned and had dug under the trap, retrieving the bait without stepping onto the trap pan. I placed new bait into the hole, reset the trap, and tidied up the snow.

The following day I checked the trap again. Same result. I repeated the process, certain I would catch the wolverine the next time. Wrong. Once again the critter dug under the trap, snatched the bait, and left. This time he urinated next to the trap. As far as I was concerned that action threw down the gauntlet, and I was determined to pinch his toes.

I rearranged the set as before, but added a new twist. I had studied the situation and noticed that the wolverine had used the same trail each time he climbed onto the beaver lodge. I chopped down a young spruce, made another drag, and dug a hole in the trail halfway up the side of the lodge. I wired a trap to the drag, buried the drag, and then dug a shallow hole for the trap. I didn't bait this trap. This was what is called a blind set. I hoped the wolverine, intent on finding the bait on top of the lodge, would step into the unbaited trap as he climbed the trail. I swept the trail with the spruce bough and moved on to check other traps on my line.

The following morning, although a blizzard howled, I headed straight for the beaver pond. Bingo! The wolverine had stepped into the blind set. The trapped animal tore up the snow for yards around as he yanked and pulled, trying to escape. The drag followed his every move. Eventually he struggled across the pond and into the woods, dragging the heavy spruce chunk behind him.

I tracked him, slogging on snowshoes through the deep snow, eager to reach the animal before the blizzard completely covered his tracks. As it was, I could still follow the rut the drag made, even though new snow covered the wolverine's tracks.

I caught up to the large male wolverine after about a mile. The blizzard began to weaken as I neared a huge clump of alders, and I spotted him in the thicket, thrashing about while trying to pull free of the trap. When he saw me approach, he bared his teeth and crouched as if preparing to leap at me. I drew my revolver from its holster, aimed, and fired. The wolverine died instantly.

Elation, sorrow, disgust, and relief all crowded together as I stood there, admiring the feisty furbearer and wishing I could undo what I had done. I saw the blood oozing from his mouth, and I pried open his jaws to see broken teeth, chipped when he tried to bite the cruel steel that bit into his leg. Flashbacks of wounded soldiers in Vietnam intruded into this wilderness scene.

That poignant moment was the beginning of the end of my trapping career. I'd find another way to make money. But before I quit trapping a year or two later, several more incidents occurred to convince me that what I was doing was wrong.

I followed a pair of fox tracks one day, and made two sets near a tree where they had stopped to urinate. I buried the traps about three feet apart and baited them with beaver meat. I covered them with a little snow and brushed away my tracks.

When I checked that branch of my line a week or so later, two beautiful red foxes struggled against the chains that held them to the tree. I killed them both with my revolver. One of the foxes had stepped into a trap while trying to dig up the beaver meat. The other one, apparently rushing to help its mate, stepped into the other trap.

On another day, I caught a hawk-owl that had been attracted by the bait near a trap that I had set for marten. A day later I retrieved a weasel from a marten set. I didn't trap weasels. Their fur brought $1.50 that year. Both animals died needlessly.

☾

I trapped a lot of animals. The income was welcome, but the emotional price that trapping wrung from me was too high to pay. I quit.

If the objective is to catch and hold an animal, and it is, then the leghold trap is the most efficient device. It's also the cruelest. Leghold traps should be banned. Snares are said to be more humane, and I used a few snares. I had little success with them, probably because of my inexperience. If an animal sticks its head into a wire snare, and if the noose tightens around its neck, the struggle will be brief. The critter strangles itself by pulling against the noose. However, sometimes the noose captures a leg as well as a neck, and the noose then cuts into the body but doesn't strangle the critter. The result must be pure agony.

Conibear traps are another type of trap. Named for the inventor, they're designed to quickly kill an animal. They work like a vise, trapping the body and squeezing the animal until it can't breathe. I never used one of those traps, but I heard that they don't work as well as advertised.

I sat on my snowmachine one day, about ten miles from my cabin, relaxing in the brief winter sunshine. I munched on a moose meat sandwich while I gazed at the West Fork of the Chulitna River. My trapline ran along both banks of that frozen river, all the way to the boundary of the Denali National Park Wilderness Area. Surrounded by silence and soothed by the sun, I pondered my life and the lives of the animals that shared my existence. Did I share their land or did they share mine? Did the land belong to them or me or all creatures? Did I depend on the animals for my existence? Or did their existence depend on my treatment of them and the land?

While I sat on the remote hilltop and chewed on that sandwich, a raven flew overhead, doing wingovers—turning itself upside down as it flew—as ravens often do. I watched that raven and decided that I had no more right to kill furbearers than I had to kill that free-flying raven. Although I would continue to hunt and fish for food, I would no longer trap.

Wild Neighbors

We learned to cope with life in the bush. Although we struggled to perform tasks that had been easy to do in our Eagle River home, we enjoyed testing our resolve against the demands of bush life. We also enjoyed watching our wild neighbors.

We shared our property with the wildlife that flitted and wandered across our land and the surrounding wilderness, but birds and animals struggled much harder than we did to survive. Their efforts often amused us, but occasionally their untimely deaths reminded us of how uncompromising life in the bush can be for humans and animals alike.

☽

Moose are long-legged critters, roughly the height of Clydesdale horses. Adult moose stride through deep snow without much difficulty during a normal winter, but in years of exceptionally heavy snowfall, wolves dine frequently on moose meat.

In the mountains and valleys near our cabin, moose make limited fall migrations, searching for thickets of their favorite willow species. In some valleys, the migration consists of little more than a meandering journey from foothills into river bottoms where spruces, willows, and a few birches march in disorderly ranks along cut banks and gravel bars. Steep-sided valleys that are oriented east and west remain without sunlight for the three months or more when the sun peeks above the southern horizon for mere minutes in midwinter. Little browse grows on the valley floor in some drainages. There, moose congregate on sloping uplands where sparse willow communities thrust gray branches into the subzero air as if begging for heat.

When browsing in willow patches, moose keep movement to a minimum to conserve strength. Nevertheless, when the hungry animals have nibbled buds and twigs from the tips of every willow branch within reach, they must move or starve. A moose plowing its way across a snow-covered valley while seeking a new food source expends lots of energy.

I flew over a dramatic scene one early March day during a winter that dumped more than 300 inches of snow on the Broad Pass region. Although it settled from its own weight, compacting as the winter progressed, almost ten feet of snow lay on the valley floors. Even though arctic winds had swept ridges nearly free of snow, no willows grew there.

I maneuvered my T-Craft above a trail, a meandering trench that wrinkled the snow-choked valley floor. That tortuous trail led to a cow moose and her two calves. The moose family had traversed halfway across the wide valley that gave birth to the East Fork of the Chulitna River. The calves, born the previous May, were almost a year old. The cow led, breaking trail, but the gaunt animal appeared exhausted. Even so, she lunged ahead for perhaps eight or ten feet; then she stopped, head down, sides heaving.

A half mile away, on the far side of the valley, a few willows poked their branch tips above the snow. I doubted if the cow moose could lead her family through the ten-foot-deep snow to that distant line of willows. I eased the throttle forward, climbed to avoid disturbing the moose, and circled.

That cow exhibited a far greater intelligence than I generally give moose credit for. Apparently nearing the end of her endurance, she moved beside, then around behind, one of the calves. She jabbed the calf in the rump with one of her forelegs, which caused the calf to lunge forward, breaking trail. I was flabbergasted. The mother allowed the calf to rest a bit then poked him again, with the same result, and repeated the procedure several times. When she apparently sensed that the calf could go no further, she lunged past the exhausted youngster and broke trail for several more feet. Whether she had used the same tactic on the other calf before I arrived I can't say. The cow didn't force the second calf into the lead while I watched. I circled for a half hour, but the plane was low on gas so I reluctantly turned away from the struggling moose family.

I flew back to the East Fork the following day to see if the moose trio had completed their journey across the valley. They had, and the emaciated family lay among some willow bushes on the lower mountainside, about 200 yards above the valley floor.

Several days later I found the family again, or at least what was left of them. Wolves had discovered the moose, and the deep snow blocked any possibility of escape. The predators killed the entire family. Tracks in the snow documented the struggle. Only some bones, stomach contents, and patches of moose hair remained, and splotches of wolf urine.

☾

Earlier that same winter, about five miles from where wolves killed the moose family, another deadly event occurred, this time involving a herd of caribou. The Chulitna River's East Fork emanated from a steep-walled valley, with the mountains on either side rising one thousand feet or more from the valley floor. Shale slides plunged down gullies between ridges that buttressed the sides of the towering mountains. Grass and lichens textured the rock-strewn ridges in summer, but snow buried the vegetation for several months. The beautiful valley was avalanche-prone, but I guess the caribou didn't know that.

I flew up that valley in February, careful to remain far enough from the mountains on either side to avoid the tremendous blast of wind that would result if an avalanche cut loose. Winds of one hundred miles an hour can develop ahead of an avalanche, and my little plane would be converted to a pile of kindling, torn cloth, and scrap metal if slammed by hurricane-force winds.

Hundreds of caribou tracks paralleled the valley floor about halfway up the mountain on the north side of the valley. The tracks ended where an avalanche had plunged to the valley bottom. Near the valley floor, many brown objects littered the path of destruction left by the recent snow slide. I flew low over the terminal area of the slide and counted twenty-five caribou in various postures. Some were buried up to their necks in the hard-packed snow, with only their heads and antlers visible. Elsewhere only antlers protruded, marking the frozen graves of several herd members. A few animals sprawled, immobile, on the surface. Some caribou slowly limped around as if dazed, which was likely under the circumstances. Others, weak and helpless, struggled unsuccessfully to stand on broken legs. One hobbled toward the valley floor. I don't know how many hapless critters lay buried. Several legs, unmoving, stuck up from the packed snow slide. The worst sight was that of one caribou lying atop the snow, still alive, hind legs sticking straight out to either side, her pelvis obviously badly shattered. Her front legs pawed weakly as she attempted to rise. The remaining survivors, perhaps seventy-five animals, floundered their way along the valley floor, away from that scene of misery. Sickened by such suffering, I turned away.

I notified a game warden of the tragic scene in the East Fork valley. He informed me that no funds were available to hire a helicopter to fly game wardens or troopers out to kill the injured animals. Besides, nature, not man, caused the event.

From my years as chairman of the Denali Fish and Game Advisory Committee, the game warden knew me well, and he gave me permission to kill any caribou that would obviously die a lingering death. He told me to report the numbers killed and to salvage as much meat as I could. The Alaska Department of Public Safety's staff would give the meat to orphanages and to others in need.

I returned to the valley with gun and ammunition, but my first priority was to find a safe place to land. I could land my ski plane almost anywhere on the valley floor, but while making a low level reconnaissance I looked up at the massive snow cornices hanging above me and realized the danger in landing there. A broad ridge about a mile away, out of the avalanche zone, offered a reasonably safe place to land my plane. Bush pilots don't become old pilots by being incautious, so I flew around awhile, giving the situation careful thought. From that ridge, I would have to snowshoe a mile through the soft snow to reach the caribou, and the daylight would be gone in two more hours. In order to get close enough to evaluate each caribou's injuries, I would be well within the path of another potential avalanche. Finally, when I fired a rifle in the confines of that narrow valley, the reverberation from the shot would quite likely trigger another massive slide. I didn't like the odds.

I flew away from that devastating sight, heart heavy, stomach churning, knowing I was making an intelligent decision, yet suspecting that the scene would be permanently etched in my mind.

I flew over the avalanche site several times after that. Surprisingly, wolves didn't discover the meat bonanza, but grizzlies discovered the feast when they emerged from their dens in April. Weasels and foxes gorged on the caribou carcasses, dodging and avoiding the bears; jays, ravens, and magpies fought over the remaining scraps. The snow melted and spring returned to the valley, with only scattered bones and ancient trails disclosing the former presence of caribou. The trails, incised deep into the tundra by centuries of caribou migrations, reminded me that caribou are survivors.

☾

Some animal species guarantee their survival by bearing large litters. One June day I installed a new trailer hitch on my three-wheeler. While enjoying the sound of the birds chirping in my backyard and the warmth of the summer sun on my back, I noticed an adult short-tailed weasel investigating the three-wheeler trailer parked near the outhouse. I paid little attention since we frequently saw weasels around our home. Then I heard chirping and squeaking noises behind me. When I turned to determine the cause of the racket, a swarm of weasels scampered in all directions.

I yelled, "Joan, come look," while the animals began to check out the three-wheeler, the outhouse, and the back steps of the cabin. A semicircle of weasels greeted my wife as she emerged onto the steps. We counted eleven: one adult, obviously the mother, and ten smaller ones about two-thirds her size.

Showing no fear and only a little caution, they separated and began to explore their new playground. Under the cabin, which sat up on pilings; into the woodshed; under the storage shed; back and forth across the yard—weasels everywhere, and very vocal.

When I ran into the cabin for my camera they scattered, but within five minutes they returned, creeping close to investigate the click of the shutter.

I took photos and enjoyed watching them for two hours. Many times four or five weasels at once scrambled from the shelter of firewood tunnels in the woodpile, but the highlight of the episode occurred when one bold youngster jumped from the woodpile onto my lap while I sat on a chopping block. He stood erect and stiff-backed on my knee, looked up at me, chirped once, and then scampered back into the woodpile.

When darkness fell, I could still see movement in and around the woodpile and hear their chirps and squeaks when they discovered something new. The next morning they were gone.

Because a family that size requires a lot of food, I decided that the mother was moving her brood to a new hunting area. Joan maintains that the poor mother simply tried unsuccessfully to run away from her large, noisy family.

☾

Searching for food occupies many of an animal's waking moments. Sometimes that search can be comical. A bird feeder sat on the front deck, and battles over food rights were always interesting and sometimes hilarious.

Joan discarded some moldy sour cream by placing it on the feeder, thinking the gray jays would enjoy it. Along came a red squirrel family instead. The two young squirrels, just little guys, had probably emerged from the nest only a couple of days before. Their size didn't limit their curiosity or enthusiasm, and they dove into that sour cream with gusto. Their eyes fairly sparkled when they tasted it, that is, for as long as we could see their eyes. In a matter of seconds, sour cream coated them from their whiskers to their tails.

They decided that chasing each other would be even more fun. Down from the feeder, across the deck, and up onto the picnic table they went, marking their route with sour cream tracks. Back to the feeder they raced, and around and around in small circles. Then they stopped, looked at each other, and started to clean up. They didn't like the cream on their feet so they licked it off. Then they rubbed their heads, which got fresh cream on their feet. So they shook their feet, spattering cream on each other. We laughed for half an hour as those squirrels tried to cope with their first experience eating "people food." The mother squirrel ignored the errant babies and daintily fed herself until the young squirrels wearied and quit their sour cream romp.

☾

I grew tired of a woodpecker that announced his arrival one spring by pecking on the cabin wall. I shooed him away, thinking no more about it. The next day we drove the 200 miles to Anchorage for our regular supply run and returned home after three days of shopping and visiting friends.

When we arrived at home, I glanced over at my shop while toting groceries into the cabin and noticed something different. It appeared that someone had found our property while we were gone and fired several loads of buckshot into the shop walls, especially into the trim around the windows. The glass didn't appear broken, though.

I took a closer look. Holes punctured every piece of window trim, and some trim looked like the colander that Joan used to clean lettuce. I heard a *rat-tat-tat* from the other side of the shop. That damned woodpecker was pecking more holes in my window trim!

The shop walls were a little uneven due to the variation in timber size, and when I had installed the exterior window trim, the irregularities created voids behind the trim pieces. These hollow spaces probably sounded like bug cavities to the woodpecker, and he vigorously pecked holes clear through the boards in search of grubs. The fact that he didn't find any didn't diminish his expectations. While we were in town, he took advantage of three days of uninterrupted time to drill holes in every board that sounded hollow.

I scared the woodpecker away several times, and he finally gave up. I still heard him in the distance, pecking on spruce trees beyond Ravenhead Pond.

❨

We enjoyed walking on the path alongside Ravenhead on sunny summer evenings. The slough about a quarter-mile away was an excellent place to watch wildlife, and we spent hours there watching moose, beavers, muskrats, and birds. Swans and a wide variety of ducks swam about on the surface or dove for food. Kingfishers perched in dead spruces overhanging the water. Arctic terns hovered overhead while searching for small fish, and hawks, ravens, eagles, gulls, snipe, plovers, phalaropes, swallows, and others filled the air with color and sound. One bird surprised me, though.

When we approached the slough one evening, I skirted an alder bush that grew alongside the trail. At that moment, something small and brown charged around the alder and came right up to my feet. Startled, I jumped back. There stood a male spruce grouse, feathers all puffed out, tail erect and fanned, clucking at me and telling me that I was not welcome in his territory. Joan joined me, but that grouse bravely stood his ground and continued scolding us.

I hurried back to the cabin for a camera, a trip that took about ten minutes. When I returned to the slough the grouse and Joan still faced each other, but my approach this time unnerved him, and he high-stepped around the alder. I sneaked around the other side of the bush and took several photos of him. He scraped a shallow depression in the dirt behind the alder, and then squatted in it, fluffing and fluttering his feathers to take a dust bath. We walked away, happy to share our property with the feisty bird.

❨

Grouse were abundant at Colorado Lake. Foxes thrived there as well. Grouse and ptarmigan frequently became fox food, but the foxes we watched spent a lot of time hunting for voles and shrews. Those plentiful rodents provided food for a variety of raptors and predators. The tiny critters scurried about all summer storing seeds and grasses for food and nesting material, and we often saw them scampering about near the cabin. In winter they scurried in tunnels they dug under the surface of the snow.

One winter day, a red fox trotted along on the snow-covered surface of Ravenhead Pond, stopped, and then pussyfooted close to our deck. We typically tossed table scraps onto a bird feeder on the deck, and when Joan noticed the fox she supposed he smelled something of interest on the feeder. He stopped again near the base of the pole that supported the feeder and, in slow motion, turned his head, first one way and then another. He appeared to look at the snow with first his right eye, then his left.

The fox stood on his hind legs, almost as if winding up, and then he pounced, thrusting his head deep into the snow. When his head emerged, a red-backed vole dangled from his mouth. He laid the vole aside, cocked his head, first one way, then another, and pounced again. For a second time he emerged with a vole, placed it beside the first one, and listened some more. We realized that's what he was doing—listening for voles—as he rotated his head from side to side.

After a few minutes the red fox quit listening, and then rolled the captured voles in the snow as if he were dipping them in batter. He sat down and with a few bites and a gulp or two, the fox devoured his catch. He then trotted off, his long red tongue making swipes completely around his lips.

❨

Swans, both trumpeter and tundra, nested on some of the many ponds and lakes that dotted the region. I hunted moose on one of the lakes that annually hosted a trumpeter swan family. The pair always paddled slowly over to inspect my campsite when I arrived each year. I felt like old friends had come visiting to welcome me back.

One evening, while I taxied my floatplane toward their end of the lake prior to taking off, one of the swans emerged from the weeds and took up a position beside me, but some thirty yards away. When I turned into the wind and applied power, the huge bird began his takeoff run. I slowly gained speed; so did the swan. I looked over at him; he flapped his wings while running on the pond's surface and looked over at me. I got the airplane up on the step as the floats began to plane across the surface; the swan's feet left the water. We continued to exchange looks. I was now going faster than the swan and pulled the plane off the water. I immediately turned right so I wouldn't interfere with his flight pattern. Looking back, I saw him bank left, away from my flight path. I gained altitude, reversing direction of flight; so did the swan. Now we were on opposite sides of the pond, paralleling each other, with me above and rapidly outdistancing him. The smile remained on my face for several minutes.

I'm certain that the swan simply decided to take off at the same time I did and probably didn't appreciate the racket my engine made. Nonetheless, I've always remembered that "formation takeoff" with a swan as my left wingman. The way we looked ahead, then across the water at each other, then ahead again, always synchronously, would have made a comical home video. I wondered if he landed later and told his mate that he'd been out flying with the big boys.

☾

Robins are not the first birds that come to mind when thinking about Alaska's wildlife, but they provided several enjoyable experiences and one rather amusing one.

The stairwell to the second floor of the cabin was quite dark, so I installed a skylight to brighten up the area. One May morning a tapping noise from the vicinity of the skylight woke us. I got up to see what was causing the racket and discovered a male robin fiercely pecking on the glass of the skylight. I waved a hand near the glass and he left. A few minutes later he was back, again pecking on the glass. This time I watched him for a few minutes to determine why he liked to peck on the skylight. He was pecking at his reflection, thinking the reflected image was a rival male. When he moved, the rival did too, and that poor bird became frantic in his efforts to chase away the competition.

Although amusing, we tired of that racket after two days and decided to eliminate the rival. Joan taped an old newspaper to the underside of the glass, effectively spoiling the reflection. I guess the robin didn't like the news; or perhaps he did, for he ceased pecking on the skylight and began singing in the adjacent tree.

☾

I built the cabin among spruce trees—one large tree on either side, and a smaller one at the rear. The one at the rear grew just outside the guest bedroom window, a mere three feet away. One year a pair of robins built a nest in that tree, perfectly situated so we could stand at the window and look into the nest. We watched the nest construction as well as the egg laying that followed. We eagerly awaited the hatching of the chicks. At the appropriate time, they pecked their way out of the blue-green shells.

Alaska summers are filled with daylight. The midnight sun provides enough light to permit participating in daytime activities twenty-four hours a day. Where we lived, the sun did dip below the horizon briefly, dimming the day to a brief period of twilight. In June, twilight lasted an hour at most.

The birds take advantage of the endless daylight to feed their babies almost nonstop; at least that's what these robins did. We couldn't believe how fast those baby robins grew. We checked on them each morning and evening, and their growth during the day was easily discernible. Their feathers seemed to appear magically, and they gained strength as we watched. The biggest surprise of all was when, eleven days after the babies hatched, they left the nest. The brief Alaska summers encouraged rapid growth in vegetation and birds alike.

☾

Moose take a lot longer to raise their young than robins do. The calves stick close to their mother's side during the first summer and venture only short distances away during their first winter. They accompany the cow throughout their second summer, although they often feed some distance away, say seventy-five yards or so. As fall approaches, the cow, preparing to breed again, changes her attitude toward her offspring. In the upper Chulitna River region, the rut, or breeding season, begins in September but doesn't hit its peak until late September or early October. Before the cows breed they banish their calf or calves from their immediate vicinity.

We watched the breakup of a moose family from the living room window. A cow with a single female calf nibbled browse alongside Ravenhead Pond one early September day. Suddenly the cow raised the roach, or mane, on the top of her neck, flattened her ears, thrust her neck forward, and charged at her calf. That young moose was completely surprised. Here was her mother, her close companion for a year and a half, suddenly attacking her. The yearling appeared totally confused, stumbled away for a few yards, and stood there looking back at her mother. The cow resumed feeding and then charged again.

Our hearts went out to the young moose, for her bewilderment was so obvious. What had she done to provoke her mother so? The cow was relentless and continued to attack her calf until the yearling moved about one hundred yards away. The mother never actually struck her, but the young cow surely got the message. When they moved into the spruces and thick willows, out of our sight, we knew we would never see the two of them close together again. We would look forward to seeing the cow's new baby next spring if she survived the severe winter just ahead. And perhaps the following year the young cow she had just driven off would have a calf of her own.

☾

Life goes on, the cycles repeat, but each year is different from the last. Nature exhibited her wonders constantly outside the cabin windows, and we never tired of what we called bush television.

We embraced the changing seasons and drama that surrounded us, but we always knew the day would come when the Alaska bush would drive us away too. It would wear us down slowly, bit by bit, the way the spring sun works on the deep snow cover, melting it one drop at a time. The long, dark, subzero winters would become less tolerable, the annual wood cutting more demanding on aging muscles, the 200-mile trip to Anchorage more difficult to contemplate. I'd have to exercise ruthless willpower to pull the trigger and kill a moose, both because the killing had become distasteful and because the drudgery involved in properly preserving the meat would weigh heavily on us as we aged. The demands of bush living would never diminish. Alaska is lavish with her displays of natural beauty and her abundant wildlife, but she extracts a price for the privilege of experiencing her many wonders.

Loon Country

Alaska hosts four varieties of loons, and three species of these large, diving birds fed in Colorado Lake and Ravenhead Pond. Some nested on our property. We came to know the red-throated loons best, but we often observed common and Pacific loons from the cabin's windows. We never saw any yellow-billed loons.

The red-throated loon, our favorite, has a gray head with a russet-red throat patch extending from under its chin to the white feathers of its lower breast. Its back is a mottled dark gray. The red-throated is smaller than the Pacific loon, and perhaps ten inches shorter than the common loon.

Most people are familiar with the saying "crazy as a loon." This expression is attributed to the call of the common loon, a wild, wailing cry. The common loon's alarm call, or tremolo, resembles someone laughing. The loons also have a private sound that seems to be used for maintaining contact between adults or between adults and chicks. It resembles the sound a duck makes when feeding—a low *kwak, kwak.*

The wail of the common loon carries surprisingly far, sometimes for miles. I heard their calls from at least two miles away while I hunted moose near lakes that were the summer homes of these loons.

The red-throated loon doesn't yodel like the common loon, and if it uses the tremolo when frightened, I never heard it do so. Instead, the red-throated loons on our lake made a drawn-out, high-pitched cry, sounding like *maaaa, maaaaaaaa.* It was not an attractive cry; the plaintive call evoked sorrow and grief, or maybe loneliness. It doesn't resemble a wolf howl, yet it brings that sound to mind.

The red-throated loons made another call, one that fooled us at first. They strung together a long series of quacks—*quackquack-quackquackquackquack*—sometimes lasting for ten or fifteen seconds. Until a loon made a low, quacking pass over the pond while we sat on the deck, we thought the sound came from a duck. We only heard that call when the loons were in flight.

Spring doesn't explode in Alaska as it does in, say, South Carolina. It warms, fizzles, bubbles, retreats, and cowers as if afraid to emerge from under the comforter of winter. When it finally arrives, meltwater floods the land. We eagerly anticipated the return of all the birds each spring, but the loons' arrival signaled that breakup was nearly over and that I would soon be lifting from Colorado Lake in my floatplane. Wind-drifted miniature icebergs still cruised on the lake when the first loon arrived. The ice chunks—floating remains of our winter trail—were thicker than the rest of the lake ice because our snowmachine-packed trail reduced the insulating value of the snow and drove temperatures lower beneath our winter thoroughfares.

A single loon arrived first, splashing onto the frigid water in late May, looking all around as he glided between the floating ice pans. If we happened to be outdoors, we heard him coming, quacking loudly to announce his arrival. Once he splashed down, he remained silent. Although the sexes look alike, we speculated that the male was the first loon on the scene, checking the conditions, staking out his claim to the nesting sites, and warding off any loon interlopers. We never knew if the arriving loons were the same ones we had enjoyed the previous year, but we assumed they were.

Often, several days passed before the mate arrived. One day a single loon swam on the pond; suddenly there were two. The loons spent their winters floating about and enduring savage storms in the Gulf of Alaska; they flew far before arriving at our pond, located more than 200 miles inland and much farther than that from loon winter feeding areas in the gulf.

The big birds rested for a week or two, making extended dives and exploring the edges of the lake and checking the islands in our pond for possible nesting sites.

The rush of the subarctic spring overtook the land as breakup washed away winter. Tiny frog voices belched and troonked almost as soon as the ice melted, causing us to wonder how the little amphibians could survive being buried in the mud for as long as eight months at a time. After winter's silence, their calls cheered us as they frantically searched for a mate, hurrying to finish mating before the yellowlegs and other frog-spearing shore birds arrived.

Bogbeans, an unappealing name for a beautiful flower, emerged from the shallow water at the pond's edge, their white and pink flower spikes filling the air with sweet aroma. Two-inch white and gold anemones speckled the muskeg at the pond's periphery, contrasting with the delicate purple of the tiny heart-shaped marsh violets. Alaska cotton pushed its narrow, grassy leaves up from marshy depressions in the tundra, waiting for warmer weather before bursting into a fluffy orb that mimicked its namesake in the southern states. Salmonberry plants, which resembled stubby anemones, opened their white flowers to reveal yellow centers. The flowers merged with the mosses and marsh grass, forming a colorful carpet as we strolled around the pond, released at last from winter's grip.

The loons seemed to enjoy their idle time, but a profusion of winged visitors flocked in from the Lower 48 and Central and South America to crowd their summer home. Arctic terns arrived, hovering sharp-eyed over the pond, inspecting its shallow depths for mottled-green fairy shrimp and mud-gray water beetle larvae, and fluttering onto the islands to test the mosses for nesting potential. The terns homesteaded annually on one of our pond's tiny islands.

A dozen or more species of web-footed transients floated about on the lake and pond, joined by tundra swans and horned grebes. Overhead, tree swallows zigzagged while snipe vibrated the air with the *woo, woo, woo* sound of their courtship flights. Periodically, one or both of the loons joined in the air show, making what appeared to be a reconnaissance flight, then quacking to announce their return shortly before they splashed ungracefully onto the pond and fractured the mountains' reflected images.

The territorial loons reluctantly shared Ravenhead Pond with goldeneyes and surf scoters. When the waterfowl first arrived in the spring the different species tolerated one another; then the loons initiated submarine warfare and shattered the truce. After slowly drifting toward an unsuspecting duck, one of the loons would quietly submerge. Thirty seconds or so later, the duck would erupt from the water, quacking and flapping as it fled from the subsurface attack. The loon, having emerged beneath the duck, simply cruised on the surface, satisfied, unless the duck didn't retreat fast enough. On those occasions, the loon viciously attacked the duck with its beak, and the duck quickly got the point. Because of that rude behavior, Joan named the loons Nasty Ned and Nelda.

One day, as I read a book while sitting on the deck, splashing from across the pond grabbed my attention. I peered across the water and spotted a porcupine swimming slowly toward me. Right behind it, a red-throated loon flayed the water with its wings and ventured dangerously close to the porky's favorite weapon—its tail. The porky, riding high in the water due to the buoyancy of the hollow quills covering its body and tail, steadily forged ahead, ignoring the loon. The loon thrashed along behind the porcupine.

When the porky cruised up to the shore directly in front of me, the loon reversed course. The porcupine beached, waddled onto the shore, slowly shook water from its pudgy body—porkys don't do anything in a hurry—and ambled along the path between the trees like a tourist strolling among totem poles in Sitka. I doubt if the loon had any effect on the porcupine's chosen route—right across the loon's territory—but the porky left loon country, nevertheless.

All the loons we observed reacted to airplanes. Each loon had an "unapproachable zone," and its response to an approaching plane depended upon the altitude and proximity of the aircraft to Ravenhead Pond.

When a plane flew within their zone they started calling loudly in a high-pitched wail, changing the noise to a mixture of wail and quack as the plane drew closer. They continued wailing and quacking until the plane departed. If a friend flew overhead, the plane flew much lower so we could identify the plane and wave from the deck. A low-flying plane energized the loons to more drastic action. Supplementing their wailing and quacking, the loons rose and ran across the pond in a manner similar to one of their courtship displays, except that with the plane overhead they flapped their wings as they scooted across the surface, beating the water to a froth. They circled frantically while walking on the water, until the plane departed.

My plane caused the loons to respond, but they were less disturbed when I idled in for a landing than when I flew overhead: they nonchalantly dived. When I taxied to either end of the lake prior to takeoff, they swam out of the way. They dived when I applied power while taking off, then surfaced and resumed their normal activities.

When I flew over remote lakes, loons below me responded to my plane, acting just like their relatives on Ravenhead did in response to approaching planes.

A couple of weeks after the second red-throated loon arrived at Ravenhead Pond, tension replaced the loons' restful interlude. They began the courtship display, using a non-aggressive posture, hiding their bills in the water, arching their necks, circling. Then one of them dived, followed closely by its mate. They surfaced together, circling, circling, peering into the water, repeatedly hiding their bills. As the days passed, they broke off the courtship to search for food and to make occasional flights, always quacking upon their return. The courtship resumed, the pace quickening to a frenzy. They circled faster and faster, then rapidly paddled their feet, forcing their bodies up onto the water's surface as they skimmed along in unison, suddenly slowing, circling, circling. Mating was imminent.

We watched this drama from the cabin windows, the pond a stage only fifty feet from the front deck. Our final summer in the bush was perhaps the best one for loon watching. As the courtship reached a climax that year, the female flopped up onto the land right in front of the cabin, struggling to move across the muskeg to a position about three feet from the pond. Loons' legs are attached well back on the body, an advantage on water but a handicap on land. They can't walk; they lunge, throwing themselves forward onto their breast, repositioning their legs under them, then lunging forward again.

The male swam frantically back and forth along the bank until he, too, awkwardly propelled himself onto the muskeg. After three or four ungraceful lunges, he arrived behind the female. After a brief rest, he mounted her. They both rested briefly, then the male returned to the water. She stayed in place, and soon he rejoined her and mated again, then both loons flopped back into the water and resumed their bill-hiding, circling behavior.

Several days passed, with a reduction in the level of courtship activity. They still peered and circled, but for briefer periods and with less intensity. The female showed great interest in one of the tiny islands, swimming back and forth, diving next to it, surfacing to continue her erratic swimming pattern. She soon lunged onto the island, flopping up onto its moss-covered surface for a distance of perhaps two feet from the water. She immediately began to turn, awkwardly flopping around and around and plucking grass and moss from her immediate vicinity with her long, pointed beak. She clumsily stuffed the nest materials under her body as she turned, but soon ceased that activity. She did very little nest construction; perhaps a better term would be depression building. Her movements merely packed down the moss a little.

Twenty-five minutes after she left the water and began to make the depression, she half stood and, with her back toward us, obviously straining, she laid an egg. She rested, sitting on the egg while the male paddled back and forth next to the island.

We don't know when she laid the other eggs, but she laid three; two is the norm. The parents alternated sitting on the eggs, and we saw them turn the eggs over and around several times. Occasionally both birds swam in the pond's waters, but never far from the nest and never for very long. We didn't see the nest unoccupied for longer than fifteen minutes.

About a month passed, and then two loon chicks emerged from the eggs. We couldn't see the chicks under the sitting loon, but within a few hours the little loons and their parent left the nest, flopped with difficulty to the water, and plopped in. They looked like little fuzzy corks as they bobbed about in the ripples of Raven-head Pond. The mother had to oil the developing feathers before they went into the water, I expect, but they surely knew how to swim at less than one day old. However, we only saw two chicks.

The following day we watched one of the red-throated loons lunge onto the nest site and pick up something in its beak. It dashed the thing against the ground, slamming it down several times. We thought perhaps a muskrat or weasel had sneaked onto the island and the loon, even though the nest appeared empty and the two chicks swam about in the pond, still instinctively protected its nest site. The adult threw the small gray object into the water, flopped into the water after it, and continued to slam it against the surface. Now we could see it better; it was a loon chick. The adult clamped its beak around the limp chick and dove. When it surfaced in the same location a short time later, its beak no longer held the chick. The loon must have jammed it into the mud at the bottom, making sure it would drown if it wasn't already dead. The little body didn't surface while we watched.

Joan and I speculated that the chick was dead before the parent began its attack. After all, the other two had left the nest the day before. However, perhaps the chick pecked its way out of the egg a day late and the parent heard it and attacked it. We just don't know.

As the days passed, the muskeg, tundra, and open spruce forest surrounding Ravenhead Pond displayed their summer beauty. The bog blueberries added their white-and-pink blossoms to the colorful carpet under our feet. Dwarf dogwood flowers reminded us of the large fluffy flakes of a late spring snowstorm, although the dogwood blossoms were much more welcome. Arctic lupine purpled the edges of our trail, and bog rosemary bowed its pink Japanese-lantern-shaped heads in the muskeg at the pond's edges. Shrubby cinquefoil's golden hues brightened bog and tundra, and the yellowish-green spores of club moss added color to the mossy carpet between the spruces. The loon chicks swam next to their parents without regard for the beauty that surrounded them.

We wondered if the small pond could sustain two chicks. Terns shared the limited food supply too. The loons aren't able to dart about like smaller birds, finding food, flying it to the chicks, and then flitting off on another foray. The loons taxied across the pond in long, half-flying runs, laboring to become airborne. They occasionally brought fish from the larger lake out back to feed to their chicks that bobbed about on the pond. However, most of the time the adults muddled about in the shallows of the pond or dove, looking for fairy shrimp, snails, or water beetle larvae.

Within a few days, we decided that one chick wouldn't survive. When a parent approached with food in its beak the same chick always reached the food first. Soon the parents ignored the other chick, and it grew weaker, finally giving up competing for the food. One morning only a single loon chick remained on Ravenhead Pond. We presume a gull or perhaps a mink ate the little body, but it wouldn't have made much of a meal.

The remaining chick grew rapidly, and then one morning there were no loons on Ravenhead. We stepped onto the dock on Colorado Lake and there, a few yards away, bobbed the loon chick and one of its parents. While we slept the parents had led that little loon across the isthmus that separated the two bodies of water. The chick must have scrambled over berry bushes, weaved through tall grass, and clambered over the twisted roots of spruce trees, all the while vulnerable to weasels and minks, or perhaps a fox. But the loon family made it and took up residence on the lake.

We so thoroughly enjoyed watching the loons that we called our property "loon country." Midway through our years in the bush we started a small woodworking business, crafting items from Alaska birch to sell at bazaars and to gift shops throughout Alaska. We named the business Loon Country Creations, in honor of the loons that nested on Ravenhead Pond and Colorado Lake. We sold the business when we left the bush, but we hope the loons will always return to loon country, splashing down onto icy Ravenhead Pond each spring, playing submarine with the ducks, and keeping the airplanes at bay while they raise their families. Loons have existed for sixty million years on this earth, and we hope they'll be around for several million more.

Northern Lights and Shadows

I peered into the subarctic night, alone, and saw a bearded face reflected on the frosty windowpane. The world beyond the glass didn't exist. Artificial light, a dim blush that would strain the eyes of an owl, oozed from the cabin. The Alaska wilderness quickly devoured the faint glow. I extinguished the propane lights and gazed out the window into boreal blackness, wondering if tonight would be showtime for the aurora. I looked forward to bush television, which is what Joan and I called nature's repertoire of amazing displays, but the schedule was iffy.

The Big Dipper lazed high aloft while the Little Dipper poured its invisible contents into the empty basin of the larger constellation. At the end of the Little Dipper's handle, the North Star pulsated in the dry, cold air. At this latitude the North Star sparkled almost straight above me, not much use as a direction indicator.

I would have stepped outside, but the thermometer reminded me it was forty degrees below zero, and a brisk breeze blew with sufficient force to slap a spruce branch against the cabin. Snow cascading from the roof had broken the branch, but it was still hanging. I hadn't taken the time to cut it off. The scraping noise sounded like a dog scratching on the door, begging to escape the cold. Maybe I would cut the branch off after I checked out the northern lights.

I studied the windchill chart tacked to the wall. My forefinger traced the estimated-wind-speed column to the appropriate intersection with the current-temperature column. Sixty-five degrees below zero. Maybe I'd wait until tomorrow to cut that branch.

When the mercury huddled near the bottom of the glass and the wind yodeled past the eaves, I went outside for only two reasons. One of them was to fetch more firewood from the woodshed, and earlier I had dumped several armfuls of wood into my indoor wood box. The wood nurtured the hungry stove that squatted on a rock hearth next to the wood box.

We didn't have an indoor toilet, and that's the second reason I braved the fierce wind that bullied the frozen land. I had done that about an hour ago and didn't take long in the doing. With an empty bladder and a full stove, I could enjoy the aurora show in comfort.

Across the snow-covered pond in front of the cabin, the Talkeetna Mountains rose like the molars and fangs from a wolf's lower jaw. Flake white against the star-sprinkled blackness, they took a bite out of the sky. Beyond the mountains, as if a poacher were searching for the wolf, a shaft of white light stabbed the darkness. The wolf's teeth glistened and sparkled and then the searchlight moved on, sweeping the northern sky. It was showtime, northern lights style.

The searchlight beam darted to the south, zipping past the cabin as if trying to catch up with the anemic sun that had disappeared hours ago. The light then dimmed like stage footlights before Act 1, retreating below the Talkeetnas. The stars trembled in the subzero night. The aurora usually built to a climax nearer midnight. I turned away from the window and waited.

In the stove the firewood popped, and the faint odor of burning pitch, pungent and pleasing, scented the cabin. The tree branch scraped the outside wall. Quiet returned.

Joan was shopping in Anchorage. I was alone in the cabin, but I wasn't lonely. I worked on a poem while I waited.

The eastern sky brightened and an invisible ray gun blasted a bluish-green shaft skyward. The shaft expanded sideways, turning into draperies of light that waved like a flag in a gentle breeze. Accordion-like, the draperies expanded and contracted as if pulled by a cord, then closed. They gently sagged toward the mountains and then zipped across the sky like a darting swallow, turning into stabbing, wispy barbs of nervous energy. Wide willow-green and arctic-white rays daubed the sky directly overhead, and on their edges a hint of blush faded into the blackness beyond.

I marveled at the speed and variety of the northern lights. I recalled a recent article that claimed a mirror image of the spectacle overhead occurred at the same time in the Antarctic, thousands of miles from my Alaska cabin. I wondered if this could be so. If it was, did another person gaze, awestruck, at the same show at the same time? I pictured a fur-clad Antarctic explorer riding a sled behind a dog team, craning his neck to watch the southern lights and seeing a copy of my overhead spectacle. The idea pleased me.

I looked to the west, at the stars and the dim outline of the Alaska Range. The sprawling mountains began to glow. Their whiteness intensified under the throbbing aurora that had now flashed clear across the dome of the sky. The western peaks came into sharp focus under the northern lights that painted green-white trails against the black velvet of the wintry sky. The light rays became agitated, skittering sideways as wave after wave of electrically charged particles sped through space on their journey from the sun.

On still nights, an observer could sometimes hear a faint crackling sound from the magnetic activity high overhead. Not tonight, and not from the warmth of my cabin. I shuffled across the floor in my sheepskin-lined moose-hide slippers, added a chunk of firewood to the coals in the stove, and looked again to the Talkeetnas. A faint rosy glob rose above the wolf's teeth, staining them the color of flesh. Like a pink dawn the colorful ball rose up, up, and chased the last of the wavering draperies from the sky. It expanded, shifted direction suddenly and fell to the west, fading as it slid down the sky dome to the western horizon. Its brief moment at center stage had ended.

I hurried from window to window, eager to see the entire show. But the climax had come and gone. Only bit players remained, presenting the epilogue to a grand performance. Smaller light beams, delicate and weak, painted faint white streaks high above the frozen scene below, then faded. A trace of greenish light flared behind the wolf jaws. The jaws overpowered the flare, devoured it, and it died.

I silently applauded the performance, but I was too tired to wait for an encore. I stuffed the woodstove with split spruce, adjusted the damper, and then climbed the stairs to bed. The wind had died and the branch no longer rasped the wall. In the silence, I thanked God for the northern lights and for the joys of bush life.

If I were lucky, I would hear wolves howl before I slept. But I wouldn't mind if they woke me with their wilderness nocturne.

The Wedding

On Christmas Day 1986 Lorraine said, "Mike and I have to change the date of our wedding." Mike's summer seasonal job was starting earlier in the spring than he had expected, which meant that he would be working on Memorial Day, the date they had originally selected as their wedding day.

Lorraine and her fiancé, Mike Elder, lived in Fairbanks at the time. Mike, a student at the University of Alaska, was earning his secondary teaching certificate, and Lorraine was the editor for the Alaska Native Language Center at the university.

"We've decided to get married during spring break, when Mike will have two days off from school," Lorraine continued. "But that means we've got to find a new location for the wedding. The Sportsman's Lodge on the banks of the Chena River in Fairbanks was a good idea for a May wedding, but it's just not the right setting when the river is frozen."

Joan looked at me, and then at Lorraine, and said, "Would you want to get married at the cabin?" Lorraine and Mike enjoyed visiting the cabin, and in March they'd have fun skiing or snowshoeing in the surrounding forest.

"I hadn't thought about that. Are you sure you can handle that many people?"

"How many guests are you inviting?" Joan asked.

"Well, Mike's mother, Louise, and his brother, Jeff. Pauline Halkett will be the maid of honor and Jeff will be the best man. Probably five or six other friends as well. What do you think, Dad?"

"I think it's a great idea," I said. "Where do you plan to spend your wedding night?"

"Do you think Towills would let us use their little cabin?"

"I'm sure they would. And I'll bet we could get permission from Jaqi Turner to put your wedding guests in her cabin for one or two nights." Jaqi's log cabin stood near the beaver dam; Towill's cabin was at the opposite end of the lake from Jaqi's, half a mile from ours. The owners, friends of ours, seldom used their recreational cabins. Getting permission would not be a problem.

"I'll call them," I said. "Who's going to perform the ceremony?"

"I'll get back to you on that, now that I know we can have our wedding here."

Several days later, Lorraine called and said she had found a justice of the peace from Nenana who agreed to come to the cabin and marry them. "However, his wife is due to deliver a baby about then, and if she does, he won't be available."

"Sounds like you need a backup plan," I said. "With everyone planning on a wedding, it'd be a shame to cancel it at the last minute." I should have known better than to raise that issue. Lorraine always had a plan.

She said, "Well, would you consider performing the ceremony in case the JP can't make it? I checked at the Fairbanks courthouse and learned that you can be appointed as a commissioner of marriage for that day, for that specific ceremony."

I pondered that proposal and finally agreed. After all, I thought, the chances were slim that I'd have to perform a wedding ceremony.

☾

Two days before the wedding, I hauled split firewood to Jaqi's cabin, shoveled off her roof and deck, and stacked the wood on the deck. After I hauled a separate load of firewood to Towills' cabin, I had to dig down through several feet of snow to get to the door, carving snow steps so I could carry firewood inside that tiny shelter. Then I shoveled off the roof so I could find their short stovepipe, hidden under several feet of snow that covered the roof and the windows. I didn't dig down to the windows to let light in, figuring the newlyweds would consider that kind of privacy an advantage.

I built a fire in each cabin the morning of March 20, the day the guests were due to arrive. En route back to our cabin, squinting through snowflakes the size of a quarter, I wondered what Mike's mother, who lived in New Jersey, would think about this unusual wedding in the wilds of Alaska, where outhouses were the norm and indoor plumbing was not. We had never met Louise or Jeff, and we didn't know what they'd think about a three-hour drive from Fairbanks followed by a short snowmachine trip to the cabin.

Meanwhile, Joan completely rearranged the room we called our office. She moved furniture, stowed items that we wouldn't need for three or four days, prepared some of the food, and made paper flowers and other decorations to create a festive air in the cabin. She moved filing cabinets together and laid a large piece of plywood on top of them to make a table big enough to hold all of the food, an impressive array that would include delicacies like smoked salmon, king crab, and wild blueberries.

When we had learned that there would be thirteen of us, we'd stopped planning for a sit-down dinner at a single table and decided to use TV trays and makeshift tables. We'd be a cozy group in that small cabin. Although most of the guests would sleep in Jaqi's cabin, they would eat in ours. We also had to prepare a gift table and attend to what seemed like a hundred other details. We finished the major preparations just in time to drive our snowmachines out to the highway to meet the arriving wedding party.

After we greeted them all, I said, "Louise, go ahead and sit on the cushion in the dogsled behind my snowmachine. I'm sorry that you won't be able to see much because of this snowstorm, but we'll be at the cabin in about twenty minutes." She got comfortable in the sled and I handed her a pair of goggles. Jeff climbed behind Joan on her machine and we prepared to head into the woods.

Louise was warmly dressed and the temperature was in the teens; frostbite wasn't a threat. "Yell at me if you want me to stop," I said, and away we went. Louise was a great sport and laughed most of the way over the trail. Snow caked on her jacket and plastered on her goggles, but she thought the ride in a dogsled was great fun even if dogs weren't pulling it.

A couple of the guests skied in, and Joan and I ferried the rest to the cabin, along with the wedding presents and coolers and boxes filled with food. Lorraine and Mike skied in alone, wearing backpacks. Several years later Lorraine said, "I don't know about Mike, but while I skied to the cabin I spent the time contemplating the big step I was about to take. I was excited and anxious and overwhelmed all at once."

At the cabin, Lorraine said, "By the way, Dad, the JP's wife went to the hospital this morning and is in labor. You get to marry us." She handed me the authorization declaring me a commissioner of marriage, along with the forms I had to fill out and sign so the marriage could be properly recorded in the borough files in Fairbanks. I began preparing appropriate remarks and discussing the ceremony with the bride-to-be.

The party that evening was a great success as we sang, told stories, and laughed until our sides ached. When the party ended, the guests headed to Jaqi's cabin for the night.

☾

The snowstorm had ceased by the next afternoon when we gathered in the living room for the wedding ceremony. I had sworn never to wear a tie again after I retired from the Army, but for this occasion I agreed to wear a white turtleneck—replacing the hated tie—with a gray sport jacket and dark gray trousers. I referred to my style of dress as bush formal.

The bride descended the spiral stairs, stepping slowly to music from our tape player. Dressed in a blue velvet jacket and skirt and white leather boots, she wore white ribbons and white carnations in her hair and carried a bouquet of white carnations and baby's breath.

The groom—wearing a tie—and I watched Lorraine as she approached and took her place next to Mike. Controlling my emotion with difficulty, I performed the ceremony and declared them husband and wife. As I spoke, my eyes met Lorraine's, our eyes filled with tears, and we looked away from each other at the same time. It was a heart-wrenching moment.

Outside, in snow that reached up to the deck railing, bottles of champagne and wine, and cans of soda and beer stood in a row, cooled and ready for the wedding toasts and subsequent festivities. Sunlight splashed a patchwork of gold through scattered clouds and onto the snow. Then the clouds lifted and the sparkling Talkeetna Mountains looked down on the happy occasion while we toasted the bride and groom and sat on the deck enjoying the lengthening daylight. The date was March 21, 1987—the first day of spring, and a wonderful day to begin a marriage.

We changed from wedding clothes into winter clothes and played outdoors, with several of the wedding party making snow angels beside the front deck. Without the happy couple's knowledge, two of the guests skied over to the honeymoon cabin and put apples and oranges inside the newlyweds' sleeping bags.

That night, after the wedding feast and lots of fun and laughter, the bride and groom put on their parkas, boots, hats, and mittens while I went outside to start Joan's snowmachine. I had sneaked out earlier under the pretense of visiting the outhouse and wired a "Just Married" sign and a string of empty cans to the snowmachine.

Mike and Lorraine left the cabin in a shower of popcorn—which we tossed instead of confetti so the birds would remove it from the snow—climbed onto the snowmachine and rode double down the trail to the honeymoon cabin. The cans rattled and clanked along behind.

Lorraine and Mike's wedding was a great example of how living in the bush taught us to deal with life differently. Of necessity, we learned to combine established traditions with our new point of view, blending them joyfully into unconventional results that shaped a lifestyle all our own.

Cabin Bears

Bears wandered through our property from time to time, undoubtedly more often than we realized. One late-spring evening while we were eating dinner, a series of woofs right outside the window grabbed our attention. We looked out and saw four grizzlies clustered on the tundra a few feet from the deck. The sow and three two-year-old cubs scattered when our chairs scraped the floor as we stood up for a better look. Their coats blended well with the tan of last year's grass, and their hair whipped back and forth as their rocking gallop carried them into thick alders along the trail that led to the beaver dam.

Out of our sight, they snarled and growled, making a terrible racket. The din reminded us of cats fighting in an alley, yowling in a whining, unpleasant tone, and we assumed the sound came from the large cubs. We didn't hear the deep-throated growls that one would expect from grizzlies that were nearly grown. However, the sow's deeper *woof, woof* was distinctive. One cub bounded along the far side of Ravenhead Pond, away from the others. The other bears grumbled their way toward the beaver dam.

I said, "Joan, I'm going to walk down to the dock and watch them cross the dam," and stepped out the back door. I had barely closed the door behind me when movement to my right caught my attention. About thirty yards away, the errant cub raced directly toward me. When I emerged from the cabin he tried to stop, but he skidded toward me in the greasy mud from a recent rain. He leaned backward in his attempt to come to a halt, with all four legs stiffly locked. When he stopped sliding, he swapped ends and bolted in the other direction, his feet slipping and churning in the mud as he tried to accelerate. Even though the cub ran away from me, I decided that I didn't need to watch the bear family cross the dam after all. Those two-year-olds were the size of adult black bears, and I wanted no more to do with them. Chuckling, I entered the cabin and closed the door securely behind me.

"Back so soon?" Joan said, with a twinkle in her eye.

"Yeah. I decided not to leave you alone with bears in the area."

☽

Two friends arrived for a visit several years later, and I rowed them across Colorado Lake to the cabin rather than leading them around the lake over the mile-long trail. That turned out to be a lucky decision. As we walked into the cabin one of them said, "Wow, look at that!"

Thinking he was referring to the breathtaking scene outside the cabin's picture window, I said, "Yeah, that's quite a view, isn't it?"

"The view's fine," he said, "but I'm talking about those bears over there!"

I looked across Ravenhead Pond and saw three grizzlies, their golden hair glowing in the summer sun. A female and her pair of two-year-old cubs nosed about in the tundra, munching on blueberries. The trail that we would have taken if I hadn't opted to row across the lake wound through the trees just beyond the bear family. If we had walked along the trail the bears probably would have left without our being aware of them, but one never knows.

The bears didn't spook when we stepped out onto the deck and watched them as they meandered and foraged. Aware of our presence, they glanced toward the cabin frequently. The sow lay down in the mossy tundra and propped her chin up on a large tussock, looking directly at us. The smaller bears continued foraging. After a half hour the sow rose and the entire bear family ambled into the brush.

❨

A black bear showed up in our yard one early-August morning and refused to leave. He ripped the tarpaper off the woodshed wall, then wandered around the cabin, sheds, shop, and outhouse. Finally, after making several attempts to scare him away by blowing a whistle, banging on pans, and bouncing small stones off his back, we decided he was too great a threat to our safety and I killed him with my .338-caliber rifle. Walking to the outhouse at night with that bold bear hanging around didn't appeal to either of us.

❨

Another black bear arrived during breakup, that miserable time of year when we couldn't travel far from the cabin. The snow was too soft for snowmachines, and snowshoes sank too deeply to be of much use. We simply laid in plenty of supplies ahead of time and waited out the three-to-four-week period until bare ground appeared. Spring comes hard at Colorado Lake, and bears emerge from their dens hungry and belligerent.

Breakup didn't deter this huge black bear, who announced his presence by standing on his hind legs and knocking a window screen onto the ground while attempting to climb into the cabin. We were in the cabin. I yelled, grabbed a .38-caliber revolver, stepped outside, and fired a shot over his head. No response. I fired another. Nothing. I shot into the ground beside the bear, thinking that the bullet's impact with the ground would scare him away. Nope. He simply shuffled around to the other side of the cabin. I fired more shots, Joan blew a whistle, we shouted—nothing bothered that bear. Sometimes when bears habituate to people, they develop an aggressive attitude. This bear sauntered toward me while I stood on the deck shooting all around him. That bellicose bruin invaded my comfort zone; I fetched my .338-caliber rifle and ended the episode. When a bear becomes as bold as that one, the only safe thing to do is eliminate the bear.

We didn't leave garbage around to attract them, and bears never rummaged in the burn barrel in which we burned our trash, so we were confident that we hadn't enticed bears in any way. We hated to kill them but, on those two occasions, prudence required that we do so. The rest of the bears we encountered—and we saw lots of them—didn't threaten us.

☾

Joan and I strolled along the lakeshore opposite our property one day in early August, looking across the ripples toward the cabin and enjoying the different vista of our acreage from that vantage point. The lake played with the sunlight, making it glint, dance, and shimmer. We looked across the lake toward the Towills' tiny recreational cabin—an old, seldom-used shelter

"Lee, look at the door to the Towills' cabin," Joan said. "Is it open?"

I peered across the lake, squinting in the bright sunlight.

"Yeah, it sure is. I wonder if someone's broken into it. We'd better go take a look," I said.

We hiked back to our property and I loaded a 12-gauge shotgun, alternating slugs with buckshot. I suspected that a wayward bear might have broken the small lock that secured the door. "I'll take a hammer and nails," Joan said, "so we can nail the door shut if the lock is broken."

We walked along the Towills' indistinct trail until we reached our friends' small hideaway perched on a knoll overlooking the lake. Wooden shutters protected the two windows, but the door hung wide open. "I'll stay behind you," Joan said, gripping her hammer. I pussyfooted up the knoll and, with muscles wound tight as a recoil starter on a snowmachine, eased toward the front door.

Because the bright sun reflected from the exterior log walls, now weathered to a silvery sheen, objects in the shutter-darkened cabin were too dim to identify from where I stood outside. I peered, squint-eyed, into the cabin and caught a fleeting glimpse of fur. I backed away, keeping the gun aimed and relatively steady despite my pounding pulse, expecting a grizzly to charge into the sunlight. I slipped the safety off, swallowed hard, listened intently.

A red squirrel bounded from the cabin and scampered up an adjacent spruce tree. I laughed with relief—a nervous, stuttering laugh. Joan laughed too, but I noticed she clutched the hammer in a death grip.

Chuckling, I said, "What were you going to do with that hammer if a grizzly charged out of the cabin?"

"Hit myself over the head with it if you couldn't stop the bear with your shotgun!"

We approached the cabin again. "That little squirrel didn't do that," I said, looking at the rows of claw marks that gouged the door's exterior. A bear had ripped the lock hasp from the doorjamb.

Stepping across the threshold, we witnessed bear destruction at close range. The black bear—we determined the species from its paw prints and claw marks—had chewed holes in most of the canned goods, knocked pans and dishes onto the floor, and torn one of the cupboard doors loose from its top hinge, leaving it askew and dangling. Flour, salt, sugar, and pepper mixed with the bedding on the floor. Tea, coffee, condiments, and dried food littered the interior. A ketchup bottle, still intact, lay against one wall.

An impressive mess indeed, but that wasn't the worst of the insults. Although I'm not an expert on the frequency of bear bowel movements, that bruin must have stayed in and around Towills' cabin for several days. Six piles of bear dung fouled the floor, and a seventh smelly mound occupied the middle of the lower bunk, a rude comment on the accommodations.

☾

One summer day we heard the constant blowing of a train whistle on the other side of Colorado Lake. When the whistle changed from a long blast to a series of toots, we wondered what caused the commotion. We hurried outside and saw a pair of grizzlies gallop down the slope on the far side of the lake and dive into the water, causing a tremendous splash. I guess the engineer saw them along the tracks and scared them out of the way with his whistle.

Bears are great swimmers, and those bears swam across the lake faster than I could row a boat. When they approached our shore, we retreated to the cabin. The grizzlies sloshed onto the shore, sent showers of gem-like drops in all directions, and disappeared into the spruces and willows.

Bear experts tell hikers that blowing a whistle or wearing bells will scare the bears away. I have fired shots over their heads, blown whistles at them, yelled unkind words, and hit them with rocks. Nothing worked on a bear that didn't want to leave. That train whistle worked but it was attached to a locomotive, which probably impressed those grizzlies more than the whistle did. A handheld whistle will alert a bear to a hiker's approach, however. I preferred to talk in a low voice to alert bears, rather than disturb the wilderness with whistle blasts.

Because bears lived in the forest around our cabin, I probably should have regularly carried a gun when hiking. Instead, I carried a gun for a week or two in the spring, when the bears had just emerged from their dens. Spring bears are often ornery. However, guns are heavy and a nuisance to carry and we just didn't bother with them. Then there's bear spray.

Bear repellent, in a spray can, consists mostly of cayenne pepper. Cayenne pepper in the eyes would cause the bear lots of misery. It might even cause him to leave the area, and probably has worked for some folks. I used bear spray once, but only in practice, not against a bear.

After a grizzly severely mauled a man just four miles away, I decided that maybe we should carry pepper spray. I bought a can of the stuff. Joan and I decided to try the spray can before we really needed it, so on a calm day we selected a stump as a target. The spray I bought was orange, I guess so the bear that has eaten you can be readily identified by the carroty dye on his lips. I stood eight feet from the stump and squeezed the trigger. A cloud of orange mist puffed out of the can, floated out about three to four feet, and slowly drifted off to one side. None of the repellent reached the stump. We were not impressed. We tried it several more times with identical results. I threw the can into our trash. Stopping a charging bear at four feet with a squirt can is more excitement than I require to maintain my interest in life. I don't claim that it won't work, but I'll let someone else perform the procedure and then tell me all about it. When a grizzly charges, I'd rather have a train whistle handy, attached to a locomotive.

❨

I hunted moose near remote lakes, using my floatplane for access. I scouted the region from the air, and if I couldn't find any legal bulls on one lake, I flew to another. Such was the case one fall when I couldn't locate any bulls near my favorite hunting grounds at a remote, nameless lake I called Shallow Lake. I searched farther north and spotted a legal moose on the narrow strip of land that separated East and West Bull Lakes. Part of West Bull Lake penetrated Denali National Park and Preserve, but East Bull Lake lay entirely outside the park boundary. A small hunting cabin nestled on one shore of the eastern lake. An air taxi service built the cabin and used it as a shelter for hunters and fishermen who paid to be flown to the lakes. The cabin squatted on state land and was therefore available for public use, although the air taxi people were prone to argue that fact.

I flew over the bull moose late in the evening, lucky to see him in the gathering dusk as he browsed in deep shadows. I banked away from the bull and flew over to the cabin, buzzed it to determine if it was occupied, decided it was vacant, and landed. I tied up the plane at the north end of the lake and bedded down in the cabin as the light went out of the day.

Up at dawn, I hunted toward the spruces where I had seen the moose the previous evening. After searching for him for several hours with no luck, I hiked back to the cabin and took a nap.

When I opened the door after awakening to the calls of migrating geese, I saw that bull moose directly across the lake from me. The lake is narrow at that spot and he presented a tempting target. Because his random nibbling along the shoreline led him toward my plane at the head of the lake, I watched him until he fed within a few yards of my T-Craft, then I pulled the trigger. He dropped, headshot. I field dressed him, cut him up into quarters and other manageable chunks, and—leaving the head, feet, and large gut pile at the kill site—flew the meat home. Moose hunting doesn't get much easier than that.

Several days later, I ran into a guide in the Cantwell post office and inquired how his hunting season was going.

"Well, pretty good," he said. "Most of my hunters have taken a moose. How about you?"

"I got mine," I replied, "and had an easy hunt too. Moose don't seem quite as plentiful this year though."

"Yeah," he said, "and this is the first year that I haven't flown meat out from Bull Lakes. I'm sure there's a bull or two in that area, but the hunters I dropped off there demanded that I get 'em out of there after one night in the cabin."

"Why's that?" I asked. I had an idea, but figured I'd better appear puzzled.

"When I landed the next day to check on 'em they were really spooked and wouldn't even leave the cabin," he said. "They claimed that a couple of grizzlies had prowled around the cabin all night. Scared 'em half to death. Don't know why the bears would hang around that area. There's lots of blueberries and these guys hadn't shot a moose so there wasn't any gut pile to attract the bears. Whatever the reason, those hunters wanted out of there right then so I had to fly 'em out. Sure was strange, those bears acting like that."

"Yup," I said, thinking about the gut pile from my moose in some bushes not far from that cabin. "That's a strange one all right. Of course, you never can tell why a bear does what he does."

The Fishin' Hole

My airplane's shadow wrinkled its way across the jagged peaks out my left window. Slipping over rock faces and hanging glaciers, the shadow seemed to seek its maker as it climbed the rising terrain beneath the airplane. Anderson Pass came into view, a gap in the Alaska Range. Below, the West Fork of the Chulitna River twisted like braided whiskers growing from West Fork Glacier's furrowed face.

Early that summer I had developed the urge to visit a slice of Alaska that I hadn't seen. A chance encounter in Anchorage with an old friend who lived in a bush village resulted in a destination and departure time. The place to go was north of Kotzebue and the fish were, according to Harry, "biting right now."

The Eskimo town of Kotzebue was more than 500 miles from my regular fishing haunts. It's located above the Arctic Circle, on the end of a spit that separates Hotham Inlet from Kotzebue Sound, which in turn leads to the Chukchi Sea, off northwest Alaska. I had been to Kotzebue several times, but had never fished in that area.

The decision made, I rushed home to the cabin, collected my gear for a remote fishing trip, and did the necessary flight route planning. To fly across hundreds of miles of unfamiliar wilderness in a tiny, two-place airplane is a delightful challenge. My 1946 wheel-equipped T-Craft had no electrical system. Therefore, the plane had no lights, no electrical navigational aids, no radio, and no starter. I swung the propeller by hand to start the engine. A magnetic compass mounted above the meager instrument panel provided me with an artificial sense of direction. A battery-operated, handheld transceiver gave a very limited communications capability—say, five miles or so. My plane was not unique; a few other bush pilots still used basic flying machines like mine.

The T-Craft squeezed through glacier-choked Anderson Pass where weather-chiseled mountain walls on either side left little maneuvering room. Once through the pass, I looked down on Wonder Lake in Denali National Park and Preserve. The lake, a favorite destination for the hordes of tourists who visit the park annually, lay in a shallow basin, framed by the rising foothills of the Alaska Range that were disappearing behind me. Ahead, low hills guarded the western boundary of the park. To my right a broad valley funneled the park road toward the lake. Another series of low hills rambled ahead of my flight path toward the great interior basin, which stretched toward the Yukon River.

The early morning sun backlighted Denali's shadowed western flanks, creating a halo effect that enhanced the mountain's mystique. Rays of sunlight stabbed the blue sky, and the snow dust from a recent avalanche still hung in the air over a rumpled heap of snow and rocks. I glanced at my compass, checked my estimated time to

Kantishna, a tiny seasonal mining settlement beyond Wonder Lake, and settled back to enjoy the scenery.

The weather was forecast to be cloudless but hazy. Smoke from forest fires would restrict visibility near the Yukon River. However, light, wispy smoke began to appear at Wonder Lake, and the smoke thickened considerably near Kantishna. The few buildings below looked gray through the haze. I was on schedule, but Kantishna appeared slightly to the right of where my compass said it should be. Probably a minor crosswind had drifted my plane slightly off course.

A two-and-one-half-gallon gas can rested on the floor of the cockpit. Fuel stops were hours apart in this section of Alaska, and the extra gas provided a safety margin. My plane's tanks held twenty-four gallons of gasoline: twelve in the main tank situated between the engine and me, and six in each wing tank. I planned to stop at Minchumina and pour the extra gas into the main tank.

Lake Minchumina had moved east according to my compass. Shrouded in smoke and haze, it materialized off to my right. I wanted to see the surrounding hills and valleys since I had never been there before, but the thick smoke discouraged sightseeing. I corrected course, frowned at the compass, and landed on the deserted dirt strip to transfer the gas. The smell of smoke stung my nostrils, another reminder of the fires still burning somewhere ahead. Lake Minchumina is one of the largest lakes in the Interior, but the smoke restricted vision to about three miles of its shoreline.

The settlement of Minchumina consisted of a few old Federal Aviation Administration buildings, now abandoned, and a small, locked shack that served as the post office for the weekly—weather permitting—mail flights. About a dozen families occupied widely scattered dwellings throughout the surrounding forest. Most of these bush residents relied on trapping or guiding for their main source of income. I added the fuel, spun the propeller, and climbed back into my plane.

On takeoff the smoke was noticeably worse, but I continued toward my next stop. Gasoline would be available at the village of Galena, on the Yukon, and I planned to rest there briefly.

The limited visibility forced me to fly lower than planned. I thought I recognized my first checkpoint—a river junction. I flew on, unsure of the second checkpoint, and I searched in vain for the mountain that was my third checkpoint. The smoke, thick now, limited visibility to between three and four miles. Flying was legal but marginal, especially over unfamiliar territory.

The twisting streams and innumerable lakes beneath me all looked alike. Each stream tried to double back on itself in that flat terrain, forming an endless series of tree-choked horseshoe bends. The oxbow lakes, formed when the streams changed course, abandoning one of the horseshoe bends, seemed identical. I stubbornly followed my compass heading, thankful I had added the extra gas at Minchumina.

Time crawled. Visibility remained severely restricted, and the swamps resembled one another. I seemed suspended over a never-changing relief map. When enough time had elapsed to indicate arrival time at Galena, I hadn't reached the Yukon River.

Mindful of countless stories about pilots who became lost and exhausted their fuel before taking corrective action, I turned the plane to a heading of magnetic north. Unless the compass was useless, I should eventually hit the Yukon River. Even in this smoke-obscured environment, I couldn't miss that huge river. More than three hours of gas remained.

I forged ahead through the smoke for three-quarters of an hour, straining for a glimpse of that mighty river. I wanted to land, set up my tent, and wait for better visibility, but the trees, swamps, and streams below precluded a safe landing. I landed on gravel bars routinely, but these bars were too short and too narrow to use as runways.

A long scar on a hillside slashed diagonally through the smoke. Turning toward it, I soon recognized it as an airstrip. And there, to my right, a village and the Yukon River slowly emerged from the smoke.

I landed immediately, checked my map, and ambled over to a construction worker who was having a smoke next to an idling bulldozer. The scent of diesel exhaust joined the smell of wood and cigarette smoke. "Is this Ruby?" I asked.

He laughed. "Yes, this is Ruby. Been lost in all that smoke?"

"Sure have. May I use a phone to extend my flight plan?"

"No problem. Where you from?"

"Colorado Lake."

"Where's that?"

"About six miles from the eastern edge of Denali National Park."

"How long you lived there?" This conversation was typical of the exchange between two strangers in the bush.

"About ten years, I guess. Great spot, but every now and then I get the urge to fly to new territory. I'm headed up Kotzebue way to do a little fishing."

"Good to meet you. Good luck, and look out for the smoke," he said as he climbed aboard the bulldozer.

I called and extended my flight plan. With that accomplished, I took off for Galena, downriver, fifty miles away. Ruby's ramshackle buildings quickly disappeared in the smoke. Downstream from the village, a sweeper—a fallen tree—luffed in the Yukon River. The tree's roots clutched the bank as if hoping to escape the tug of the powerful current. That struggle would end when the river inevitably won, pulling the tree toward the Bering Sea.

The Yukon flows through the heart of Alaska, fed by tributaries with names like Koyukuk, Melozitna, Innoko, and Atchuelinguk. Prosaic creeks spill into the river too: Stink Creek, Marten Creek, Big Creek, Birch Creek. The wide river guided me downstream during my uneventful hop to Galena.

An Athabascan Indian village, Galena hosted an assortment of visitors in summer. The Galena airfield, appearing through a gray smokescreen, bustled with activity. Firefighters gathered around planes that would transport them upriver to Hughes to ply their trade. Air taxis took off with miners and engineers aboard, heading into the smoke for unknown destinations. An odd mix of ancient and modern planes, including U.S. Air Force jets, buzzed in and out. Tankers took on loads of slurry to be dropped on the fires to the northeast. I flew my tiny airplane into the middle of this confusion, grateful to have a place to land and stretch.

Commercial fishing for the millions of salmon that swim up the Yukon River to spawn brought welcome cash to the Galena residents. Firefighting provided another money source. Each year lightning ignited dry grass and dead spruces, burning hundreds of thousands of acres of tundra and taiga—small clusters of trees isolated by the surrounding tundra. The tundra, consisting of grasses and tussocks atop peat moss, sometimes smoldered underneath the winter's snows, erupting again in the heat and dryness of the Interior Alaska summer. The fires burned unchecked unless they threatened a community, and then the Athabascans went to work as firefighters for the Bureau of Land Management.

Ten miles upstream from Galena the U.S. Air Force occupied a small ridge, its cluster of buildings providing shelter and recreation for the pilots and support personnel who guarded Alaska's periphery against Russian intrusion. Their dollars contributed to the local economy too.

Fueled and rested, I departed for Kotzebue. I resolved to monitor my compass closely and not miss a checkpoint this time. At these high latitudes the magnetic declination was more than twenty degrees; that is, the compass needle pointed approximately twenty-two degrees to the east of true north. Knowing that, I had factored it into my planning, but I checked my work before takeoff just in case. My calculations proved correct.

Thirty minutes later, lost again, I quit searching for my checkpoints. I knew by now that my compass led me off course, but the reduced visibility prevented me from taking a bearing on a distant-enough landmark to determine the magnitude of the compass error.

Oh well, I had lots of gas and at the worst I would eventually arrive at the Bering Sea. At that point, I'd fly up or down the beach until I came to a village. Or I would land on the beach and camp until the visibility improved. The terrain below became increasingly hilly, and I strained my eyes to see as far ahead as possible. I didn't want a mountain to sneak in front of me in the smoky air. Spruce and birch poked up from the hills, and rivers squiggled through the valleys.

The Granite Mountain radar site thrust its huge towers up out of the smoke a long time later. I recognized the site from a previous visit when I was an advisor to the Alaska National Guard. I turned north, the prevailing wind scrubbed the air clean, and I easily flew on to Kotzebue.

About 2,500 people, mostly Eskimos, lived in this Northwest Alaska hub. The air force occupied a radar site on the hills to the south. Kotzebue also housed the headquarters of the Alaska National Guard's Third Battalion of the 207th Infantry Group (Eskimo Scouts), and several government agencies occupied space in the weather-beaten buildings that made up the town.

The Baldwin Peninsula leads slightly northwest from the mainland, and I followed it to the airfield, which appeared to end in the sea. It didn't; the only road leading out of town separated the end of the airfield from the icy waters of Kotzebue Sound. The road ends at the air force site ten miles away. Airplanes provide the only access to Kotzebue from the rest of Alaska, unless you include the barges that supply the town during the brief ice-free summer.

I landed, happy to climb down from the tiny cockpit and stretch and smell the sea salt blowing in from the sound. In the early evening hush, the only sounds were the occasional squawk from a mew gull and the gentle slap of the tiny waves washing ashore. Then an Eskimo child, maybe ten years old, wearing blue jeans, knee-high rubber boots, and a nylon anorak, zoomed up to me on a three-wheeler and asked, "Where you from?"

"Denali," I replied, knowing he wouldn't be familiar with Colorado Lake.

"Oh," he said and squeezed the throttle, performing a wheelie for me as he headed back into town. His long, black hair floated out behind him, then whipped sideways as he swerved around a mongrel dog lapping at a mud puddle.

I spent the night in Harry's home and told him about my navigation problem. "Harry, I've got a compass problem, and I suspect it's off by several degrees."

"Well," he said, "we'll push your plane over to the Alaska National Guard hangar tomorrow morning. There's a compass rose painted on the ramp there, and we can check your compass against the rose."

"Sounds good." Tired from the tension of flying through the smoke, I excused myself, rolled out my sleeping bag in Harry's den, and went to sleep with visions of an endless expanse of tundra slowly passing beneath me.

We wheeled the plane to the ramp the next morning, and the results shocked me.

When we aligned the plane with north, the compass pointed exactly to north. However, when we turned the plane to a heading of 270 degrees, or west, the compass pointed to 240 degrees, or southwest.

"No wonder you missed checkpoints," Harry said. Because the flight from my cabin to Kotzebue followed a northwesterly heading, the compass led me south of my checkpoints. The deviation from the desired course widened in relation to the distance from my last known location. "Let's tweak it with this brass screwdriver." Harry adjusted the compass.

"Thanks, my friend, and thanks, too, for sharing your house with me last night."

"No problem. Stop in anytime. Have a safe flight."

☾

I left Kotzebue and flew up the beautiful Noatak River, so clear in places it seemed polished. A sweeping bend in the wide river ate away at the gravel bluffs below the Eskimo village of Noatak, exposing cones of permafrost. Although I had visited Noatak in winter and learned of the erosion threatening the village, this was the first time I had seen it in summer. Some of the small weather-scrubbed houses appeared to be on the verge of plunging into the encroaching river.

Upstream from the village the river straightened out, passing through a treeless landscape that rose gently to the Maiyumerak Mountains on my right. Only low vegetation covered the perma-frost, which was spotted with small pools of water that hosted a variety of floating dots that I took to be waterfowl. The Noatak led me on toward the Brooks Range.

A river I'll call Fish Creek flows into the Noatak many miles above the village, deep in the Brooks Range. At that juncture, I left the Noatak and followed the river, looking into the crystal-clear river for fish. Fish Creek flows out of the Brooks Range and wanders through a broad, sparse boreal spruce forest. At this time of year its low banks confined the stream, but the wide, dry, braided riverbed on either side of the flowing water told of violent floods during spring breakup. The dry gravel bars offered a choice of landing places.

Flying perhaps one hundred feet above the river, I could easily see fish finning in the pools and riffles. I spotted hundreds of them and turned back to the pool that contained the most fish. A conve-nient gravel bar sloped gently away from the pool.

I landed and set up camp next to that silvery pool, high above the Arctic Circle. I tied the plane to a log that had drifted downstream during the spring floods and pitched my tent next to the plane. Fish Creek flowed sweet and clear about twenty feet from my orange tent, tinkling as it gathered speed over the riffles, gurgling around the large boulders that provided rest stops for the fish, bubbling when the water swirled over hidden rocks. A few mosquitoes buzzed about, mere remnants of the bloodthirsty hordes present in early summer. A yellow warbler added a splash of color to a spruce snag across the stream, about fifty feet away. A lesser yellowlegs strolled along the far bank, yodeling at me as it teetered back and forth. A golden-crowned sparrow hopped along the gravel bar, and a raven swished overhead. Spruces scented the air. I began to let the tensions of life flow downstream with the murmuring river.

I gathered driftwood for a fire, made a fire ring from rocks, and then changed my mind. I couldn't stand it any longer; I had to go fishing. After what I'd been through to get here, the minor discomfort of an empty belly seemed an unimportant distraction. I munched on a granola bar and rigged my tackle. Casting a fly toward the lower end of the pool, I watched an arctic grayling explode from the water beside the fly, arc through the air, and grab the fly on its way down. The strain of navigating through smoke disappeared at that moment.

For three days, I caught and released fish until my arms ached. In that one pool alone, three different species provided the thrills. Grayling tailed slowly in the riffles at the lower end of the pool. The middle, deeper section contained fresh chum salmon with jaws like bolt cutters. At the upper end, just below three large boulders that made the stream stumble into the pool, arctic char scissored behind one another across the current.

The char, spectacular fighters, preferred to dance on the surface until exhausted. Silver with fluorescent pink spots, they're a beautiful challenge on light tackle. They reminded me of the eastern brook trout of my boyhood, although these char were much larger, weighing perhaps five pounds.

The grayling were great fighters in their weight class and often leaped from the water to take my tiny fly on the way down. At other times, they gently sucked the fly into their mouths as if sipping an after-dinner cordial. These iridescent fish with the big dorsal fin averaged fifteen inches in length, with an occasional fish stretching to seventeen inches.

The heavy chums preferred to slug it out in deeper water, slowly shaking their heads, then stripping line from the reel in sizzling, pool-long runs. My whoops as I raced alongside trying to retrieve line would have amused any observer. Weighing in at ten pounds or more, these salmon exceeded two feet in length, their deep, heavy bodies toned and shiny from their years at sea.

Taking breaks from fighting so many fish, I explored the sparse forest and open glades that extended from the stream banks, stretching my legs and enjoying the stillness away from the rippling water. Berries grew in clusters, offering a taste and scent of blueberry, cloudberry, and mossberry. The green club moss with its tiny spikes of orange made a silent carpet for my boots, and the hum of insects and the chirps of warblers and sparrows kept me company.

Two visitors arrived during my stay on Fish Creek. A loud *woof!* spun me around one evening while I rummaged in my plane for some fishing gear. A grizzly growled at me from across the narrow stream. He shifted his weight from one front foot to the other as if trying to decide whether to fuss at me from his side of the stream or splash across and confront me on a more personal basis. He didn't pop his jaws or make any false charges, so I decided he just wanted to lodge a complaint. I shouted, waving one arm and hanging on to my survival gun, just in case. He muttered several more threats in bear talk and grumbled off into the bushes. His rump, getting fat from eating salmon, waddled and rolled with each step. I didn't see him again until I took off from the gravel bar on my way home.

The next morning a movement below the bank across the pool caught my eye. The cut bank below the skinny spruces gave way to a narrow, sandy beach. A silver fox lapped at his image in a still pool, then hunted along that strand, looking for his breakfast while I prepared mine. His black coat glistened in the soft sunshine and when he turned and caught the reflected light from the pool, I could see the silver guard hairs that gave his coloration its name. Aware of my presence, the fox only occasionally looked at me during his morning hunt and soon disappeared into the brush. The smell of salmon sizzling in my pan brought me back to the important task of refueling for another day of fishing.

I fished, explored, napped, took photographs, rested, read a book, and spent some time just reminiscing. I ate my fill of grayling and char, drank the clear water of Fish Creek, and breathed the smells of boreal forest, tart and fresh on the gentle breeze.

The midnight sun beckoned, impossible to ignore, and I crawled from my sleeping bag at 2:00 A.M., mesmerized by long shadows that stretched across the stream like phantom pontoon footbridges, their wavering shapes seeming to float on the current. Subdued patches of arctic summer sunshine dappled the stream between the shadows, flashing on the ripples like a swarm of fireflies. Only the burbling water interrupted the stillness. I fished for a while, then crawled back into my tent and slept some more. Life doesn't get any better than that.

I left that pool on Fish Creek with reluctance. The fishing had been the best I had ever experienced, the solitude and scenery superb, and the weather perfect. But I had to attend a meeting at Denali National Park and Preserve in a couple of days, so I took a few more photos, loaded my gear into the plane, and spun the prop.

I saw the grizzly about a quarter mile from my campsite as I lifted from the gravel bar. I nodded, mentally returning the river to his guardianship, grateful for having shared one of his fishin' holes.

❆

After a fuel stop in Kotzebue, my old T-Craft and I were ready for the challenge of finding Galena again. The wrinkled hills east of Kotzebue led me onward, and the Great Kobuk Sand Dunes slowly materialized off my left wingtip.

This rippling sheet of sand seems completely foreign to this land of blizzards, permafrost, and rolling tundra. About twenty-five square miles of barren sand scars the open stands of birch and spruce, looking like an oasis in reverse, nature's joke moved here from the Middle East. Originally deposited by ancient glaciers, the sands still resist revegetation millions of years later. Why?

The prevailing wind from the east keeps the dunes in motion and the north wind maintains them, blowing the sand against the Waring Mountains to the south, depositing fresh grains atop the shifting sands of the ancient dunes. These same winds blast any plant life that grabs a foothold, blowing it into the distant arctic landscape.

When the dunes disappeared behind my plane, I turned my attention back to navigation. The checkpoints appeared exactly where I had plotted them, but I arrived at each checkpoint late because of headwinds, those same winds that shaped the dunes. The winds, however, had cleared the area of smoke. Violent gusts rocked me severely when I passed the last ridge before arriving at the Koyukuk River, which flows clear, dumping into the muddy Yukon. The crosswind landing at Galena required all of my attention.

After refueling at Galena, I followed the Yukon River upstream, passing over Alaska Native fish camps with their slowly revolving fish wheels anchored just off shore. A black bear poked about in the

Yukon backwaters. Debris, piled on islands in the river, gave evidence of the power of this tremendous body of water. Entire trees, roots and all, made breastworks on the fortress-like islands. A barge plowed slowly through the current upstream from Ruby. Low, spruce-covered hills flanked the huge river on either side, gently herding it toward its rendezvous with the Bering Sea.

At the Native village of Tanana I left the Yukon, following the twisting Tanana River to its confluence with the Kantishna River. The low sun gave a golden glow to the entire panorama, broken only by an occasional local shower. Scattered rainbows layered pastel colors upon the scene. Moose strolled the marshes, and at one point I maneuvered around a soaring golden eagle.

Turning south, I watched the river village of Nenana slide past my left window. I now followed the Parks Highway, the main route from Anchorage to Fairbanks. The high barrier of the Alaska Range looked formidable, impassible, as I viewed it from fifty miles away. Nearer, the flat willow-and-birch plain below glistened from the multitude of tiny potholes that offered nesting places to thousands of waterfowl.

The route through the Alaska Range revealed itself as I approached the coal-mining village of Healy, and I tightened my seat belt a notch. The usual turbulence bounced me through aptly named Windy Pass, spitting me out on the south side as if glad to see the last of me. I flew over wide, lake-dotted Broad Pass and soon touched down a mile from our cabin.

After tying down my T-Craft on the dirt airstrip and toting my camping gear to our cabin, I walked onto the dock for a look at Colorado Lake. A large arctic grayling, barely ten feet from me, jumped clear of the water, grabbed a mosquito, and splashed back into the lake, sending silver scales of water into the air. My own fishin' hole offered some mighty fine fishin' too, come to think of it.

Frostbite and Flashlights

Daggers of wind stabbed my nose and cheeks. Ten miles from my cabin and without a facemask, I had a problem. I turned my back to the fierce gusts, seeking relief from the cutting wind that assaulted my unprotected skin. Unless I shielded my nose and cheeks, I faced permanent scarring from severe frostbite.

I had been checking my trapline, mindful that the temperature was well below zero, yet unconcerned. Only a slight breeze ruffled my parka hood when I left my cabin in the January morning darkness. In the busy final moments before I departed, I checked my gas supply, attached the trapping sled to the snowmachine hitch and started the machine, but I forgot to take my facemask. Normally, it rode in the small backpack I carried while trapping, but I had used the mask the day before and hung it next to the woodstove to dry; there it remained.

Now, out on the trail in midafternoon, darkness descended, the temperature plunged, and the wind slammed me with little warning. I donned my goggles and turned toward home, hoping to arrive without too much damage to my face. My heavy beard protected most of my cheeks and chin, but the bare skin between my goggles and beard, plus my nose, quickly suffered from minor frostbite.

My breath, condensing all day in the subzero cold, formed frost feathers and icicles that dangled from my three-inch-long beard like chandelier crystals. An insulated beaver hat covered my head, and military-surplus arctic mittens, worn over a pair of woolen gloves, shielded my hands. Synthetic fur, sewn to the backs of the mittens, was handy for wiping a runny nose. Green woolen pants, worn over thermal long johns, warmed my legs. I wore a thermal pullover underneath a wool shirt, a down vest, and a heavy parka that resisted the wind and gave me flexibility. On my feet, my bunny boots were waterproof and warm. I needed only my facemask to be impervious to the numbing wind. Lacking it, my exposed skin suffered as I drove into the icy gusts on my trip home.

Holding the throttle down with my right thumb, I steered the snowmachine with my right hand while pressing the false-furred back of my mittened left hand against my nose and exposed cheeks. Resting periodically, I removed a mitten to hold a warm hand against my freezing nose to keep the frostbite from worsening.

Drifting snow, which the arctic blasts packed into speed bumps that angled across the trail, made one-handed steering difficult as I ricocheted along the trail. The snowmachine headlight pierced the darkness, lighting the rough trail—that is, until the bulb burned out.

Working in the frigid wind and the dim light of a headlamp, I struggled to install a spare bulb, a simple but frustrating job that I couldn't accomplish with my mittens on. Now my fingers lost their feeling, and the replacement bulb fell into the snow twice before I managed to insert it into the spring-loaded headlight socket. With the new bulb installed, I warmed my hands on the engine and then resumed my bouncing journey along the rough trail.

Our frost-covered cabin windows glowed in the distance, cheery spots of warmth that beckoned in the cold darkness. A day on the trail was hard work, but the cabin lights always urged me on when I rounded the last turn in the trail and straightened out for home.

Joan greeted me with a concerned look when I entered the cabin. "Froze your face again, huh?"

"Just a little frostbite."

"It doesn't look so little to me. I noticed your facemask was still here after you left this morning. I thought you'd be back for it."

"I didn't notice it was missing until I needed it."

I stood next to the woodstove, giving the frost and icicles in my beard time to melt and drip. I looked into a mirror to see a white, frostbitten nose centered like a bull's-eye on a cold-puffy, bearded face. Two smaller white spots accented my cheeks between my beard and the oval groove that the goggles had engraved on my skin. Within minutes my frosted nose and cheeks, thawing now, ached with a sharp, cutting pain that made my eyes water. The sensation was nothing new; I had frozen my face before. When a dull ache replaced the sharp edge of the pain and the icicles in my beard turned to water, I removed my outer clothing.

Joan handed me a cup of hot chocolate. "Here. This will help you thaw out."

"Thanks."

I felt like purring in the cabin's cozy heat. My face suffered no permanent damage, and I expected that sometime in the future I would again experience frostbite. Such was life on a trapline during an Alaska winter.

❨

Friends in the Lower 48 often asked us how we survived the cold Alaska winters without thermostats and electric blankets, using only a woodstove for heat. We planned. Regardless of conflicting demands on our time, we filled our two woodsheds with dry wood each spring. As a result, when fall freeze-up gripped the land and slowed the rhythm of our lives, we were prepared for the change of seasons. Our heat source, carefully stacked in tiers, was mere steps from the back door.

I split the wood as we needed it, swinging a splitting maul high over my head, driving the sharp blade deep into the dry spruce. Knots in the swirl-grained, uncompromising spruce sometimes resisted my fiercest blows. Occasionally, a stubborn spruce chunk won the skirmish, refusing to surrender. When that happened, I declared a truce with that chunk of stubbornness and tossed it aside. I knew, although the tree segment didn't, that it had just volunteered to burn to ashes in my shop's barrel stove.

I toted firewood into the cabin one armful at a time and, with a thunder-like rumble, dumped latent warmth into our huge wood box.

The Earth Stove was efficient and the cabin well insulated; we burned only four cords of split spruce during an average winter. An additional cord or two kept my shop reasonably warm while I skinned my catch, repaired sleds, mended broken tool handles, or designed and made birch trinkets that we sold to gift shops.

Because we lived near the upper end of the Matanuska-Susitna Valley, almost in Broad Pass, we were south of the Alaska Range. Therefore, we enjoyed more moderate temperatures than those in Fairbanks, which, located north of the range, shivered in a depression where the cold lingers and numbs. However, our warmer climate came with a cost: wind.

Fairbanks experienced low temperatures of minus fifty and minus sixty degrees, but our lows ranged from minus thirty to minus forty-five degrees. Most of the time at Colorado Lake, at those temperatures, frost crystals hung nearly motionless in the still air. Tree limbs, stressed from a load of snow and ice, fractured with a silence-splitting crack under the combination of weight and severe cold.

Thirty below zero was not T-shirt weather, but, depending on your frame of reference, it was tolerable. I quit flying at minus twenty degrees and quit using my snowmachine at minus twenty-five. I checked my trapline down to minus twenty-five, but below that I stayed home, wrote letters and poetry, and composed articles that I sold to magazines. Joan liked to crochet and knit, among other hobbies, and we read lots of books over the years.

The frost-filled air glistened and glittered in the weak midday sun while we skied on our cross-country skis during cold, calm spells, staying within a mile or two of the cabin. Red polls twittered overhead and ravens croaked as we slid silently along on our skis or squeak-trudged on our snowshoes. In the trees, grosbeaks cracked spruce cones and chickadees, puffed and rounded against the temperature, sang to us.

When the temperature dropped to minus forty degrees and wind attacked from the north, funneling through Windy Pass and spreading across loon country like a whirling, screaming ice fiend, we surrendered. We shut down all outdoor activities, except for two: We still had to go to the outhouse, and I had to split and carry firewood into the cabin. Even those brief excursions required planning. Because I froze my nose several times over the years, and previously frozen flesh freezes more quickly the next time, I had to wear a down facemask when facing such windy conditions. We saw windchill factors plummet lower than one hundred degrees below zero several times. Skin exposed to those temperatures freezes in seconds. Even for trips to the outhouse, we dressed as if we were going for a snowmachine ride. The walls of the little house out back sheltered us from the rampaging wind, but we concluded our activities there with impressive speed.

We adjusted our activities to the cold rather than trying to fight it. We didn't have to be anywhere at a certain time, unlike city dwellers who worked outside their homes. We lived on land that we loved, a plentiful food supply occupied our shelves and filled our natural outdoor freezer, and our shelves held lots of good books.

Wind rattled the cabin, pelted ice crystals against the walls and windows, shrieked around the eaves, moaned around the chimney, and drove an occasional puff of smoke back down the chimney into the cabin. Hoarfrost grew like ferns on the insides of our windows, building up until we couldn't see out, and the daylight hours were short. Darkness made the cold seem more penetrating, and after a three-day blow we were ready for some moderate temperatures of, say, twenty below, with no wind.

We scheduled our infrequent trips to town around the weather. If heavy snow or severe cold was forecast, we stayed home. We were well prepared to withstand nature's fury. Gas lamps illuminated our cabin, and we stored at least four one-hundred-pound propane tanks that were filled to capacity. Our woodstove warmed us. During our first five years there, we melted snow for water and boiled the water that we drank. In later years, we hired a well driller to install a well that could suck water up through a metal pipe and disgorge it into our cabin, a real luxury even though the pipe froze now and then.

Three or more days of severe wind pricked at us like a tight boot rubbing against a blister—annoying, aggravating, maddening. Sleeping became difficult.

Our bedroom, located upstairs, seldom reached a temperature above forty-five degrees during the rare one-hundred-degree-below-zero windstorms. Flannel sheets, heavy wool blankets, and down comforters—all welcome against the night's chill—pressed us firmly onto the mattress. A nightcap protected my bald head, and wool socks warmed our feet. However, getting up and putting my feet into cold moose-hide slippers before descending the stairs to stoke the fire was a guaranteed eye-opener.

Downstairs, we wore long johns under wool shirts and flannel-lined jeans, and staked out claims in the living room, not far from the hard-working woodstove. Heavy, wool-lined slippers over wool socks kept our feet warm. We maintained a living room temperature of around sixty-five degrees when winds spawned at the North Pole sped and swirled across our land. Encouraging our stove to raise the cabin's temperature higher, although possible, forced it to devour wood at an alarming rate.

When the wind beast completed its rampage, silence returned to the land. A frozen, wind-tossed ocean of snowdrifts awaited us when we stepped through our door. Packed into strange shapes and nearly as hard as ice, the drifts rearranged the landscape into a futuristic moonscape. We gazed at a mosaic of semi-circular craters, sloping inclines that peaked then dropped cliff-like, ice-smooth plateaus, ripples resembling an old-fashioned scrub board, and dimpled areas that reminded us of the topping on a lemon-meringue pie. We trudged without snowshoes or skis across open, wind-whipped areas, but we floundered in snow up to our armpits in areas screened by spruce trees. We bounced over the hard drifts on snowmachines, rebounding from the seats the way a tenderfoot horseback rider bobs in the saddle. The constant lurching and bouncing was as hard on the machines as on us, and we began hoping for fresh snow to cushion the rough trails.

When it did snow again, chances were good that a two-foot snowfall would maroon us in our cabin. We would endure each snowstorm, eager to be released from weather-imposed idleness. Winter made the rules; we obeyed them.

❨

Perhaps the greatest irritant was the darkness. We could deal with the cold by remaining indoors or dressing appropriately, but the darkness was pervasive, difficult to defeat. At first, we didn't pay much attention to the long nights as we adjusted to bush life and eagerly accumulated knowledge about the animals and climate. But darkness sneaked up on us in the fall, captured us in winter, and retreated grudgingly when spring approached.

Joan described our winter existence as "life on the end of a flashlight." Flashlights and headlamps accompanied us everywhere. The headlamps—lightweight, battery-operated versions of those worn by miners—were helpful when a task required the use of both hands, such as toting wood from the woodshed or hitching a sled to a snowmachine. We accumulated flashlights like beavers collect willow bushes for a winter feed bed. We stored flashlights of various sizes in every room, in my shop, in the cargo compartment of each snowmachine, in my airplane, and in our parka pockets. Headlamps hung on hooks near the back door, ready to illuminate the trail to the outhouse. More flashlights awaited the call to duty in our pickup truck out at the highway. Our battery supply was a cache of stored energy, ready to provide temporary relief from the enclosing darkness.

Despite owning that many lights, we still lost items from the dog sled. I secured boxes and bags with bungee cords and with ropes, and then threw a tarp over the entire load and lashed it down. Even so, items, including flashlights, shook free somehow, not to be seen again until they poked up through the melting snow at breakup.

After ten years or so, the winters seemed darker for longer periods. Each winter trip to Anchorage or Fairbanks started and ended in the dark, and the brief half hour of daily sunlight we enjoyed at year's end appeared even less illuminating. The darkness was in control until the first days of February when the sun came back from exile. The returning sun diminished the darkness by five to six minutes a day, impelling it northward. The snowscape glittered when the sun finally found our valley, but warmth was more elusive. Soon the cold surrendered to the persistent sun and our favorite season arrived.

Sunshine poured into our April days, and the temperature climbed above zero. Sun arrows ricocheted from millions of snow crystals, flashing into our eyes. Sunglasses replaced flashlights. From one mountain range to the next, sunshine flooded the valleys, washing the land with scintillating sparkle. Joan and I eagerly emerged from the cabin.

Our snowmachines carried us into the Alaska Range, where we reveled in release from the demands of a harsh winter. Sun-drenched alabaster mountains surrounded us. We ate picnic lunches as we lay back on the seats of our snowmachines, letting the returning warmth and light soak away the cold and darkness. Even though the snow would be with us well into May, or even into early June, the sense of having survived another Alaska winter was cause to rejoice in April.

If lunchtime found us at home, we sat on the front deck, blinking in the brightness of the spring sun. We ate on wooden benches, absorbing heat from the sun-warmed wall at our backs. We shared our food with the gray jays that once again behaved territorially, signaling the onset of their courtship season. Those tough camp robbers were year-round companions, braving the terrible winds and bitter temperatures. Their antics cheered us as they prepared to nest with three feet of snow remaining on the ground. Their young often appeared at our feeder before the sun defeated the last of winter's snow cover. We knew when the baby jays appeared that winter was a memory, at least for the next four or five months.

The Cabin Sitter

As much as we loved the bush life, we occasionally flew to the Lower 48 to visit relatives and friends. Each excursion Outside made us appreciate even more the wonderful and challenging life we led. We were so relieved to return to our cabin that we wondered why we left in the first place. Crowds and traffic tired and frustrated us.

We planned our trips Outside during the coldest part of the winter, for why would an Alaskan want to leave the state in the summer when the salmon are torpedoing their way upstream to spawn, and the midnight sun floods the land with constant daylight? We ventured away from Alaska three times in sixteen years, with the first two winter departures from the bush presenting no problems. Our luck ran out while preparing for the third trip.

Unless we wanted to return from a vacation to a frozen mess, we had to find a cabin sitter to keep the fire going. Otherwise, our canned and bottled goods would freeze and burst.

It's not easy to locate someone who wants to take on the rigors of bush living for two or three weeks in the coldest part of the winter. Amazingly, we found two wonderful cabin sitters.

The first sitter was a delightful blonde woman about twenty-two years old. Laura grew up in the state, was an accomplished outdoors person, and knew our area quite well. She just wanted a place to spend a couple of weeks where the rent and food were free. She had no problem operating woodstoves, using an outhouse, or spending time alone. One of her friends visited once or twice during her stay, and together they explored the wild country to the west of our place, reveling in the solitude.

Our second cabin sitter came from Fairbanks. Virgil ran a home for recovering alcoholics and needed to spend a few days away from the demands of his job. He, too, was a skilled outdoorsman, and he later told us he felt like he had died and gone to heaven at our cabin. He loved every aspect of our lifestyle and hated to leave when we returned.

For our third trip, we decided to go to Costa Rica one January to see if perhaps we wanted to move there when we eventually left the bush. I advertised in the Fairbanks newspaper for a cabin sitter and received several calls. I settled on one man, an Alaska Native, who, unfortunately, hurt his back seriously shortly before we were to depart. Then there was the man I'll call Elmer.

Elmer had responded to the same ad, and I kept his number as a backup. I called him, determined to learn more about him and find out whether he still wanted the job.

He claimed he had lived in Fairbanks for six years, long enough to convince me he was no cheechako. Fairbanks in the winter is grim, plagued with ice fog and temperatures of minus fifty to minus sixty degrees. Anyone who had survived that for six years and still claimed he loved winter had to be a tough guy, or so I thought.

Elmer told me he was a retired cab driver from a large city in the Lower 48, a city that saw snow occasionally, but was, generally speaking, located in a mild climate. He said he absolutely loved winter and the colder the better. He didn't drive in the winter, he said, but placed his car in storage until spring. He walked to the store for his groceries no matter the temperature. He wanted to experience a three-week stay in the Alaska bush in January.

I held nothing back, telling him he would have to split wood, start a generator occasionally, ride a snowmachine or use snowshoes if he wanted to travel away from the cabin, and that he would be all alone and isolated. He would have to shovel the snow from our cabin and shop roofs, keep my two airplanes' wings free of snow, feed the birds and marten. "You'll have lots of time to read," I said.

"It's exactly what I'm looking for," Elmer told me over the phone.

I wanted to meet this man, but since he didn't drive in winter and I had no time to drive to Fairbanks just to talk with him, I hired him over the phone, sight unseen. I made a list of his dietary likes and dislikes, and because we had to travel to Anchorage the next day for dental appointments, we were able to buy food that he preferred.

I called him on Friday, finalizing our plans and verifying his desire to live in the bush for a while. I told him what to expect for temperatures, suggested the type of clothing he should bring, and told him the current temperature was fifteen degrees below zero, which would be a warm day in Fairbanks.

"Elmer," I told him, "board the train in Fairbanks on Sunday and tell the conductor you want to get off at Colorado siding. He'll know where that is, and I'll meet you at the railroad tracks and transport you to our cabin in a sled attached to my snowmachine."

"What if you're not there?"

"I'll be there," I assured him. "If for some reason I'm not, just stay put until I get there. The snowmachine could break down, but I have two of them and will certainly be there within a few minutes of one thirty, which is when you're due to arrive."

"What about the bears?"

"Bears?" I said. This was my first inkling that maybe Elmer wasn't all he claimed to be. "The bears are all sleeping, Elmer, and have been for three months. No bear in his right mind comes out of a warm den to subzero weather and nothing to eat."

"If a bear comes along, and he's hungry, he might attack me and eat me."

"Elmer," I said, "take my word for it. Bears are the least of your problems at this time of year."

Joan stood beside me, a puzzled expression on her face. I shrugged and turned back to the phone.

"Wear warm clothes," I said, "and I'll see you at the tracks on Sunday at one thirty. I'll be there fifteen minutes early, although the Alaska Railroad has seldom been accused of being on time."

He agreed and I hung up and turned to Joan. "I'm afraid we have a problem. Anybody who worries about bears in January is one ski short of a pair. I suspect he's someone who thinks living in the bush is as simple as driving to the mall for an ice cream sundae." She agreed, but we were committed now.

I enjoyed the scenery, watching my breath steam and coil into the cold as it drifted away on the breeze in the minus-ten-degree air while I waited for the blue and yellow Alaska Railroad engine to appear. Dressed properly for the temperature, I was toasty warm. The tepid sun sat on the horizon, completing its customary low pass across the mountains to the south. It would disappear less than two hours after it rose.

A bright headlight signaled the train's approach as it rounded the bend three miles up the tracks. I wondered if Elmer would be on board. As the train approached, the engineer tooted the whistle twice, letting me know that the train would be stopping, and I waved so he would know that I understood.

The train slowed to a stop, steam curling from the giant wheels that had warmed slightly from the braking action. The conductor slid back the door to the baggage car and a bearded man wearing a knit cap, multi-colored lightweight jacket, and red-and-white-striped seersucker pants stood in the open door, peering down at me.

"Lee?"

"You must be Elmer," I said.

"Aloha," Elmer said. "We're near Honolulu, right?"

Honolulu was the name of a deserted whistle-stop ten miles farther south, but the way this character was dressed I wondered if he thought he had arrived at a tropical beach.

He jumped down, landing in the soft snow on his desert-boot-clad feet. His light driving gloves completed his paltry defense against the chilly day.

I grabbed the green Samsonite suitcase the conductor handed me and toted it to the dog sled attached behind my snowmachine. While I lashed it down, two tourists, one from South Africa, jumped down from the baggage car and asked if I would join them on my sled for a photo. I consented and the conductor assumed the role of photographer. When he had the opportunity, he rolled his eyes in Elmer's direction, shrugging his shoulders. I got the message. Our visitors usually arrived with backpacks. The Samsonite luggage was not a good omen.

Although I didn't know it, a journalist and a photographer were aboard the train, researching an article about the unique Alaska Railroad. They had met and talked with Elmer during the trip from Fairbanks. He had proclaimed to anyone who would listen that he was going to cabin-sit in a bush cabin.

In the article the writer quotes Elmer, in part: "I haven't met these people, and I just hope and pray that he's there to meet me, because I don't want to pitch camp there in the spruce trees. I don't want to be eaten by bears. I'm sure there's at least one bear that's not hibernating, that's waiting for me."

According to the article, as the train starts up again the conductor, referring to Elmer, says, "He's not dressed for that. His testicles are going to be ice cubes."

I shook hands with Elmer and told him to relax and look around for a minute while I oriented him. I showed him the Alaska Range to our west, pointed to north, and then indicated the direction to our cabin, which was east.

"You can't get lost here because you can always orient on the Talkeetna Mountains over there. See those jagged peaks? I call them Cathedral Spires. You can see them from the cabin's front window."

Elmer was too busy shivering to pay much attention. Because the view from the high snow bank beside the railroad tracks was excellent, I wanted him to know how to reach the highway if necessary.

"The trail to the highway is in that direction. Just follow my snowmachine trail and you'll eventually reach the road."

Elmer's teeth rattled like castanets in a marimba band. The slight breeze probably felt like liquid ice pouring through his thin seersucker pants. His fingers, he said, were turning numb inside his thin driving gloves, and his feet were already clumps of ice surrounded by shoes that were little more than loafers.

"I've only got on a short-sleeve shirt under this jacket too," he informed me. "How far is it to the cabin?"

"It's only a mile or so. Climb aboard the sled and hang on. I'll have you there in no time."

"Can I ride on the snowmachine with you?"

I hated riding double on a snowmachine, but I saw his point. He could use me for a windbreak, but on the sled he'd be exposed to a brisk breeze as we went down the trail and across the lake. I pulled the starter rope.

"OK, get on and hang on to my waist."

I could hear his teeth rattling behind me as we pulled up to the cabin's back door. He didn't stop for his suitcase; he practically ran into the cabin. I followed and introduced him to Joan, whose eyes were rounded in surprise as they slowly looked this stranger over. Those red-and-white-striped seersucker pants would be attention grabbers on a Hawaiian golf course. Out here, at ten degrees below zero, Joan was hard pressed to keep from bursting out laughing. I avoided eye contact with her, knowing the result if our eyes met.

"Elmer, let's go back outside so I can show you around and brief you on the generator, woodshed, and other details. It'll be dark soon," I said.

It took a powerful lot of persuasion and two cups of hot coffee before I could pry him loose from the hearth in front of the woodstove.

I demonstrated how to start the generator, a necessary chore if he wanted to charge the batteries that powered some of the lights. He was nonplussed. Three demonstrations later I gave up. *Let him spend his time in the dark*, I thought. I didn't dare tell him about my propane lights for fear he'd burn the cabin down trying to light them.

We walked over to the woodshed where I had stacked a winter's supply of firewood. His only task was to split and carry what he needed into the cabin. He told me he had never split firewood.

I grabbed my eight-pound splitting maul, balanced a piece of spruce on the chopping block, and showed him how to swing the maul, splitting the chunk into two pieces.

"Oh, my," he said. "I've never done anything like that before."

"Here." I handed him the maul. "Try it. Just place the chunk on the block, put your hands on the maul like this, then swing it over your head and bring it down onto the chunk. Spread your feet far enough apart for good balance and so you won't chop your leg off if you miss the chunk completely."

Elmer gingerly took the maul from my hands and spread his feet so far apart I was afraid he'd dislocate his hips. He lifted the maul about a foot above the chunk, and gave the spruce a love tap that probably wouldn't have broken the skin on my fingers if I'd had them in the way. A woodpecker hits harder than he did, and with better results. After he pecked twice more at the piece of spruce, I figured I knew how he'd spend his time while we were gone. At the rate he was bruising that piece of wood, he'd use up all the daylight splitting enough wood to keep him warm until the next day, when he could do it all over again. We trudged back into the cabin, accompanied by the sound of teeth castanets.

I showed him how the inverter system worked, inverting 12-volt battery DC power to 110-volt AC power for our lights. Charging the batteries about once every five days kept the system in good working order. Elmer was awed as well as odd.

At dinner, a wonderful meal of roast moose, potatoes, vegetables, gravy, and pie, he insisted on relating stories of his life as a cab driver, a topic that failed to excite me. He simply couldn't comprehend the tasks it took to live in the bush, even though I kept steering the conversation back to the essentials of bush living. Every now and then he remembered the bears though, and I doubted if he would brave the short distance to the outhouse in the dark. Shortly after dinner he went upstairs and to bed.

Joan and I hadn't had a chance to pack for our Costa Rica trip, so we took care of that chore before we went to bed. We weren't leaving until Tuesday, but the train ran south only on Sundays, which is why Elmer arrived early. I still had another day to try to get him squared away and familiar with the simple chores he'd have to perform. It seemed a daunting task.

I rose on Monday about 6:00 A.M. and went downstairs to stoke the fire. Joan soon joined me and we prepared breakfast.

"Lee?" came the timid voice from the guest room.

"Yes?"

"Can you come up here a minute?"

I went up the stairs, knowing it was all over.

"Yes, Elmer, what can I do for you?"

"I haven't slept a wink all night. I had chest pains and nearly called you a couple of times. I guess I shouldn't have come out here. The doctor told me I was OK, but it's only been two weeks since I was in the hospital with chest pains. And I'm worried about starting the generator, and I don't understand the inverter, and I don't know if I can split wood, and I don't know where I am, and I don't know where the highway is, and I can't drive a snowmachine, and . . ."

I was not pleased, to put it mildly. "You mean you came out here two weeks after having chest pains? Why on earth didn't you tell me all this over the phone?"

"Well, I wanted to come, and I guess I didn't understand what bush living was all about. I know you have your tickets and will probably have to cancel your trip because of me, but I guess I've got to go back to Fairbanks."

"OK, but I don't have time to take you to Fairbanks. I'll take you to the highway where you'll have to catch a ride any way you can. Because you're leaving, I've got a lot to do."

I turned and went down to the living room, where Joan, having heard every word, squinted her eyes and looked disgusted. She was a woman who had spent many days alone in the cabin while I was gone, sometimes as much as ten days at a time. She didn't have much sympathy for our retired taxi driver.

I decided we were going to Costa Rica in spite of this setback, and to that end we had a lot of work to do in one short day. I called friends, Mark and Gale Borman, who graciously agreed to store our perishables—items that couldn't be frozen—at their place. That meant we had to box up all our food, which was in plentiful supply for Elmer to enjoy, and load it onto the sled to take to our truck out at the highway. We started packing.

Elmer came down, refused to eat much for breakfast, and wisely kept out of our way. He walked around the yard for a few minutes and then came in and said, "Can I use the phone to call a friend in Fairbanks? Maybe he'll come get me and I won't have to hitchhike."

"Sure."

He called. I could, of course, hear only his side of the conversation: "Can you come get me at the Igloo? It's a gas station twenty-five miles south of Cantwell. Well, go see Martha and borrow ten dollars from her for gas. Oh. Well, tell her I'll pay her back when I get to town. Lee owes me forty dollars for the train ticket down here. Call me back."

Within a half hour his friend called back, saying he would meet Elmer at the Igloo sometime around 11:30 A.M. I was relieved that he had found a ride and agreed to get him to the Igloo in plenty of time. I would have taken him there right then, but I didn't want to impose my problem on someone else.

I eventually loaded Elmer onto the sled, tied down his suitcase, and hauled him out to the highway, then along the highway to the Igloo, where I left him. I promptly turned around and sped back to the cabin to start hauling our food out to my pickup. I loaded the boxes onto the truck and drove to the Bormans' house, where Gale told me to call my wife at once.

"Yeah, what's up?" I said.

"You're not going to believe this," Joan said.

"Now what?"

"I just got a call from Elmer's friend. He's in Healy, at the food mart. His truck caught on fire about five miles north of Healy and a wrecker is hauling it in to Healy now. Burned it completely, including the tires."

Healy was a coal-mining village about sixty miles north of us on the route to Fairbanks.

"OK. I'll tell Elmer, but I doubt if he'll believe me."

I finished unloading my food and drove back to the Igloo, finding Elmer walking around outside, looking anxiously north along the Parks Highway.

"Elmer, you're friend isn't going to make it."

"Oh, he'll be here all right."

"No," I said, "he can't make it. His truck burned up."

Elmer looked at me as if I had just told him, for the first time, that the Tooth Fairy didn't exist. "No, he's got a good truck. He'll be along."

"No, he won't. I'm serious. He called Joan from Healy. He's presently hitchhiking back to Fairbanks. I suggest you do the same."

Elmer was having another bad day.

He finally accepted the facts, and the last I ever saw of Elmer, he was bent over in his red-and-white-striped pants, looking in the window of a car parked at the gas pumps and asking the driver if he could catch a ride to Fairbanks. I figured my forty dollars for his one-way train ticket was a small price to pay to move him out of our lives.

As it turned out, other than seeing some pretty country, watching fascinating wildlife, and enjoying the warm climate in Costa Rica, the trip wasn't worth the effort it took to get there. We didn't like the country well enough to move there. I guess I had seen enough jungle in Vietnam.

Our cabin managed just fine without us for three weeks, but when we arrived home at night, the temperature inside matched that outside: twenty degrees below zero. We slept with our long johns on and every blanket we owned piled atop the bed. At that temperature, the woodstove took a long time to drive the cold out of the walls and raise the inside temperature to a comfortable level.

I took even longer to stop chuckling over our would-be cabin sitter. Seersucker trousers and desert boots in the Alaska bush in January? I sure wish I had taken a photo of that apparition. That train conductor was right. Elmer probably did freeze his testicles into ice cubes.

The Untouchables

I poked around in some decrepit abandoned buildings in the central Alaska Range one frigid February day. The snow-covered, tumble-down derelicts, the only remnants of the defunct Dunkle coal mine were tucked into a narrow valley several miles from my cabin. Snow mushrooms grew on the roofs, softening the jagged, splintered boards and ruptured ridgepoles. Snow lay deep in the valley, more than head high. The only sound was the wind whistling through cavities in the decaying remains of deserted dreams. I was alone.

I climbed steps buried under wind-packed snow and entered the old kitchen and communal dining hall, exploring with casual interest. Porcupine droppings, owls' regurgitations of vole hair and mouse bones, and torpedo-shaped rodent parts strained through a fox revealed the identities of temporary intruders into humans' former domain. The worn and scarred table on which miners had rested their elbows while they munched on moose meat was littered with the scatological commentary of the critters that benefited from the coal miners' departure and the mess they left behind.

After finding little of interest, I turned away, walked outside, and snowshoed to the last cabin in the row. I unbuckled my snowshoes and slid down a snowdrift that spilled through an empty window opening and onto the floor of the nearly collapsed cabin. In the semi-darkness of that weathered old cabin, something moved in the shadows.

I jumped back, stumbled over an empty coal scuttle, and landed on my butt in the snowdrift. After I scrambled to my feet, I calmed down and peered into a dark corner at the far end of the narrow room. As my eyes became accustomed to the gloom, I saw a porcupine bristling at me. It raised and flared its quills and shuffled back and forth, giving ample indication of its intent to leave. I got the message and sidled out of its way. The porcupine's quills rustled as the critter waddled up the drift, climbed out through the opening in the sagging wall, and struggled up onto the surface of the deep snow.

I followed the large, clumsy rodent outside to see where it would go in such a bleak and barren landscape. I had noticed only a few willow bushes poking their tops above the snow; no other vegetation interrupted the drifts.

The porky knew the area better than I did. Halfway up a steep hill that rose above the old mining settlement stood a solitary aspen. The determined critter clawed its way toward the tree, often sliding backward as it struggled upward through the loose snow between drifts. It finally reached the tree, climbed to the first branches, and stared down the hill at me.

The ten-below-zero temperature and brisk wind drove me back into the shelter of the building. The porcupine, on the other hand, seemed perfectly contented and unaware of the winter's chill.

☾

Porcupines have thick, yellowish-brown hair with a sprinkling of black and white hairs mixed in. Underneath, the fairly long, soft underfur is brown. This underfur protects them from the icy north wind during the severe Alaska winters.

A different kind of hair—quills—provides protection from predators. These hard spines are needle-sharp, hollow, and barbed for about one-fourth their length. The barbs prevent easy extraction of an embedded quill, a fact many animals have discovered the hard way. Bears, wolverines, and other predators occasionally attack porcupines. The predator usually ends up with an empty belly and a face and mouth full of quills, a painful lesson that lingers. The temptation of a fat porcupine for dinner can confound the judgment of even the supposedly intelligent wolf.

I once shot two wolves that had recently encountered a porcupine. Quills bristled from each wolf's lips and gums, and several quills protruded from their tongues. A quill stabbed into one wolf's tongue so far back in its mouth that swallowing must have been torture. I couldn't remove the slippery spines by gripping them with my fingers because the tiny barbs caught at my flesh, grabbing me just as they had grabbed the wolves. I ended up yanking the quills out with pliers. I wondered what fate would have awaited the wolves had they not been shot. I suspect they would have starved.

Other animals also succumb to the attraction of fresh porky. I found a few quills lying between the flesh and the hide on some of the foxes I skinned. I once skinned a mink that had a quill in its side. Those subcutaneous quills were soft, suggesting that perhaps after the quill works its way under the skin, it softens and then lies parallel to the body at that point, causing little further discomfort. The quill's location probably determines the degree of misery the unwilling host suffers. Usually, initial contact with quills causes pain severe enough to force a predator to abandon the attack.

Legend has it that porcupines throw their quills. Not so. When threatened, a porky raises the quills on its back and sides and swings its tail back and forth. The loosely attached quills release at a mere touch. The heavily quilled, thrashing tail does the greatest damage, driving the little spears deep into the predator.

Porcupines can cause damage in other ways. They have an affinity for salt, and many remote Alaska cabins exhibit porky teeth marks at places where salt has contacted the wood. Sweaty hands implant salt into wooden tool handles, turning the handles into a favorite porcupine snack. Road slush contains salt that sticks to vehicle tires. Porkys love to chew on salty tires. A porcupine chewed partway through the wall of my fuel shed, apparently liking the taste of the redwood stain that protected the plywood. Little wonder that porcupines aren't very welcome around rural homesteads.

Trees, too, undergo the bite of the porky's sharp, orange-colored incisors. The inner bark of aspen, birch, and spruce provides the bulk of their winter diet. A porky will sometimes remain in one tree for several days or even weeks, eating its way around the trunk and branches. The result is usually a dead tree. Porcupines don't travel far in deep snow, and their hungry gnawing often kills several trees in a small area.

The buds and leaves of bushes and trees constitute their summer diet, but because porkys are more mobile in summer, the damage isn't as severe.

Porcupines in Alaska breed in late fall, typically in November. The solitary animals then go their own way. The female gives birth to a single baby in a den located in a ledge, a small cave, or an abandoned building, usually in March. The quills are fully developed at birth, although soft. Quills harden as they dry, and little porcupines are not any easier to deal with than their larger parents.

A young porky grows quickly and soon leaves its mother. When fully grown, porcupines can attain a weight of up to forty pounds, but most are smaller. Their three-foot length includes their six-inch, quill-covered tail. They have four claws on their front feet, rather sloth-like in appearance, and five claws on their hind feet.

Today few people eat porcupines, although some older Alaska Natives use them as an occasional food source. Because porcupines are slow and easy to kill with a club, many hunters refer to them as survival food, although I've never met a hunter or anyone else who claims to have killed and eaten a porky in a survival situation. I suspect that snaring a rabbit would be easier than trying to find a porcupine. They're mostly nocturnal, but do move about some in the daytime. I spent many weeks in the woods and only occasionally encountered porcupines. Most sightings of porcupines occur along highways, where cars take a toll of the prickly mammals.

A porky doesn't ask for much in life. A tender spruce or aspen keeps it healthy and contented for a long time. A porcupine stoically endures the worst weather Alaska can throw at it. It'll avoid people if possible, but if someone insists on challenging it, the prickly critter will respond with a many-barbed reply.

Porcupines remind me of old Alaska sourdoughs I've known.

Meeting the Challenges

Murphy's Law "If anything can go wrong it will, and at the most inappropriate time" convinced me that Murphy must have lived in the Alaska bush at some point.

I chose to think of certain situations as challenges rather than problems, since I prefer meeting challenges to solving problems. I met lots of challenges and so did Joan. We've forgotten many of the routine difficulties, but some stick with us.

☾

When we moved into the cabin in March, I shoveled down through six feet of snow and then used an ice chisel to chop through three feet of lake ice behind the cabin. The lake water, under the tremendous pressure of the heavy snow lying on the ice, erupted like a geyser when I poked that ice chisel through the remaining two inches of ice. That ice water drenched me—nature's chilly initiation into bush life.

We used the water just as it came from the lake for dishes, baths, and laundry. Joan boiled it for drinking.

The following year, we discovered that the lake near the shoreline froze nearly to the bottom by January. When I broke through the ice with my chisel, I unintentionally stirred up the mucky lake bottom, muddying the water. I had to look elsewhere for a clean water supply.

I found a section of the Middle Fork of the Chulitna River, about two miles away, that didn't freeze over until the temperature remained on the south side of minus twenty degrees for several days. Even then, the ice never got thick in one spot. I would lash a new, galvanized thirty-gallon trash can to my sled, hitch the sled to my snowmachine, and haul water from the river. Even with the cover secured firmly in place with bungee cords, about one-third of the water slopped out of the can while I drove over the rough trail. Laundry day required lots of trips. Actually, I hauled the water two days prior to Joan's scheduled washday. She couldn't immerse her arms in the icy water for more than a few seconds, so we heated water in a pot on the woodstove—a slow process—and added it to the washer and rinse tubs to raise the water temperature.

I started a small gas generator and ran an extension cord in through a window. Joan plugged in the old wringer washer and washed the laundry to the swish, swish of the washer agitator slopping clothes back and forth. She ran the clothes through the wringer, and then hung the wet clothes out on a line I had strung between two spruce trees.

We packed the yard with our snowmachines and snowshoes instead of shoveling pathways, and by spring we often walked around with our heads level with the eaves of the cabin, sometimes higher. The clothesline, strung high enough so we could walk under it in summer, disappeared, and I dug down to it so Joan could hang out the wet clothes to freeze. She didn't hang up clothes; she hung them down.

Our sink drained gray water into a dry well, which was a deep hole in the ground lined with logs woven together similar to the way a log cabin is constructed, but without the notches. The wastewater drained into the well, then seeped slowly between the logs into the surrounding soil. The logs kept the soil from collapsing into the hole. Concerned that a sudden large volume of water would overwhelm the well, we emptied the washing machine one bucket of dirty water at a time, and dumped the water on the ground some distance from the cabin. We delayed doing the laundry until we were down to our last set of clean clothes.

☾

A snow belt extended from twenty or thirty miles south of Colorado Lake to ten miles north of our location. Prevailing winds blew moisture north from the Gulf of Alaska until it hit the summit at Broad Pass, where it dumped on the area as snow. Consequently, we received much more snow than most regions of Alaska, excluding the Valdez area. More than 200 inches of total snowfall was common. It settled, but by midwinter at least six feet of snow lay on the land. One year the snow depth measured ten feet.

A steep roof crowned our cabin so the snow would slide off, or so I thought. Our woodstove's chimney emerged about six feet up the roof from the eaves, centered on the length of the cabin. Twelve feet of roof stretched between the chimney and the ridge—lots of room for snow to accumulate, compact itself, and wait for just the right time to release its grip. Six feet of snow built up on the roof before it avalanched.

Joan and I were sound asleep when the damnedest racket woke us. Slide! Rip! Boom! Thump! Then all was quiet.

"I guess the roof dumped its snow load," I said, proud I'd had the foresight to build a steep roof and avoid all that shoveling. We went back to sleep.

Looking out the living room window the next morning, with visibility restricted by darkness and swirling snowflakes, I noticed the huge pile of snow that reached nearly halfway up the window. Something black protruded from the top of the pile, sticking up about three or four inches. The fresh snowfall would soon bury the object; I idly wondered what it was. The woodstove seemed a little smoky as I ate breakfast, but because the outdoor air was thick with snowflakes swirling in a slight breeze, I didn't think the smoke was out of the ordinary.

Daylight finally arrived at 10:00 A.M., allowing me to see farther than a few feet. I strapped on my snowshoes and inspected the snow pile, still curious about the black object I had seen through the window earlier. Fresh snow covered it, but I probed and dug and eventually found it. It was our outdoor section of stovepipe. I looked at the roof. A gaping hole looked back at me, a hole where the chimney was supposed to be. Most of the smoke from the stove curled lazily upward, disappearing into the snowflakes. A smoky puff, boosted by an erratic breeze, curled back into the attic every now and then, which explained the smoky odor inside.

When snow compacts from an avalanche, it's nearly as solidly packed as ice. Not only did I have to shovel all that snow away from twelve feet of chimney, I had to use an ax to loosen the snow before I could shovel it. Finding all the sections of my stovepipe, which had scattered like a flock of fox-spooked ptarmigan, wasn't how I had planned to spend my morning. But I did it, reinstalled the battered chimney, and made a note to buy some heavy conduit to use for a chimney brace. I also made a mental note to shovel the roof above the chimney after each significant snowfall. Murphy won that round, but I figured he wouldn't win another round if chimneys were his targets. Wrong.

We both hated to go to Anchorage and occasionally drew straws; the loser had to make the trip and buy the supplies scribbled on our list that had been two or more months in the making. On one occasion, Joan drove to town while I, having won the drawing, stayed behind. A major snowstorm smothered loon country while she was gone. Busy making crafts in my shop, I didn't realize how much snow had fallen. I eventually noticed how unusually dark it was for 5:00 P.M. in March, and I stepped outside to look around. There was no wind, but snow swirled in the flashlight's beam like white butterflies, so thick I couldn't see the cabin thirty feet away. I shined the beam onto the shop's chimney and decided I'd better get up there and remove the snow above the chimney before the roof dumped its load. I almost made it, but Murphy got there first. When I set the ladder against the eaves, down came the snow, and the chimney rode right along with it. The storm collar where the chimney exited from the roof was badly torn and crumpled— nearly beyond repair. I began digging out the buried chimney. At 8:00 P.M., soaked and weary, I finally completed repairs to the chimney and patched the roof collar.

☾

I tethered my airplanes on the shore of Colorado Lake. Keeping the wings clear of snow during snowstorms consumed a lot of time; I swept the wings just before bedtime, then got up once or twice during the night and did it again. In spite of my best efforts, Murphy managed to outfox me.

On one occasion when we went shopping together in Anchorage, heavy snow fell on loon country. Although no snow fell in town, as we drove home we noticed that the snowbanks alongside the highway increased in height the closer we got to our destination. About forty miles south of Colorado Lake, we ran into a heavy snowstorm that nearly obliterated the road. We crept along in the darkness at fifteen miles an hour in snow that was hubcap deep. When we eventually reached the place where we parked our pickup, we loaded both sleds with groceries and other supplies and towed the sleds behind our snowmachines. I led as we started down the trail in the total darkness. The fresh snowfall had obliterated the trail, but I was confident that I would find the cabin with no problem as long as my snowmachine didn't get stuck.

Huge snowflakes plastered onto my goggles, making them useless, so I drove, squint-eyed, without them. The snowmachine's headlight sliced a narrow cone of light into the chaos of whirling snowflakes. At the head of the lake, the trail made a slight jog to the right and then continued down the lake to our cabin. Adrift in a featureless landscape at night in a blizzard, I didn't recognize the place where I should have turned right, and I continued straight ahead instead.

I became aware of trees on my right where there should have been only open space on the lake. Uh-oh. I couldn't turn around in a short circle because of the twelve-foot sled I towed. If I stopped, the snowmachine wouldn't be able to budge the sled from a dead stop in the loose snow. I kept the throttle down, weaved my way through the trees in a gradual turn, and finally rejoined my back trail. Joan followed. After I reached the point that I figured was well beyond where I should have veered right, I stopped on the trail and unhitched the sled. Joan stayed there while I set off again, and this time I found the lake.

I passed in front of my floatplane just before I reached the cabin and thought it looked rather odd, but I concentrated on breaking trail, giving it little thought. I circled several times to pack the snow at the back door of our home, and then went back for Joan and the sled. We arrived at the cabin, built a fire in the woodstove, and unloaded the sleds. I lashed on my snowshoes and mushed out to the lakeshore to examine the floatplane.

Murphy had struck again. Over three feet of snow had fallen while we were in town, and the right wing strut had buckled under the weight. The floatplane looked like a ptarmigan dragging a broken wing as it squatted, nearly buried, in the blizzard. My ski plane was buried as well, but fortunately the wing struts held and that plane suffered no damage. I began shoveling the accumulated snow from both planes immediately, a task that took more than an hour, and I rose from bed to sweep the planes once more during the night.

Repairing the wing required the services of a certified airplane mechanic, and Larry and I repaired the floatplane when the weather turned warmer in the spring. Before leaving for town in the winters following that expensive lesson, I braced the wings with two-by-fours set vertically under the lift struts.

☾

One early November weekend, I drove to Anchorage to sell our crafts at a bazaar, while Joan traveled to Fairbanks for the same reason.

I drove home in another heavy snowstorm, arriving at the cold cabin at noon. Joan planned to arrive home the next day.

My unfortunate wife had a tough trip. She ran off the road north of Cantwell and got stuck in the ditch. It was snowing so heavily that she simply couldn't see where she was going, but she was afraid to stop because she knew a semi-trailer followed not far behind her and she feared being run over by the big truck.

The trucker crept along, following Joan's tire tracks in the snow. He realized there was a problem when he saw her taillights at an odd angle in front of him, and he stopped just in time. He pulled her out of the ditch and she drove as far as Cantwell, twenty-five miles from our cabin, and called it quits. She spent the night in a motel.

The next day was sunny and reasonably warm. I knew Joan would be coming in, and I tried to break a trail out to the highway so she could ride her machine in on my snowmachine trail. I labored for two hours to travel about 300 yards from the cabin. The trail I had made when I came home was buried under thirty inches of new snow, and the snowmachine would travel only a few feet before it bogged down. I had to turn it around manually, heaving and tugging on the heavy machine, drive back to the cabin where I had packed the yard, turn, then speed back over the packed trail, blasting a few feet of new trail before the snow swallowed the machine again. I finally gave up, strapped on my snowshoes, and fought my way to the railroad tracks about a mile away.

When I arrived at the tracks two hours later, my efforts had left me exhausted and thoroughly soaked. I knew that Joan could walk along the plowed railroad tracks without too much difficulty, but first she would have to break trail to the tracks from the highway, an almost impossible job in that new snow, even though she carried snowshoes in the pickup. I simply couldn't help her; the distance was too far and I was too worn out. When she called from Cantwell to tell me she was on her way, I warned her of the ordeal that lay ahead.

Joan didn't leave Cantwell until 2:00 P.M., after the snowplows had cleared the road south of that town. Hoping to let the new snow settle a little before she started her trek, she had let as much time pass as she could and still start out with some daylight remaining.

The tremendous effort to snowshoe to the railroad tracks nearly wore her out, but she did it. Once at the tracks, she had another three-and-one-half miles to go. She left the highway about 2:45 P.M. and finally arrived at the cabin at 8:00 P.M. She had to scramble over the berm alongside the tracks and allow a train to pass and then struggle back over the eight-foot high berm to reach the tracks again.

Darkness arrives early in November, and she had run out of daylight long before she reached the tracks. We always carried headlamps in winter and she used hers occasionally on this trip, but the clear night and new snow offered good visibility. For most of the journey along the railroad tracks, she trudged along with the light off, conserving the batteries. She was very happy to discover the trail I had snowshoed earlier in the day, but she had to use her light to follow the trail through the woods.

She was one exhausted lady by the time I saw her light bobbing through the trees across the pond out front. I put on my snowshoes and hurried to join her, and she gratefully put her pack on my back for the remaining distance to our cabin. We worked hard for the money we made at the bazaars that weekend.

☾

The deep snows caused us many challenges, but somehow we managed to meet them all. I once broke a ski on my snowmachine while checking the trapline. I cut a branch with my hatchet, wired it to the machine in place of the ski, and drove it home. It didn't steer well, but I made it.

On another occasion, I was breaking trail in unfamiliar territory and ended up plunging over a bank and down into a deep depression. I couldn't drive the snowmachine up out of there and back onto level ground; the spinning track merely dug a hole and the suspended machine sat there while the track spun uselessly. I took a coil of rope from my trapping sled, tied one end to the snowmachine track and the other end to a tree up on level ground. I started the engine, eased the throttle down, and the rotating track acted like a windlass, allowing the machine to pull itself up the hill.

Sometimes our snowmachines broke through the snow cover on lakes and into the water, called overflow, that lay atop the ice under the snow. The heavy snow load on the ice, in part, causes overflow. The ice contracts, cracking in the process, and the weight of the snow forces water up through the cracks. The snow acts as insulation, preventing the water from freezing for hours or even days, and the unsuspecting snowmachiner can't detect that water lies beneath the snow and on top of the ice. The ice is safe enough, but the water freezes quickly when exposed to the subzero air and can rapidly immobilize a snowmachine.

Standing knee-deep in water with the air temperature at minus twenty degrees, trying to extricate machine and sled before the water freezes solid, reminded me of a cleaner but more frigid version of mud wrestling. We developed a healthy respect for overflow after digging our machines out of the slush on several occasions.

☾

We used skis more for recreation than for serious travel. When daylight and relative warmth returned in the spring, we skied through the woods at a leisurely pace, enjoying the outdoors. On crust, we covered many miles easily. That is, unless a volcano erupted.

Mount Redoubt, 150 miles from Colorado Lake, blew its top one winter. Volcanic ash dumped on us a couple of days later, and until it snowed again, covering the half inch of ash, the fallout confined us to the cabin. Ash sucked into a snowmachine's carburetor, and thence into the engine, can quickly ruin the cylinders. Skis and snowshoes don't perform well in ash either.

The volcano erupted twice more that winter. The three ashfalls were a nuisance, but nothing more, and then breakup was upon us. The spring sun licked at the snow until the layer of volcanic ash from the last eruption emerged. The dark ash retained the sun's heat, and it quickly ate its way down to the next ash layer, and repeated the process down to the final layer.

At night the sun-dampened snow froze, forming a concrete-like crust to ski on. While skiing down a steep, shaded hill where the sun hadn't yet nibbled down to the volcanic layers, we zoomed out of the shadows, hit a patch of volcanic ash, and came to an abrupt halt, or at least our skis did. We kept going, headfirst, sliding on the crust, skis still attached to our feet and dragging along behind, until we reached the bottom. Hitting that ash was like running into a giant sheet of sandpaper.

As breakup progressed, increasingly larger areas of ash forced us to detour until skiing became impossible. Ash covered everything, but it was worth it. Volcanic ash is good fertilizer, and a prodigious crop of blueberries purpled the tundra when summer arrived.

☾

One year the ice didn't go out of Colorado Lake until June 14. That was the year snow fell every month of the year; we had only forty-seven frost-free days between the last spring frost and the first frost in late summer. Winter arrived early and lingered long at Colorado Lake.

I referred to breakup as "the annual agony." For a minimum of three weeks each spring, and usually longer, breakup confined us as winter collapsed around us. The snow became too soft for snowmachines, and our snowshoes sank down deep, with the slushy snow falling on top of them. Each step sapped our strength. When the snow melted to a depth of two feet we hiked in hip boots, but lifting our legs two feet in the air at every step removed the pleasure from the day. In planning for breakup, we hauled in lots of supplies in late April because we knew we wouldn't travel to town again before the first or second week in June. Mail would wait in the Cantwell post office until we could retrieve it.

A Chinook blew into our region one year at the end of April, on the day after we left the cabin on our last trip to Anchorage prior to breakup. We had left one snowmachine at the cabin because the clutch was badly worn, and ridden double on the other machine out to the highway. We would buy a new clutch in Anchorage.

Although breakup had never before arrived that early, spring was threatening to become summer when we returned two days later. The temperature was in the low forties when we left the groceries and other supplies on our pickup and, riding double, began our worst trip ever over the winter trail to the cabin.

The trail was a five-foot-deep track of slumping slush that thwarted our best attempts to stay upright and on the trail. We couldn't shift our bodies on the machine at the same instant in order to balance the snowmachine on the melting trail, and the soft snow off the trail embraced us in a sloppy, wet hug each time we toppled. We struggled like that for about two miles; then I gave up, realizing that we would never make it to our cabin riding double.

Joan didn't have the strength to muscle the snowmachine out of the melting snow alone, so I said, "Honey, why don't you stay here while I drive to the cabin and get our snowshoes? Then you can either walk on them or drive the machine to the cabin."

"OK. See you in a half hour or so."

We hadn't taken our snowshoes with us, contrary to our normal routine, because before we left for Anchorage the cold nights had been freezing the melting snow into a thick crust.

The honeycombed snow bogged me down several times en route to the cabin. Consequently, the trip took much longer than I anticipated. Rotten snow and slush covered the lake, making it impossible to drive along our regular trail. I had to break a new trail through the woods and down the isthmus, spending lots of time digging out from the wet snow that nearly defeated me.

I decided I couldn't drive back over that miserable trail. Instead, I strapped my snowshoes onto my feet at the cabin and set out across the lake, knowing that I'd make better time on the railroad tracks. The slush and water made for tough traveling, but I eventually reached the far shore and struggled up the hill that led to the tracks. There, I stepped out of my snowshoes and carried them as I trudged along the snow-free railroad bed. Nearly two hours had passed since I had left Joan behind.

A couple of miles up the track, I began to hear Joan calling, "Lee, Leeeee."

I yelled back, but she didn't hear me.

Joan, thinking something serious must have happened to me, had tried to walk on our deteriorating snowmachine trail. One leg would plunge hip-deep into the sloppy snow, and when she tried to lift that leg, the other leg would plunge into the snow at an angle so she ended up standing on her own foot. Wet snow collapsed on top of her feet, and she had to dig it away with her hands so she could free her legs. She finally gave up and crawled on her hands and knees. However, when she shifted her weight from her knees to her hands, her arms plunged into the mushy snow up to her armpits, driving her face into the sodden snow.

She slung her purse strap around her neck and tossed the purse onto her back out of her way, but it swung around in front each time her arms punched deep holes into the remnants of winter. It hung down from her neck like the small brandy flask that swung from the neck of a Saint Bernard dog. Joan, normally a mild-mannered and cheerful bush resident, continued to call my name. The warm breeze blew toward me, so she couldn't hear my return shouts.

When I arrived opposite where I thought she was on the trail, trees blocked my view, but I hollered to tell her that I was coming and she stopped calling. I strapped on my snowshoes and trudged away from the railroad tracks, slogging through the snow until I saw her on her hands and knees with the purse dangling from her neck. I chuckled but made no comment. Although I knew she was nearly exhausted and I felt sorry for her, the picture she presented was too funny to allow me to keep a straight face. I expected to pay dearly for chuckling, but at least I didn't guffaw.

Rather than carry her snowshoes and mine, I had decided that she could step onto my shoes behind me. Then, stepping in unison, we could make it to the railroad tracks along the trail I had just made. Wrong.

"Where are my snowshoes?" she asked.

I explained. Her face, as red as a boiled crab, reflected her disgust at my decision in particular and with the entire trip in general. In all of the years we lived out there, I never saw her as angry and frustrated as she was at that moment.

"Come on," I said. "Step onto the back of my snowshoes, hold me around my waist, and we'll make it."

We tried, but the waterlogged snow collapsed and we plunged sideways off the trail with every step. I tried counting cadence, left…right… Nothing worked. I finally gave up, removed the snowshoes and gave them to Joan, then struggled to reach the railroad tracks about one hundred and fifty yards away. We finally made it and walked along the tracks, not speaking.

"Wait here while I cross the lake and get your snowshoes," I said. Joan didn't say a word. I donned my snowshoes, crossed the lake and carried her snowshoes back across, and together we trekked across the lake on snowshoes, sloshing occasionally in meltwater between defrosting drifts.

In the cabin, Joan decided to speak to me and said, "Well, I'm never going to town again in the winter without snowshoes. I'm not walking double on snowshoes, either."

"Good idea." I felt guilty for not having taken the snowshoes with us when we left for Anchorage, I truly did. But I had to turn away so she couldn't see the grin on my face from remembering how she reminded me of a Saint Bernard with a brandy flask hanging from its neck when I saw her on her hands and knees with the purse dangling from her neck.

❲

We performed our wood-gathering chores in early spring. The area where we lived offered only spruce for firewood, although hardwood, such as birch, would have been a better heat source. Birch was scarce, widely scattered. An adequate supply of standing dead spruce trees, aged by weather to a silver finish, poked their silhouettes against the sky among the live spruces, and those gray skeletons provided our firewood. Tangles of pesky, head-high willows and alders as dense as steel wool intermingled with the trees, making access to the spruces difficult in summer. Vortices of mosquitoes discouraged summer woodcutting, as did the difficulty of getting the wood to the cabin without cutting trails. Therefore, I cut our firewood in the spring when snow still smoothed the forest floor, having buried most of the bushes.

The majority of the dead spruces straggled across the hillside beyond Ravenhead Pond. To get to them, the day before I planned to cut firewood I packed trails by snowmachine to and around each tree. The trails compacted well overnight, and the following day I could haul a loaded sled with little difficulty. That was the easy part.

Arriving at a dead tree, I stepped off the packed snowmachine trail, sinking up to my armpits. Then I packed the snow close to the tree with my feet, widening the area around the base of the tree enough to allow room for my chain saw. Even tramping and compacting the snow as much as I could, and then cutting the trees level with the top of the packed snow, I still left stumps sometimes as high as four feet above ground. When the snow finally disappeared in late May, those silver stump memorials to departed forest members chronicled my chainsaw's erratic passage across the hillside.

The chainsaw disturbed the quiet, but it couldn't be helped. After I felled a tree, the deep snow compounded the challenge of removing the limbs and cutting the trunk to stove-length pieces. Joan was a great helper, and she stacked the heavy chunks in piles next to the trail so I could load the folding sled without constantly having to move the snowmachine. Otherwise, if I cut the fallen tree into chunks and left them where they lay, I had to either start the machine and move it alongside the cut-up tree or tote each chunk to the sled, with each one lying farther from the sled than the last. She piled the pieces while I hauled each load back to the cabin and stored the chunks in our woodsheds. Snow-soaked and weary by the end of the day, we crawled into bed by 8:00 P.M., groaning as sore muscles punished us for making them work so hard.

Each year we had to travel farther from the cabin to obtain dead trees, traveling more than a mile in search of firewood by the time our years in the bush ended. Nevertheless, each spring we filled two woodsheds with dry firewood before the snow softened too much for travel. We then had the freedom to enjoy the brief summers that went by so quickly.

☾

Hauling supplies from Anchorage or Fairbanks presented minor challenges. In summer, we used large coolers to prevent the perishables from spoiling during the four-hour trip on the highway. Then we used a three-wheeler to transfer everything from our pickup to the cabin. I attached a small trailer to the three-wheeler and made many trips over the trail after each visit to town, towing our purchases to our home.

We continued to use the coolers in winter, although I guess we should have called them "warmers" then. We wrapped them in heavy quilts and never lost any produce due to freezing. We transferred our supplies and groceries from the pickup to the dogsled and folding sled, lashed everything down, and pulled the sleds behind our snow-machines. We carried the boxes and containers into the cabin, then unpacked, sorted, and stored the goods—some in the cabin and some out in the shop. We had become closely acquainted with our groceries by the time we consumed them.

We ate lots of fresh fruits and vegetables for a couple of weeks after a town trip, and then we reverted to frozen foods stored in our propane refrigerator, and canned goods that crowded the shelves of our pantry. Wild game anchored our diet, whether fresh, frozen, or canned. Fresh moose liver and onions was a tradition on the day after I killed our annual moose, and fresh salmon, grayling, and trout were available all summer, just a short walk or brief flight from the cabin. We smoked and canned the salmon we caught, and canned berries and some of our bear and moose meat.

We seldom encountered insurmountable challenges, but when they occurred, we dismissed them as probably a bad idea in the first place. We quickly forgot the minor challenges, and the major ones became part of our memories of life in the Alaska bush.

Hard Splendor

In spite of the many challenges, we loved our life in the bush. Sometimes the land fell asleep before snow arrived to tuck it in. Under the anemic light of a dying sun, summer hardened into autumn. Cold, exiled to the Arctic Ocean in the summer, crept south and seized the land. Ravenhead Pond evicted its feathered summer tenants as subarctic cold sealed its surface. Liquid transformed to hard splendor. We laced on our ice skates in the comfort of the cabin, wobbled down the stairs leading from the front deck, stepped onto the tundra, and toe-walked to the pond. There, we skated onto the surface and glided on clear, petrified water.

We skated, scritching our way around the pond, documenting our passage in long, bold strokes, surrounded by autumn-bright trees. Beyond the ridge, tundra as red as wine stained the mountains, swallowed by termination dust partway up.

Ravenhead's irregular shoreline and the several islands that protruded above the icy surface beckoned, and we followed the meandering edges, looking down through clear ice and wondering if we might spot a frog's nose protruding from the mud. We never did. Marten and mink tracks marked the margins of the pond—dark splotches in the frost that whitewashed the tundra.

Out in the center of the pond we skated fast, slow, forward, backward, and around and around, two middle-aged children reliving a favorite New England winter pastime.

Eventually, ankle-weary and foot-numb, we wobbled back into the cabin, removed our skates and massaged our aching feet and calf muscles, looking forward to the next day, when Colorado Lake should be safe enough to support us. It was, and we toured the perimeter on skates, arms swinging back and forth and legs stroking long, white, staggered chevrons onto the icy surface. Our breath gusted into the cold air, our noses reddened, and frost outlined my mouth as my breath condensed and froze on mustache and beard. Smiles seldom left our faces.

Only the scritch and muffled rattle-rumble of our skates parted the silence, which closed behind us as we glided and coasted across a mirror. Puffy clouds floated in the blue sky and duplicated themselves beneath us on the clear ice—the white breath of early winter mirroring our breath clouds.

☾

The delightful snowless interlude didn't happen every year, and it seldom lasted more than a few days before clouds grayed the scene and decreasing daylight condensed into winter darkness. Storms moved in and drapes of heavy snowfall blocked our view of the Talkeetna Mountains, erasing autumn.

When the sun lost its desire to share its heat, stubborn and unyielding winter clamped down on us. However, nature refused to be left in the dark, and the stars, northern lights, and winter moon replaced the long daylight of summer, at least on clear nights. We peered out our windows, watching the full moon announce its impending arrival by transforming black sky to increasingly lighter shades of gray behind the northeast shoulders of the Talkeetnas. Glowing slowly brighter, the moon burst over the peaks with a surprising swiftness. Pale, surreal moonglow reflecting from the snowy surfaces of mountain, lake, and tundra illuminated our entire valley. The moon could not be ignored; it demanded attention, required us to applaud its efforts. No artificial light or gas-engine smog interfered with nature's extravagant light show.

☾

We dressed warmly, laced on our ski boots, and out we went, eagerly stepping into our cross-country skis that were cached beside the cabin steps. Gliding over our trails, with only the moon and stars for light, we felt as if we were floating in a new and strange and fantastically beautiful world. Puffs of specter-like breath hung above our tracks, slowly falling to join the ski-pole-punctuated tracks on the snow.

On other nights, northern lights waved and beckoned as we took advantage of the respite they provided from winter's chokehold. On snowshoes or skis, depending on snow conditions, we traversed the lake or glided through the surrounding forest, startling an occasional snowshoe rabbit or disturbing an owl that perched on a branch while waiting for a meal to hop or scurry into sight. Overhead, shivering curtains of white-green light pulsated in the frosty sky.

During the brief daylight hours, if the winds had deserted the land, we packed our Coleman stove, moose burgers, and vacuum bottles of hot chocolate into our backpacks and snowmachined to a vantage point high in the Alaska Range. The scenery, accentuated by the midday sun creeping along the horizon, was awe-inspiring. The low sun angle of late November cast a pink glow on the hills and mountains, causing them to blush as if embarrassed that their beauty had been detected. The snow sparkled like sequins and the only sound was the wind, and perhaps a flock of redpolls chirping as they passed overhead. No tracks other than ours disturbed the snow, and for a time neither of us spoke. Moose burgers cooked on the camp stove tasted extra special as we gazed across trackless wilderness and deep into Denali National Park and Preserve.

☾

I occasionally attached my sled to my snowmachine and hauled friends and their skis up to the old Golden Zone gold mine, twelve miles from our cabin. From the mountain that crested above the mine, skiers enjoyed a six-mile downhill run, ending at the West Fork of the Chulitna River. On sunny days in early spring, with temperatures in the low teens, the exhilaration of skiing in wilderness— away from the crowds that crammed the slopes at Mount Alyeska, near Girdwood, and at Arctic Valley, near Anchorage—compensated for the windstorms and darkness and other winter challenges that we accepted as part of bush living.

☾

When April's warm days and freezing nights crusted winter's surface, we mounted our three-wheelers and roamed freely almost anywhere, the rubber tires cushioning our ride over the crust. Unlike snowmachines, the wheeled machines had no windshield, and the rush of spring air past ears no longer covered by hats held the promise of the arrival of loons, ducks, and other winged migrants.

We took care to head toward home before the temperature warmed and softened the crust; three-wheelers bog down in soft snow. But as long as the crust remained hard, we enjoyed the freedom of traveling into areas that were difficult to reach in summer, and we left no tracks.

Unpredictable Bears

Of all the bears we observed or encountered during our bush years, the one thing they had in common was their unpredictability.

I came across bear tracks many times during my journeys through the surrounding forest and on hunting forays far from the cabin. I seldom paid much attention to the tracks, other than to note the species of bear and its apparent size. If a track seemed especially fresh, with water still seeping into it from surrounding mud, for example, I became more alert than a marmot watching an eagle circling overhead.

☾

I hunted moose one year near a large lake about twelve miles from our cabin. Spruces, willows, and some devil's club comprised most of the vegetation, and a few frost-withered berries dangled from scattered cranberry bushes. I eased through the forest, alert, stepping quietly on moss. Eventually I came to a cluster of bushes that blocked my view ahead. I fought my way through the thick clump, making more noise than I preferred, and stumbled into a twenty-five-foot circle that was bare of vegetation except for a loosely structured pile of grass, moss, and small bushes. In the center of the scraped area, protruding from the bottom of that shoulder-high mound, a moose leg pointed directly at me.

Bear tracks in the dirt told the story. A grizzly had killed the moose and buried the uneaten portion, a common habit. Often a grizzly will lie on top of the mound, protecting its kill, but not this time. Perhaps the bear heard me or caught my scent and left before I stumbled onto his kill site. Perhaps he waited in ambush, content to merely watch his kill unless I trespassed closer.

I retreated, walking backward into the brush, facing the kill but swiveling my head in all directions, expecting a charge at any moment. My luck held, and I left the area without incident, convinced that moose hunting would be more productive on the other side of the lake. Besides, I planned to catch an arctic grayling for my lunch and now seemed a good time to accomplish that pleasant chore.

☾

Joan's sister, Martha, and her teen-age son, Jason, visited us one summer, just in time for the salmon run. They caught one or two fish locally, then drove down the Parks Highway to try their luck in Byers Creek. Jason, wading around a bend downstream from the rest of the party, came upon a young grizzly. The bear, perhaps two years old, reacted by running in the opposite direction, splashing from the stream and disappearing into thick bushes that grew on the bank.

Jason reversed his direction, running upstream in hip boots, lifting his knees so high they seemed to rise above his ears. The lad made excellent time against the swift current. "A... A... A... b... b... b... bear!" he shouted, his eyes wide.

"Don't run!" Joan said, though it was rather late for that warning, since Jason was abreast of the group and still high-stepping upstream. I continue to call Jason "Bear Bait," a moniker he'd just as soon I'd forget.

☾

Our daughter visited us one year in late May. We met Lorraine at the highway, and as we bounced over the trail on our three-wheelers, we came upon a cow moose standing in the middle of the trail that crossed the beaver dam half a mile from our cabin. On the ground around the moose, in a tangled mess, lay a long section of my phone line, broken in several places.

Moose normally ran from our approaching three-wheelers, but this cow just stood there, intently gazing toward the south, away from the lake. We stopped, afraid to approach, but within five minutes she moved far enough from the trail to allow us to pass. I looked at the snarled wire and decided the cow somehow got tangled in it and broke it.

I gathered some splicing tools and materials from my shop, and Lorraine and I drove our three-wheelers back over the trail, intending to repair the phone line. The moose had moved fifty yards away from the dam while we were gone, but she still peered intently toward a large clump of alders. I sorted out the twisted mess and started splicing the wire. One end of the unbroken section of wire lay some six to eight feet away from the trail, three feet below us and down in a marshy area. While I spliced the other breaks, I asked Lorraine to retrieve the end of the line. She jumped off the trail and promptly let out a yell. I said, "What's wrong?" and ran over to where she stood.

"Look!" she said. "Look at what I landed on when I jumped!"

I looked down and saw the freshly killed moose calf that lay at her feet, a tiny portion of the head eaten and the body still warm. No wonder the moose cow refused to leave the area. After nervously scanning the bushes for any sign of the bear that killed the calf, we promptly jumped on the three-wheelers and sped to the cabin.

We pieced the story together in the safety of the living room. A bear came upon the cow and calf in the vicinity of the dam. While the cow tried to protect her calf and the bear maneuvered to kill it, they got tangled in my phone line and broke it. The bear won the argument and killed the calf. I can only guess, but I suspect we happened along within five minutes of the kill. The noise of our three-wheelers spooked the bear, and it retreated to the nearby alders to wait until we passed. The cow was staring at the bear's location when we first arrived, although we didn't know it. Most bears will defend a fresh kill, and we were lucky it didn't attack as we crossed the dam. And then we returned, jumped on top of the kill, and still didn't provoke an attack. The bear must have been in a good mood.

I slung my rifle over my shoulder and Lorraine and I went back to finish the splicing job. She stood watch while I worked, but I spent nearly as much time looking at that alder patch as I spent splicing the wire. We didn't see the bear.

We repaired the phone line that evening because, living in bear country, we refused to let the possibility of a bear attack control our lives. We remained alert, but we went about our business and hoped the bears would do the same. When the infrequent encounters occurred, we handled them according to the situation and we survived. Most of the time, the bears did too. Usually they avoided us. I don't know how often a bear let us pass unmolested within a few yards of its concealed location, but I suspect that happened several times.

❅

I hunted for moose with a friend near the old Dunkle Mine one year. We separated and he hiked up the trail to a bare hilltop. I moseyed around an old beaver pond below the hill, hoping to spot a bull moose. I failed to find any fresh moose sign, so I sauntered back to the trail and slowly climbed up to my friend's location. A sort of half smile wrinkled his whiskered face when I approached.

"What are you grinning at?" I said, wondering what could be so amusing about watching me climb a hill.

"Do you know you passed within twenty-five feet of a black bear?" he asked.

"You've got to be kidding! Where?"

"See the patch of alders at the base of that knoll? He was behind the alders, feeding on blueberries. I watched him for a long time, then his head came up and he stood up on his hind legs, looking toward the trail. I saw you walking up the trail and that bear just stood there and watched you pass by on the other side of the alder patch."

I looked down at the alders, but the bear had departed. My friend couldn't have warned me with a shout—the distance was too great—and a warning shot would only have caused me to stop and try to figure out what he was shooting at. Stopping might not have been a good idea, so a savvy friend did the right thing by doing nothing. Fortunately, so did the bear.

❅

I frequently fished in the nearby Middle Fork of the Chulitna River. Salmon, rainbow trout, and large grayling swam in the cold, clear water. To arrive at my favorite fishing hole, about four miles downstream from our home and adjacent to an old, abandoned cabin, I had to travel the final yards through a dense tangle of alders that choked the former trail. One July day, as I emerged from the entanglement, I nearly stepped on a salmon, 300 feet from the river, still bleeding from the teeth marks on its back and sides. I never saw the bear, but I decided that I had important business elsewhere. I assume the noise I had made by deliberately talking and whistling while I picked my way through the alders alerted the bear to my approach and it left. So did I.

❰

Unfortunately, some bear encounters don't end happily. Four miles north of our cabin, near the Middle Fork of the Chulitna River, a man armed with only a hatchet was looking for some property markers. Hearing a noise behind him, he turned and faced a charging grizzly. He managed to hit the beast in the skull with one blow from the hatchet before the bear knocked him down. The bear ripped into the man's neck, scalp, and back, then picked him up in its jaws, shaking him as a dog shakes a rawhide bone. After the grizzly dropped him, it moved away, then returned to attack again, chewing on the poor man's head before leaving for good.

The victim crawled a half mile to the highway, where a passing motorist picked him up and took him to a filling station. A medevac helicopter evacuated him from the gas station to a Fairbanks hospital, where doctors sutured his wounds, using nearly 2,000 stitches during a nine-and-one-half-hour operation.

That encounter, so close to us and on the same river that I fished, reminded me that unpredictability is the only predictable bear trait.

Rapids Landing

I smelled the smoke before I saw it. Unusual cockpit odors were commonplace while I piloted my plane through Alaska skies. The fishy smell of salmon, grayling, and rainbow trout accompanied me during fishing season. In the fall, the blood smell of fresh moose meat and the musty odor of wet camping gear often filled the cockpit, replaced in winter by the damp musk of fresh furs. Nevertheless, the list of acceptable odors in my airplane did not include oil smoke.

I flicked my eyes across the instrument panel, scanning the gauges, and I simultaneously listened for any change from the engine compartment. Streams of smoke began pouring into the cockpit through small holes in the firewall, holes designed to provide passage for the cables and vacuum lines and wires that led to the instrument panel. The smoke filled the entire cockpit, reducing my outside visibility to near zero.

I was on my way home after helping an old friend, Drew Dix, who lived in Manley and had asked if I could give him a hand working on his new log cabin.

❨

Glad of any excuse to fly over some beautiful wilderness and pleased with the opportunity to help Drew, I had climbed into my floatplane at Colorado Lake two days earlier and flown north through Windy Pass. I passed the entrance to Denali National Park and Preserve, gazing down at tour buses, at rafts hauling loads of tourists down the Nenana River, and at the hodge-podge of gift shops, hotels and jammed parking lots that littered Glitter Gulch, the commercial area outside the park boundary.

I skirted the coal-mining town of Healy, altered my course to a more northwesterly heading, and flew across miles of twisted rivers, open muskeg, spruce forest, and marshy meadows. Below, moose browsed knee-deep in lakes, wobbling their heads under the constant torment of mosquitoes. Ducks and swans dimpled the waters of potholes and small lakes, and a swimming beaver created a vee across a mirror-smooth pond.

I landed on the slough at Manley, tied down the plane, and spent a pleasant weekend working on the cabin with Drew and a mutual friend, Jack. I built a door out of spruce and helped frame a window, among other tasks. In the evening, we gathered in a small bar near the airstrip and swapped old war stories and hunting tales. The weather remained clear and warm, and I worked until early Sunday evening.

I inspected my Taylorcraft carefully, said goodbye to my friends, and climbed in. After a routine takeoff, I pointed the nose toward the Alaska Range,

❨

I was approaching Windy Pass, with Otto Lake about ten miles ahead, cruising along against a slight headwind and contented with life, when the smoke-filled cockpit caused an abrupt change in my outlook.

Instinct and experience take over in emergencies. I immediately reduced power to idle, while wildly glancing about the cockpit for evidence of flames. The instruments all registered in the green, or normal.

Coughing from the thick smoke, squinting through smarting eyes, I opened the windows, stomped on the left rudder pedal, and applied right aileron, causing a slip. Slipping the airplane, which allows a rapid loss of altitude without an increase in airspeed, cleared the smoke from the cockpit. I seldom flew very high, but—wouldn't you know it—now, when I needed to land immediately, I had to lose about 2,500 feet of altitude.

With visibility restored, I looked around for a place to land. Otto Lake, obviously the best choice for a floatplane, was too far away. The engine purred smoothly at idle, and I no longer detected smoke. Still, I had to diagnose the cause of the problem, and stepping out onto the floats to open the cowling cover while 2,000 feet in the air didn't appeal to me.

The Nenana River flowed north about a mile to my left as I flew south directly over the Parks Highway. Between the highway and the river, the Alaska Railroad tracks paralleled the highway. If my T-Craft had been wheel-equipped, I would have landed on the highway. The floats canceled that option.

I chose the Nenana River. I identified the railroad bridge at Ferry, a whistle stop on the railroad. Upstream from the bridge the river doglegged to the east, and then ran straight for half a mile or so. I aimed for that inviting straight stretch of river. From my height above it, the water looked smooth and inviting.

In addition to eyeballing the stretch of river I had decided to land on, I also noted the distance and direction I'd have to travel to get to a phone, provided I could walk away from the plane after landing.

I approached low over the bridge, engine still at an idle, followed the river around the bend, and clearly saw, for the first time, the turbulent, frothy water below. Water-scoured boulders interrupted the river, causing two-foot waves.

If I landed and failed to beach the plane before it lost its forward momentum, the swift current would take me back downstream and into the tree-choked bend. A small slough that angled away from the river had appeared, from altitude, to be an ideal exit from the river. I now saw, from close range, that trees crowded the water's edge on each side of the slough; the wings would be destroyed if I tried to enter that backwater. Of course all this time I was gliding and losing altitude, looking at rough rapids, and evaluating remaining options. There were few left.

I looked about 500 yards upriver and spotted a break in the trees that lined the riverbanks on both sides. A sandy beach ran from the river's edge back to a small marshy area. It looked great. Problem was, I was too low to glide that far, and if I landed too far downriver from that beach, I would lose forward momentum in midstream, stop, and float back down the river with the swift current.

My options were now down to two. I could head into the first slough, tearing both wings from the plane as I hit the trees on each side. Not a good option, but one that I felt certain I could walk away from.

The second option was chancy and depended on whether the engine would respond if I applied full power. A short burst of power would allow me to reach that attractive piece of beach. I decided to gamble, and shoved the throttle to the full open position. The engine roared to life. Smoke entered the cockpit.

Trying to see through the smoke while judging distance to my selected point of touchdown, gauging height above those rough rapids, maintaining directional control—all the time worrying again about being on fire—well, life doesn't get much more exciting than that.

Somehow, I put that old T-Crate down on the river, every muscle tense as I bounded across the tops of the waves and walked on the rudder pedals to maintain directional control. I gripped the yoke, clenched my teeth, pointed the plane toward the beach, gave the throttle one last nudge, and rocketed up onto that lovely bit of sand. The force of the floats hitting the sand rocked the plane forward, lifting the tail into the air, but the prop didn't strike the ground and the plane recovered nicely and stopped. I shut off the engine, dove out the door, and raced away from the smoking cowling before the plane quit rocking. Safely away from any possible explosion, I turned and looked back.

Streaks of black oil smeared the underside of the nose cowling. Oil dripped onto the sand below, and tendrils of smoke drifted from the air intake holes and through the cowl hinges. However, the plane wasn't burning.

Swatting mosquitoes, I returned to the T-Craft and opened the cowling. Oil drenched the engine, drizzled and dripped from the hoses and vacuum lines, and fouled the inside of the cover. Regardless, I had landed safely and the airplane remained in one piece. Any landing you walk away from is a good landing. If you can use the airplane again, it's a great landing.

I carefully inspected the engine compartment and found the cause of my problem, a faulty oil pressure line. My mechanic, Larry Draveling, had installed a brand new oil line two days before I flew to Manley. The rubber hose had held together for about four hours of flight time, then a factory defect caused it to burst. The smoke resulted from the oil splashing onto the hot muffler and exhaust pipe. When the plane was under power, the pressure sprayed the oil through the break. When the engine idled, the hose resealed and the oil quit splattering onto the exhaust system. Fortunately, I had responded correctly and the engine suffered no damage because of loss of oil. I don't know why the oil didn't ignite.

I stood in sunshine on the sandy edge of the slough at 9:30 on a June evening, about a mile and a half from the nearest house, and with Joan expecting me home in a half hour. Could have been an awful lot worse. I might have been out over that wild country with no river to land on, facing a wilderness hike of many miles.

I donned my bug jacket—a piece of mesh clothing soaked in insect repellent—pulled its hood over my head, grabbed my gun and survival pack, wove through the trees and meandered around marshy spots, aiming for the railroad tracks. Once on the tracks, I increased my pace and soon reached the small house I had spotted from the air.

When I flew in the summertime, I donned an old olive-drab beret that I wore for a time while in the Army. Unlike the average baseball cap, the beret didn't have a button on top, which made it more comfortable to wear beneath headphones.

I hiked up to the house, holding a shotgun and wearing an olive-drab mosquito jacket with the hood pulled over an army beret. My three-inch beard completed the picture. I must have looked like a fugitive from a terrorist training camp. I knocked on the door.

I have to give the woman who answered my knock a lot of credit for courage. Here I stood, looking like a member of Fidel Castro's militia, and there she stood, all alone and miles from the nearest neighbor. She did jump back a couple of feet, but recovered nicely when I explained that I had just made an emergency landing on the river about a mile and a half away. She was an emergency medical technician, she said, and volunteered to go with me to help the injured. She was a true Alaskan, eager to help a pilot in trouble.

I said, "I was the only one on board and I'm not hurt. Sure would like to use a phone, though."

She looked me over very carefully and said, "OK, come on in," and showed me the phone.

I called Joan, explained my situation, gave her the number I was calling from, and asked her to call Larry and have him call me.

"What's up?" the mechanic said when he called.

I explained. Larry asked, "How risky is the river to land on?"

"Forget it," I said. "Land at Otto Lake. We'll meet you there. This nice lady has offered to drive me down to get you. And by the way, bring four quarts of oil and some new oil line."

Larry gave me an estimated time of arrival, and we left in time to drive the eight miles to the lake and be there when he landed. By this time—1:30 A.M.—it was a bit dusky. She drove us back to her house, and then Larry and I hiked to my plane. He installed a new oil line while I swatted mosquitoes. Then I added the new oil to the oil tank.

I had a brilliant idea. "Larry," I said, "why don't you fly my plane back to Otto Lake? That way, you won't have to walk all the way back to that house."

He looked at the river and then at me and declared, "There's not enough money on earth to get me onto those rapids."

Oh well. It was worth a try.

I walked along that section of riverbank three times, figuring out how best to attempt a takeoff. I would have to dodge several rocks while bouncing downstream and downwind. The wind direction favored an upstream takeoff, but there wasn't enough straight river between the sandbar and the sharp bend. Also, the current ran too swiftly to permit an upstream takeoff. I studied the straight run, the ninety-degree bend below it, and the short straight stretch beyond that bend, at the end of which stood the railroad bridge. The takeoff threatened to be as exciting as the landing had been.

In order to lighten the load so I could get airborne as soon as possible, I added tools, ammo, clothing and other assorted gear to my survival pack, which I handed to Larry. Being a gracious kind of guy, I again offered to carry the load and walk back to the woman's house while he flew the plane off the rapids. Being an intelligent kind of guy, he declined.

The ride down those rapids scared the hell out of me. Each wave threw me into the air, but without enough airspeed to fly, the plane plopped back onto the river, only to be tossed into the air again as it hit the next wave. As the plane stumbled through those rapids, I worked the rudder rapidly, steering around the rocks that protruded above the surface, zigzagging like a skier charging down a slalom course.

One final bounce and the T-Craft flew. Dead ahead lay the dogleg, approaching rapidly. Tension mounted. I banked the Taylorcraft hard right, concerned about catching a wingtip on the rapids a few feet below. Gaining speed and altitude, I rounded the bend. The railroad bridge, dead ahead, seemed twice as tall as it had from the riverbank.

For a split second I considered going under it, but the piers that supported the span seemed awfully close together. Planes don't fly well with a couple of feet of wingtip missing on each side. I had to go over the bridge.

I held the plane level for as long as I dared in order to allow the airspeed to build, then hauled back on the yoke and shot upward. I cleared that bridge with ten feet to spare, leveled out, and headed for Otto Lake.

On approach to the lake in the 2:30 A.M. dusk, at the last moment I spotted red warning balls on some electrical wires strung along the road next to the lake. I added power, cleared the wires, and landed. Rain began falling. For some reason I felt a little tired.

An hour later the kind lady drove up with Larry and dropped him off.

Now the wind increased and swirled the rain around us. I'd had about enough fun for one day. Larry and I climbed into my plane to get out of the weather and munched on some granola bars. I said, "Larry, I almost didn't see those wires next to the road on short final approach. I just barely cleared them."

Larry said, "What wires?"

We emerged from the plane and I pointed to the wires. Larry, now speechless, hadn't seen the wires at all when he had landed. We agreed that things could only improve from here on out. We were wrong.

Since we were both tired and the weather was bad, we agreed it'd be best for Larry to follow me home and eat breakfast and take a nap at our cabin before flying another hour and a half south to his home. Larry's T-Craft, like mine, didn't have an electrical system. That meant no navigation lights on either plane. Visibility was improving, and we could see well enough to fly, but we didn't know what kind of weather we would encounter in the pass.

The weather improved somewhat and a helicopter passed overhead, entering Windy Pass. When it didn't turn around and come back out, we decided we, too, could safely take off and fly into the pass. My plane flew about five miles per hour faster than Larry's, so we decided I would fly high and right, leading, and he would fly low and left, behind me.

We flew into the Alaska Range in that formation. Halfway through Windy Pass, we ran into a rainsquall and heavy wind. Flying the airplane required every bit of skill I possessed, and I wondered about Larry's progress behind me. Turbulence walloped the plane, dropping it with such force in the sudden downdrafts that at times my feet came completely off the rudder pedals. My knees slammed into the instrument panel. The fire-hose stream of rain and wind did its best to blast me into the sheer mountain walls, first on one side, then on the other. And somewhere in the air behind me flew Larry. I could only hope his plane hadn't suddenly acquired faster flight characteristics. Too busy to look back for him, I flew onward, fighting the storm.

That trip through appropriately named Windy Pass was one of the roughest rides of my life. Below me, the Nenana River raced through the gorge in a liquid panic. There were no smooth stretches, and landing in that wind would have been impossible anyway in such a light airplane. I could only hang on and hope the wings would too.

To avoid smashing into the canyon walls, I flew the T-Craft in such a crab—that is, with the nose pointed in a different direction from the flight track over the ground—that I approached the south end of Windy Pass flying sideways. My knees ached from being slammed against the instrument panel, and my knuckles, gripping the yoke, were as white as a January snowdrift. Pilots are normally cool and calm, but this pilot was about out of cool.

After a monstrous cough of wind spat me out of Windy Pass, I gained better control and straightened out, sashaying toward home thirty miles away.

Colorado Lake boiled with two-foot whitecaps and the wind peeled water from the wave tops, sending ragged froth whipping down the lake. I buzzed the cabin to wake Joan, since it was 5:30 A.M. Her help would be crucial in holding the plane against the wind while I tied it down.

Normally I would have flown to another, calmer lake and waited out the wind. Nothing had been normal about this whole affair. Because I hadn't slept in twenty-four hours, and because I worried about Larry, I landed on the unruly, lumpy lake. A crosswind hissed against the plane's vertical stabilizer, slewing the plane sidewise, causing it to stagger, shudder, and shiver.

When I reached the dock I leaped from the plane, dug in my heels, and clung to the wing strut with all the strength left in my trembling arms to keep the plane from being blown into the trees. Joan realized that the wind would cause me serious problems, and my savvy wife arrived at the dock about as soon as I did. Between us, we muscled the plane into its position beside the dock and I threaded the ropes through the tie-down rings, tying the knots with extra care.

Larry landed about five minutes later. I helped him tie his plane down, we walked into the cabin, downed a stiff shot of scotch to calm our frazzled nerves, and sat down to breakfast.

We discussed the flight while we ate, agreeing that we had never before encountered such turbulence. Larry's legs still shook as he climbed the stairs to the guest room. So did mine. We both slept until well after noon, and then Larry flew home in calm conditions.

☾

Flying in Alaska takes skill, courage, experience, and a good measure of luck. I flew in Alaska for many years and probably used up most of my luck. Fortunately, as a pilot acquires flying hours, experience takes over and luck plays a lesser role. Entries in my logbook describe difficulties encountered while negotiating Alaska's skies, but this flight is the one Larry and I still talk about. And each time we discuss that unforgettable night, he shakes his head over the unseen wires at Otto Lake, and he wonders how I managed to control my plane while I bounced downriver during that pogo stick takeoff.

Defining Wilderness

Nature prefers wilderness; humans prefer comfort. Joan and I
wanted to live in wilderness, yet we wanted to be comfortable. We
walked lightly on the land, and the effort seemed worthwhile, but
we strode across the land as if we owned it all. We tried to protect
something that wasn't ours. We resented the intrusion of others
who blasted the hush with the roar of snowmachines. We turned
away those who would trample our property—thoughtless, rude
people who sought fleeting pleasure in the weekend destruction of a
wilderness landscape that had taken thousands of years to compose.

We were selfish, protective, unyielding. And yet, we welcomed
friends to our cabin, and even strangers whom friends recommended.
We were eager to share a few special places with those who could keep

secret an untrammeled, special place, or a pool aboil with salmon, or the aerial spectacle of a mountainside crawling with caribou.

When Joan and I moved to the bush, we weren't fully aware of the impact our presence could have on the future of the lands that surrounded us. We slowly realized that we could protect or destroy, and we chose the former. We used the resources that nature provided, and began to understand the difference between visiting wilderness and living in it. Many visitors charge into wilderness like a williwaw blasting down a mountain valley. The intruders slam to a halt, pull the trigger or click the shutter and leave. A few pause long enough to drink a toast, or perhaps several, and then too many christen the land with the empty containers of their temporary euphoria. They leave, the proud owners of bragging rights. They have challenged wilderness and won, leaving their litter and their thoughtlessness behind.

At some point during our stay in the bush, motor homes became the recreational vehicle of choice. Huge homes on wheels towed huge snowmachine trailers that held four or more snowmachines, and they parked at every turnout along the highways, from Seward to Fairbanks and beyond. The air, particularly on weekends, snarled and whined with the sounds of the snowmachine hordes. Low, stinking clouds of exhaust clung to the turnouts on still days, but still the hordes came, eager to add their contribution to the foul air.

Trails that we carefully groomed to ease our passage while toting groceries from our pickup to our cabin became a series of moguls that jounced our supplies and us as if we were riding a mechanical bull. We left vast areas of snow unmarked because we preferred animal tracks to snowmachine tracks. The weekenders gouged circles and trenches everywhere and, after they left, the slashes hardened and remained, slowing our travel to a crawl.

High-marking became popular, a new way to acquire bragging rights while slashing across wilderness. High-marking is a simple, senseless activity, which consists of determining which snow-machiner can leave the highest track on the targeted mountain. Willows, small spruces, and other bushes that struggle to survive under the harshest of conditions become victims as snowmachines growl over them and snap them off, scattering bits and pieces in their wake. The tracks remain until summer, mute commentary on the insensitivity of a group of people who roared across wilderness on a Saturday afternoon, whooping and hollering and scattering a few ptarmigan, an occasional rabbit, and winter-exhausted moose. Flat-topped trees and clipped bushes tattle on them, lasting monuments to a few minutes of exhilaration and thoughtlessness.

Not only city dwellers ravage the wilderness. Some residents in small villages adjacent to wilderness can't abide having to dismount from mechanical steeds and walk. They hack a trail to a downed moose rather than pack its meat a few hundred yards. Year after year, they slash new trails. Some of those people rely on the subsistence excuse to justify the destruction they cause.

In Alaska, relatively few people live a true subsistence lifestyle, Alaska Natives included. Alaska Native villages in remote regions do rely on subsistence hunting and fishing for a major portion of their diet, and so did we. But even in places with names like Anaktuvuk Pass, Stony River, Tooksook, and others, mail planes visit regularly, depending on weather conditions. The pilots drop off groceries, supplies, and fuel to land-bound villages. Riverboats and barges haul tons of supplies to villages that perch on banks above the Yukon, Kuskokwim, and other major rivers.

How far from those clusters of humanity must one travel to enter wilderness? The distance varies, and some would say the wilderness vanished with the introduction of the snowmachine and off-road vehicles (ORVs). Perhaps it vanished when the Alaska Natives, too, learned to rely on snowmachines and ORVs.

ORV owners have slashed thousands of trails where none existed, creating bogs that constantly widen as hunters seek a drier route around tire-trashed tundra trails that destroy the vegetation that insulates the permafrost. Each time hunters kill a moose or caribou or bear, they hack new trails through the brush and taiga. A few hunters still pack meat on their backs, but, perhaps surprisingly, most of them are sport hunters whom bush pilots drop off, or hunters who own their own planes. Even those who hunt from a riverboat may carry an ORV in their vessel so they won't have to pack game animals any great distance. Hunters seldom use horses and dogs to pack meat anymore.

The few trappers who still use dog power to transport them along their traplines are becoming an endangered species. Whether they travel by dog team, snowmachine, or ORV, the drivers hack trails to ease their entry into wilderness.

My snowmachine transported me along my trapline, but neither the machine nor I cut new trails. I found ways to dodge around alder thickets or through stands of black spruce. I snowshoed many miles in copses where snowmachines couldn't penetrate. However, I left only tracks that would disappear under the spring sun. No evidence remains of my several years of trapping in wilderness.

Because I trapped in it, did it cease to become wilderness? I'm uncertain. I left no visible traces, so perhaps the wilderness was undisturbed, although killing beavers, marten, mink, weasels, foxes and wolves certainly disturbed those animals. The killing disturbed me, too, and that's why I quit trapping. However, the death of an animal doesn't destroy wilderness, any more than the death of a human destroys a society. In my view, greed and the destruction of habitat destroys wilderness.

❨

Firewood, harvested from the forest and burned in our stove, kept us from freezing during the months of subzero temperatures and blasts of subarctic wind. However, I seldom cut a live tree. Tree skeletons, ghostly reminders that nothing lasts forever, hopscotched upright across the state land that abutted our property—trees that had succumbed to old age or insect infestation. The standing, dry trees made excellent firewood. We undoubtedly destroyed lots of potential woodpecker homes when we felled those dead trees, but we limited our impact to a small patch of wilderness.

❨

August is an ambivalent month, uncertain whether to preserve the quiet of a summer evening or shatter the brief summer season with the honking of geese and sandhill cranes or the rattle of musketry when hunters invade. The first frosts nipped the tundra in late August, and by the end of the month, and usually sooner, our woodstove returned to work after a brief summer vacation. The woodstove heralded hunting season.

I gave up on hunting moose near our cabin because the annual hunter invasion spoiled the essence of the hunt. Instead, I climbed into my floatplane and flew to Shallow Lake, about a twenty-minute flight away. Within three minutes of taking off, I had outdistanced the hunters and was puttering along above wilderness, spotting grizzly bears, black bears, moose, and swans as they passed beneath my wings.

When I landed on the lake and taxied to shore to set up my tent, true wilderness surrounded me. My plane left no tracks. The next day I would hunt for a moose, which would supply us with our meat for an entire year. Alone in my tent at night, surrounded by wilderness and the muffled sounds of murmuring ducks, I reflected on my good fortune and savored my opportunity to experience wilderness while that option remained open, unsullied by so-called progress.

Some folks are engineered for city life—where crowds and the rumble of daily routine overwhelm the senses. I lean toward the elbowroom that wilderness offers, and toward silence and solitude and heightened awareness of all of my senses.

I carried mental baggage into the wilderness and, violating my personal code of leaving only tracks, I left that baggage behind. Wilderness absorbed my invisible demons, lifting them from my shoulders and locking them away in a file perhaps labeled "Superfluous." I figured no one would ever know that remnants of Vietnam are filed in the Alaska wilderness.

Looking back on nights spent alone on the shores of wilderness lakes and streams, or on mountainsides, or in abandoned cabins, I can see how wilderness changed me, causing me to rethink my life's goals. I tried not to transform much wilderness during my transformation into a conservationist. I enjoyed wilderness and took what I needed from it, but I left wilderness untouched much as possible. Wilderness fulfilled me.

Song of the Wolves

Gazing from our cabin window one mid-October day, I spotted what I thought was a dog team trotting along the trail beyond Ravenhead Pond. Clumps of snow clung to leafless alder patches, partially screening my view of the team.

The two-foot snow cover offered excellent mushing conditions, but we didn't allow mushers to use our property. Joan and I didn't like stepping on the piles of droppings the teams leave behind. I started to open the door to get the musher's attention when the "dog team" separated into eight individuals, each one nosing about in a different direction.

"Wolves!" I said.

Joan came running to join me at the window. "How many?"

"I'm still counting . . .six, seven, eight. I count four adults and four pups."

The animals ranged in color from ivory to midnight black. "I guess that big white one is the leader," I said. "Those pups must have been born last spring." The smaller wolves were about two-thirds the size of the adults. Wolf pups are born in May and grow rapidly, reaching adult size in less than a year.

We watched while they sniffed the snow that covered some scattered moose bones, the remains of a bull I had shot two years before. "How can those wolves smell bleached-out old bones under two feet of snow?" Joan said.

"I have no idea." The ravens, jays, and shrews had picked those bones clean a long time ago.

The adult wolves poked their noses into the snow, and one of them sneezed. Perhaps the sneeze was a signal because the pack trotted into the spruces, working their way toward the ridge that rose just two hundred yards beyond the pond.

Ten minutes passed, and then the howls of two wolves drifted through the trees. The wild, mournful sound flowed down the ridge and across the open pond, penetrating our cabin walls. Shivers crawled up our spines, and the back of my neck tingled—not from fear, but from delight and awe.

That night I awoke to the sound of wailing sirens. Groggy and half awake, I wondered how somebody could have driven an ambulance to the ridgetop. The ululation penetrated our sleep-numbed brains slowly, the way a dripping faucet eventually screams for attention.

"Joan," I whispered, "listen to the wolves."

The wolf pack serenaded us with a group howl. Wolf song—a caterwauling, rising, falling moaning—reached us from across the pond. First one, then a second wolf would howl, their voices not at all synchronous, but somehow harmonious. The others, not to be left out, yodeled the chorus of the song, their voices trailing off to a low murmur, then rising in a crescendo that suggested hunger and longing and freedom.

We lay in a warm bed, surrounded by the sounds of wilderness Alaska. Few people ever hear the live song of the wolf, and fewer still listen to that wild music from the comfort of a snug cabin.

The pack serenaded us for perhaps three minutes or so, and then silence returned to the night. I wondered how the howls affected prey species such as moose, caribou, or rabbits. Did a different kind of tingle crawl along their spines?

☾

Lone wolves often travel long distances, crossing formidable mountain ranges and swimming swift glacial streams. A moose hunter shot one of these loners about ten miles north of our cabin. Alaska Fish and Game Department biologists had tagged that wolf the previous year on the Kenai Peninsula, a distance of maybe 400 miles the way the wolf would have traveled. He had to detour around Turnagain Arm, a three-mile-wide expanse of tidal water that joins Cook Inlet. The thirty-foot tides in that dangerous body of water would prevent a wolf from swimming across. That barrier cost him many extra miles of travel, but I suppose since he had no destination it didn't make any difference to him. He crossed the rugged Chugach Mountains, skirted the city of Anchorage, traveled through the broad Matanuska-Susitna Valley, crossed an unknown number of rivers, including the Twentymile, Matanuska, Susitna, and Chulitna, and certainly avoided many people and dogs along the way.

His luck ran out and his journey ended when he reached Broad Pass and failed to avoid the moose hunter.

❮

One twenty-below-zero February day another single wolf, marked with the gray and white pattern of Alaska timber wolves, trotted across Ravenhead Pond and nearly up to our front deck. His huge size and his lack of concern in the proximity of our cabin surprised us. Hunting, he sniffed all around the cabin, the shop, the wood-sheds, and my plane tied down on Colorado Lake in back. He cir-cled the cabin and eventually headed back in the direction he had come from. The snow measured six feet deep and, although it had compacted a great deal since the last snowfall, I needed snowshoes to walk on it. The wolf's huge paws served as his snowshoes, and he had no trouble trotting along nearly as easily as he would have on bare ground. I envied his ease of movement.

❮

One crisp, sunny October day with the temperature in the teens, Joan and I strolled along the isthmus between Ravenhead Pond and Colorado Lake. Ahead of us, one end of the beaver dam was an-chored to the isthmus, forming a shoulder-high mound above the frozen ground that we walked on. A three-inch snow cover softened the noise of our passage through berry bushes and over mossy hummocks. Compressed by our boots, blueberries, moss berries, and cloudberries—insulated by the snow cover—oozed juice, stain-ing our footprints bright red and purple. Scattered willows retained a few yellow leaves, but with most of the leaves gone, visibility into the surrounding forest was unimpeded.

As the level of our heads rose above the end of the dam, we came face to face with a gray and white wolf. He was as startled as we were. He spun around and raced away from us, leaving puffs of powdery snow hanging in the air as he zigzagged through the trees. The mental image of that wolf's startled expression has remained with us, a re-minder of a delightful surprise on a gorgeous fall day in the bush.

❨

Another incident with a single wolf occurred while I hunted moose on Shallow Lake. A single, dark gray wolf trotted to the shore at the south end of the lake one afternoon, a distance of 600 yards from our campsite. My hunting partner noticed the wolf first. Mark howled. The wolf howled back. Each wolf howl was a single drawn-out wail, followed by silence. Then Mark howled again, and so did the wolf. This routine continued for perhaps thirty minutes, but the wolf wouldn't come any closer. Wise wolf. He tired of the duet and eventually disappeared into the willow bushes near the lake's outlet. Perhaps Mark howled in the wrong key.

❨

Different wolves react to people differently. For example, I wondered why some wolves ignored our cabin on their infrequent forays across our property. A wolf's nose is an awesome appendage that informs the animal about current events and ancient history, so I assume that human scent notified the wolves that people occupied the cabin. If so, we never understood why some of them weren't bothered by our scent. Wolf tracks in the nearby forest indicated that most wolves detoured around our property.

Some wolves that don't stray from Denali National Park and Preserve—especially the packs whose territory is near the headquarters or encompasses the road to the tiny mining town of Kantishna—become habituated to humans and allow fairly close approaches. Wolf packs whose territory extends both in and out of the park tend to be more wary, the result of being shot at or trapped.

❨

For several years after Alaska outlawed killing wolves from the air, a game law referred to as "land-and-shoot" was in effect. Under the land-and-shoot rules, a pilot had to land the airplane and step out of it before he could legally shoot a wolf caught in a trap. Except for access to a few remote valleys that I couldn't reach by snowmachine, I seldom used my plane to check my trapline.

While flying, I carried my rifle in a scabbard attached to my plane's left wing strut. The only way I could reach it was to land, step out, and extract it from the scabbard. I had to land before I could shoot.

Because I served on several fish and game committees and commissions, I needed to learn about the land-and-shoot process in order to make informed recommendations to the Alaska Board of Game.

While hunting wolves under the land-and-shoot rules one wintry day, I flew low over a spruce-topped ridge and descended into the Ohio Creek drainage about five miles from the southeast boundary of Denali National Park and Preserve. Ohio Creek emanates from one of the many stretch-marked, snow-covered glaciers that incise the valleys of the Alaska Range. Beyond the creek, the mountains stairstep their way higher until they run into Denali—The High One—boldly occupying the top step of the wrinkled, icy staircase.

On the snow-covered river bottom lay a moose carcass. A pack of seven wolves gnawed on the frozen meat.

I reduced power and prepared to land. My plane, on skis, had no brakes. The engine idled so quietly that the wolves didn't hear me and I landed short of them, but the plane's momentum to carried me right into the pack. The Taylorcraft divided the pack; three wolves scrambled away on one side of me and four wolves dashed across the snow on the other side. Trees lined the riverbanks, about 200 yards away on either side. By the time the plane stopped and I jumped out, those wolves had raced into the timber. I had barely jerked the rifle from its scabbard before they disappeared.

I decided right then that killing a wolf legally by the land-and-shoot rules was almost impossible, at least in timbered areas where landing possibilities were limited.

After my plane had glided to a stop and the wolf pack had scattered, I released my snowshoes from the bungee cords that secured them to the right wing strut and lashed them to my feet. I wondered how far from the dead moose the pack would go while I hung around. Upon reaching the spruces that crowded the riverbanks, I marveled at the size of the area the wolves had packed down under the trees. It was the size of a football field, with spruce trees and willow bushes interrupting the packed area. I concluded that the pack retreated to the cover of the trees when not crunching on the moose carcass.

The wolves not only rested among the spruces; they used the area as a sheltered playground. I found several spruce sticks about eight to twelve inches long that were devoid of bark, splintered on the ends, and punctured by teeth marks. The many skid marks indicated extensive play activity, with the sticks used as toys. Wolves play, just as dogs do, and claw marks where the wolves skidded to a stop and changed direction told me that the wolves played their version of tag between meals of moose.

A wolf had scratched out a hole under one tree, and I assumed that a female chose that location for a den. She had dug down through about five feet of snow and eighteen inches of frozen ground.

About the time I began inspecting the hole, the pack began to pour howl after howl down the mountainside right above me. It's difficult to judge the distance and direction of a wolf's song. The notes quaver, rise, fall, and echo. When other wolves join in, the resulting blend sometimes seems to surround the listener. Nevertheless, I judged the distance to be no more than a large parking lot away, but because of the spruces, willows, and alders I couldn't see very far. The howling lasted perhaps for perhaps one minute.

The pack became separated when I landed and spooked them, and their howls probably reunited the scattered individuals. I leaned against a spruce tree, silent, watching, listening. Even though I heard nothing and saw no more wolves, the experience pleased me.

I snowshoed back to my plane and took off, having learned a little more about wolves and a lot about the land-and-shoot technique, which is why I landed among wolves in the first place. I've always wondered if the digger wolf returned, deepening the hole into a den.

☽

Why did pilots risk having their planes confiscated if they were caught shooting wolves illegally? The thrill of the chase drove some pilots to kill wolves from the air. Some hunters simply hated wolves, blaming them for declining populations of moose and caribou. And some broke the law for the money they could receive from selling wolf pelts. The pelts were worth an average of $350 to $450 each, depending on the condition of the pelt, the color, and whether the hide had been properly stretched. Shooting two or three wolves in a period of a few minutes could provide significant income.

I heard tales of unscrupulous pilots harassing wolves from the air until the harried beasts became exhausted. The outlaws then landed and shot the wolves. I remained skeptical of those stories because anyone who would illegally harass a wolf that way would not bother to land first. He would shoot from the air instead, using a shotgun. Nine pellets of buckshot in a shotgun shell increased the odds of hitting a wolf. Killing a wolf with a single bullet from a rifle was difficult.

I never killed a wolf by landing and shooting, although I didn't devote a lot of time to attempting it. I never shot them from the air when it was legal to do so, either; therefore I can't comment on the efficiency of that technique. I've heard it's deadly, but I just didn't believe in that type of hunting. I mention my personal experience merely to illustrate that the *legal* taking of a wolf by airplane is not as easy as some groups would have people believe. Perhaps pilots more skilled than I, or hunters who flew the wide-open spaces of arctic Alaska, were able to legally take wolves by landing and making long shots on running wolves. I have some doubts.

❨

Different wolves react differently to airplanes. Denali wolf packs pay little attention to an airplane overhead. Wolves living outside Denali and other preserves usually run for the timber, if there is any, at the sound of a low-flying plane.

One year a nature photographer hired me to fly him over wilderness for several days in March. I modified the passenger window so he could more easily aim his camera, and he proved to be one tough guy, withstanding the subzero wind that lashed his face while his upper body hung out the window. Joel Bennett and I covered several thousand square miles in our search for wolves to photograph.

Surprisingly, wolves like high places. Except for Dall sheep and mountain goats on specific mountains, no prey species occupy most of the windswept peaks. Nevertheless, wolves often climbed the steep sides of barren mountains. Sometimes wolf tracks led right over the top.

We found one wolf pack high on a mountain that rose nearly straight up from the Nenana River.

"Lee," Joel said, "can you make a pass near that pack?"

"Sure. Get ready."

I banked the plane and flew parallel to the six wolves that lay scattered about on a boulder-strewn ledge. They looked at the plane but showed no other reaction to it.

"Can you get closer? Maybe you could fly straight toward the pack and then bank close to them. That would make a great shot," Joel said.

"OK. I'm afraid they may spook, but here goes."

I circled, lined up with the pack, and followed Joel's instructions. I headed straight for the mountain, rolling the plane into a sharp bank at the last second. The wolves simply ignored us.

"Great!" Joel shouted above the engine noise and rush of the wind past the open window. "Do it again!"

I complied, and shook my head in amazement at the wolves' attitude toward the plane. I could see collars on two of the animals, which told me that this was probably the Headquarters Pack from Denali National Park and Preserve. Because a biologist checked them frequently in his plane, the pack didn't fear planes. Actually, their current location, which was outside the park, made them vulnerable to hunters and trappers, but they didn't know that.

We flew away from that pack and over the great Susitna River basin, a broad valley that encompasses thousands of square miles of wildlife habitat and little human habitation. The Susitna River drains one of central Alaska's most productive areas for moose and caribou. Grizzlies and black bears roam its vastness; wolverines, otters, minks, weasels, and beavers abound. In summer, millions of waterfowl nest in its many potholes, tiny lakes, and river backwaters. Ptarmigan and grouse raise their broods amid the spruce, birch, and alders that cluster on the rolling tundra. Wolves like the area too, and we saw many trails weaving in and out of thickets along brushy hillsides.

"Lee, can you follow that wolf trail?" Joel pointed ahead of the plane to a wavering line of wolf tracks that entered a spruce thicket, came out the other side, and turned to climb a steep, barren hill. Wolves tend to travel one behind the other, and their trails in soft snow are easy to spot from the air.

"Sure, but I expect we'll lose them on top of that hill." I followed the trail until the tracks disappeared on the hard-packed, windswept hilltop. "See what I mean, Joel?"

"Yeah. Can't pick up the tracks on that crust. Oh well, let's head east to Wrangell-St. Elias."

We covered vast sections of Wrangell-St. Elias National Park, flew along treeless ridges, dropped into deep, tree-choked valleys, circled 16,000-foot Mount Drum, and explored the shoulders of Mount

Sanford. Abundant wolf tracks dimpled the snow within the park, but we soon could not distinguish them among the caribou tracks that churned the snow. We gave up looking for wolves in that area.

We had intended to land and spend the night at Chistochina Lodge on the Tok Cut-Off, but the plane rocked violently in crosswinds that were too strong for my tiny plane. I gave up after two landing attempts and flew west, landing on Lake Louise. I dodged a caribou that wandered across the ice just ahead of us, and taxied to Evergreen Lodge. Weary from hours of weaving and bouncing through windy skies, we looked forward to relaxing.

I tied down the plane, and Joel and I walked into the welcome warmth of the lodge. Backing up to the fireplace, we removed layers of arctic clothing while the fire drove the chill from our bones.

"Got reindeer steak for dinner, fellas," the waitress said when we sat down at the family-style table.

"Make mine medium, and bring a carafe of red wine," Joel said.

"I'd like a reindeer steak too," I said. "Medium, please."

"You men out wolf hunting?" the owner said.

Joel and I looked at each other, and I decided to let him handle this one. He was paying the bill so he might as well answer the questions. Joel hunted, but he adamantly objected to aerial wolf hunting.

"Yeah," he said, leaving it at that.

The next day, my tiny plane poked its nose into the Ohio Creek drainage, wandered back and forth across Broad Pass, searched Caribou Pass, climbed into the hanging valley that leads to oddly named Honolulu Pass, and ended the odyssey in Denali National Park and Preserve.

The rangers at the park knew Joel and me and directed us to one of the wolf packs they were studying. We were grateful, for their kindness saved us fuel and perhaps several hours of searching. We also secured permission to fly lower than the minimum legal altitude when flying inside the park boundaries.

When we first sighted the wolf pack, I expected them to run from the airplane like wolves did that lived outside the park. Not these wolves. They were a pack of six, loosely spread out in a rough triangle, slowly padding across the snow-packed tundra. A band of perhaps thirty caribou slowly grazed about a half mile ahead of the pack, pawing down through the snow for lichens. The watchful caribou stared at the wolves, between efforts to paw through the snow to reach the frozen caribou moss that makes up the bulk of their winter diet.

I reduced power, Joel opened the window, and we passed over the wolves at 200 feet, low enough to spook most wolves that I had previously encountered. These wolves merely glanced casually up at the plane and kept moving steadily in the direction of the caribou. I was astonished.

"Let's make the next pass lower," Joel shouted above the engine roar and screaming wind.

"OK," I shouted in reply.

I cranked the plane around in a tight turn, chopped power, and descended to about a hundred feet. Joel recorded the scene on his movie camera, and I figured this would be his last chance at this wolf pack. But once again the wolves paid us little attention.

"Lower!" Joel screamed. I shrugged, made another circle, lined up on the pack, and dropped down to 50 feet. Same result. Of course, photographers are never satisfied, always wanting one more shot, or a different angle, or maybe the light would be better over there...

Joel, one of the best in the business, convinced me to fly lower. Now he wanted me to bank the plane as we flew by the pack, allowing him to extend the shot as we came around in front of the wolves. "Pretend your wingtip is the camera," he said. "The shot will be much more impressive if you rotate around the pack."

Airplanes are not capable of ninety-degree banks at slow speed close to the ground, at least not the ones I flew. Nevertheless, I complied with his wishes—within allowable safety limits—and on the next pass my right wingtip sliced the air within twenty-five feet of the ground as I banked in front of the pack's leader. Unbelievably, that leader stopped and sat down. I guess he figured he'd take a break while the idiots in that airplane finished whatever they were doing.

We made pass after pass, and the wolves took it all in stride. A wolf biologist had been studying them from a plane for several years, and they had become so accustomed to seeing airplanes that for them it was just another day on the tundra. Besides, that caribou herd interested them more than an airplane on skis. Joel finished filming and I took the plane up to a more reasonable altitude. We wanted to see what would happen when the wolves narrowed the distance between themselves and the caribou.

The wolves slowly fanned out, one beside the other, spaced roughly thirty feet apart. They picked up the pace from a walk to a slow trot, and at that instant every caribou head in the herd came up and swiveled toward the wolf pack. A long look, a mass turning of the herd, and the caribou began their strange, bouncing trot away from the wolves.

The wolves seemed in no hurry, but we were, and we had to leave before the drama concluded. A dwindling fuel supply limited our time above the wolves. I banked the plane onto a course for home.

As we flew through brilliant sunshine in the scoop-shaped hollow that was Foggy Pass, needles of light surrounded us, flashing off snow that had been wind-ruffled into frozen fleece. I looked at Joel, who was as entranced by the sparkling scene as I was. His face resembled the fiery blush of a boiled Alaska king crab. His long exposure to the wind and below-zero temperatures concerned me, but he recovered with no lasting problems.

My mind retains a lasting image of the wolves on line, the caribou trotting away from them, and the entire drama a mere speck upon mile after mile of rolling tundra.

❨

For a time in the mid 1980s, Denali National Park and Preserve wolves were magnets for poachers. The vastness of the park makes it impossible for one airborne park ranger to cover the entire area. The rangers sometimes use dog teams, but ground patrols aren't much of a deterrent to illegal aerial activity. I detest poachers. They're lowly thieves who steal wildlife from legitimate hunters and wildlife observers and can harm endangered species.

The eastern park boundary meandered through the mountains only six miles east of the cabin. I spent a lot of my own time and money patrolling the West Fork of the Chulitna River, Easy Pass, the Bull River drainage, and as far south as the Eldridge Glacier. I burned many tanks of gas on my private patrols while on the lookout for poachers.

While flying up the West Fork of the Chulitna River in Denali National Park and Preserve one beautiful day in late winter, hoping to show a friend a wolf pack I had seen the day before, I met a low-flying Super Cub. The mountains rose steeply on either side of us, leading us up the river toward Anderson Pass on the left and Easy Pass on the right. The Dunkle Hills eased the transition from mountain to plain behind us. The snow-packed valley sparkled and twinkled in the bright sun.

Ahead, a dead wolf sprawled on the snow in the middle of the river bottom. Human footprints mingled with the tracks from a ski-equipped airplane, telling the story. After a low pass to look things over, I turned and flew back out of the valley, headed for a telephone.

I landed on Colorado Lake, rushed to the phone, and described the situation to the chief park ranger. He asked me to return to the scene and keep an eye on things until they could get a plane into the air and begin their investigation.

I returned to the kill site, but too late. Apparently the poacher, on the ground, had heard me coming during my first trip up the valley and took off. His was the plane I saw when I first approached the crime scene. He probably circled above the Dunkle Hills, a treeless area just north of the West Fork, waiting to see what I would do. When I flew back out of the valley, he returned to the West Fork, landed, and picked up the dead wolf. The wolf carcass had disappeared by the time I arrived the second time, so I flew home.

Two hours later, the park rangers landed on my lake and told me what they'd found. They recovered two skinned wolves that they discovered buried in the snow after they landed at the kill site. My arrival interrupted the poacher's illegal activity, and he hadn't had time to skin the last animal. He buried two of the carcasses, but had to take off before skinning and burying the third. When he returned after I departed, he landed, threw that unskinned wolf into his plane, and left.

He probably carried a gunner with a shotgun in the backseat of his Super Cub. The two recovered wolves had been killed by buckshot, indicating they were gunned down from the air.

That poaching incident illustrates how difficult it is to stop a determined poacher.

☾

Poacher patrolling was not without its amusing moments. Flying up the West Fork on another occasion, I again met a low-flying Super Cub. The Piper Super Cub is the poacher's plane of choice because of its maneuverability and short-field takeoff and landing capability. Since this one flew low as it exited Denali National Park and Preserve, I became suspicious. I passed beyond him far enough to make him think I had no interest in him, and then turned. I gained a little altitude and followed him. By maintaining my position above and behind him, I stayed in his blind spot and he didn't know I was there.

I followed that Cub for miles, up and down valleys, over ridges, and along river drainages. The pilot circled, flew erratically, banked first one way then another, and I had a tough time remaining in his blind spot. I felt like the Red Baron, or maybe Snoopy. He was obviously looking for game and probably for wolves. I already had noted his registration number; all I needed was to witness the poaching I knew would occur if he found wolves.

Eventually he straightened his flight path, headed south towards Wasilla, and gained altitude. I assumed he was heading for home, and I turned and did the same.

On landing at my cabin, I checked his registration number against a list of known and suspected poachers. I also maintained a list of numbers for enforcement officials' planes. My face turned more than a little red when I discovered I'd been chasing an Alaska game warden. The next time I saw him I told him about it, and he had a great laugh at my expense. Turns out his flight objectives mirrored mine; we both had been looking for wolves and poachers.

☾

Wolves kill and eat a lot of animals, but in the area where I lived I think grizzlies were responsible for more kills than wolves, at least of moose. I can't prove it, but my years of observations left me with that feeling. Bears are more efficient killers than wolves. I saw both species making kills, and the bear attacks seldom lasted long. Wolves, on the other hand, sometimes took days to complete an attack.

Near the southern entrance to Easy Pass, I flew over a kill in progress. Five wolves surrounded a cow moose and her calf. A spruce-strewn plateau inclined gently from the valley floor to a mountain that rose abruptly from the edge of the slope, a distance of some 500 yards. The moose and wolves occupied a position halfway up the incline, in a ragged clearing encircled by stunted spruces. The calf, torn and bloody from the attack, lay dead on the battle-scarred, bloodstained snow.

The cow still guarded her dead calf. Her head hung low, and blood drizzled down her torn face and dripped from her tattered nose. Blood also stained her coat in various places, and patches of moose hair littered the surrounding snow. The wolves, content to sit and watch the moose, showed little concern for the plane. They merely acted skittish when I flew a little too low.

Circling was a challenge because of the proximity of the mountain immediately east of the kill site. A pilot can become so engrossed in the scene below that he or she forgets about mountains and other hazards while watching such a sight. Nearly every year, one or two Alaska pilots lose their lives during moose season because of crashing into a mountain or succumbing to a condition known as a "moose hunter's stall."

In a tight turn close to the ground, a pilot who is distracted by animals below has a tendency to tighten the turn, keeping the animal in sight off his wingtip. The wing that's pointed down toward the ground is moving slower than the upper wing, and if airflow becomes too slow over the low wing, it stalls. The plane then noses toward the ground, often turning upside down, a deadly event at low altitude. Between keeping an eye on the mountain and on my airspeed while trying to make a detailed observation of the activity below, I was a busy pilot.

The tracks in the snow indicated that the moose had made little attempt to run away, probably for a combination of reasons. First, by April the winter-long struggle to find nourishment left the moose weak and vulnerable. Second, the still-deep snow limited the moose's ability to maneuver. And third, the cow might have escaped, but she wouldn't leave her nearly year-old calf.

As I circled, the wolves took turns making false rushes at the cow. Perhaps they intended to wear her down even more, thus reducing the possibility of her injuring a wolf. In any event, the pack made no concentrated effort to complete the kill while I flew overhead.

I returned the next day for another look, and the scene seemed frozen in time. The cow remained on her feet, head still down, although blood no longer dripped from her nose. She continued to guard the dead calf. The wolves maintained their loose circle around the moose. The outcome wasn't in doubt, but the pack seemed in no hurry to claim victory. Whether they had made attempts during my absence I can't say.

When I returned on the third day, the wolves were feeding on the cow's carcass, and the young calf had been reduced to hide, skull, and other inedible scraps.

Although I observed other wolf attacks, no others lasted this long. A solitary bear would have made short work of both moose, eaten his fill immediately, covered the remains with snow and brush, and then lain down either on top of the pile or in some brush nearby. This difference between the bear and wolf attacks that I observed leads me to conclude that bears kill more efficiently than do wolves.

☾

I recall an incident that occurred at Denali National Park and Preserve headquarters one spring day. The story involves a bear instead of wolves, but it illustrates not only my point about the killing efficiency of bears, but how shocking it is to witness an animal attack.

A commotion out front grabbed the attention of the tourists browsing for books in the small headquarters building. A tiny moose calf, probably no more than a week old, dashed around the corner and scrambled up onto the porch. About six jumps behind galloped an adult grizzly bear in hot pursuit. The poor calf had nowhere else to go, and the grizzly attacked and killed it within a few seconds.

Inside, the tourists—who moments earlier were prepared to marvel at all the wonderful, natural, unspoiled scenery available in the park, including animals going about their daily routines—clamored for the rangers to kill the bear. When the rangers responded by doing nothing, exactly as they are mandated to do, the tourists verbally abused them for failing to prevent the death of that cute little defenseless moose calf. The bear ate some of the calf right there on the porch and then carried the carcass off into the nearby woods.

❰

Wolf populations fluctuated in the areas I observed regularly. I suspect that hunting and trapping pressure was the primary cause of wolf mortality. Biologists told me that wolves occasionally kill other wolves, but I never observed such an event.

In years of unusually heavy snowfall, wolf predation on moose and caribou increased dramatically, and it seemed to me that wolf litter size increased after those winters. More sightings and more tracks in areas where I hadn't seen much wolf sign in the past led to that conclusion. With an increase in wolf sightings, hunters and trappers increased their efforts to kill wolves, and the population decreased. However, wolves recovered from population declines much more quickly than herbivores like moose and caribou, and I never felt that wolves were endangered in my "backyard."

Wolves are magnificent animals. Those lucky enough to observe even a fleeting glimpse of a retreating wolf will remember the experience for a lifetime. The location where one saw a wolf remains forever special. Wolves have become a symbol of the earth's wild places, and I'm grateful for having had the opportunity to share their space, and the space of every other animal I encountered during our years in the Alaska bush.

Cabin Shenanigans

I wandered the hills near some gold claims on Colorado Creek, but not poking and picking for gold. I hunted moose there occasionally, and in the winter—during the early years—I ran a trapline up the West Fork and set traps near a tilted, deserted structure called the Colorado Creek cabin. I also set traps near a beaver pond that nestled in a hollow beside the old, nearly impassible road that led to the Dunkle mine. I trapped both sides of the valley, which led to Ruby Creek, and ended my line short of the original Denali National Park (DNP) boundary.

One day while I set traps near the Bull River a man suddenly appeared around an alder tangle, walking and pulling a child's orange plastic sled that was covered with a lashed-down canvas tarp. He was heading east, away from the West Fork and the park boundary.

I greeted the stranger, surprised to see anyone in that part of the country, especially in October when the snow had normally driven hikers back to the warmth of city life.

"Howdy," I said.

"Howdy."

"Coming from the Golden Zone gold mine?" I asked.

"Nope. From up the West Fork."

"Trapping?" I was concerned that perhaps he intended to horn in on my trapline.

"No. I've been looking for a place to build a cabin and thought Ruby Creek would be a good spot. Been camped out up there for a month or so."

"Ruby Creek? That's inside the hard park. You can't build a cabin there." We locals referred to the original DNP as the hard park because it was a wilderness area; trapping, hunting, and off-road motorized access were prohibited.

He toed a clump of snow. "Yeah, well, nobody ever checks," he said.

"My name's Lee Basnar. What's yours?"

"Lawrence."

"Where you from?"

"Cantwell," he replied. "Got to keep moving if I'm going to get to the highway before dark." He picked up the towrope and shuffled along the trail I had just come over, pulling his little sled behind him. He exerted less effort hiking along my packed trail, but he didn't walk any faster as he plodded toward the highway.

Perhaps a foot of snow covered the ground, and I was breaking trail with my snowmachine, checking animal sign and setting traps. The West Fork hadn't completely frozen over yet, so I was restricted to the north side of the river. I wanted to follow his tracks to see where he had really come from, but the river sloshed hard against a cliff and cut me off about two miles short of Ruby Creek. His tracks indicated that he had likely hopped across the river on scattered boulders and probably dragged the sled through the water. I decided to check out his campsite after the river froze and I could drive my snowmachine closer to Ruby Creek. Besides, lots of trapline work awaited me that day. I turned around.

Time passed and winter got deeper and colder. Busy with my trapline, I hadn't bothered to make a run to Ruby Creek, although it was only a dozen miles from our cabin. Daylight was scarce and sunlight absent between the mountains that formed the West Fork valley, and I couldn't afford to waste any of the precious light searching for a campsite now buried under five feet of snow.

Then the park rangers showed up. As I split firewood one morning, I heard someone shout, "Haw! Haw!" and turned to see two dog teams mushing along the lake and turning left onto our property. "Whoa!" The teams halted at the cabin's back door, and I walked over to greet the mushers. The chief ranger and another ranger from DNP said, "Hello."

"Welcome," I said, and invited them in to thaw out.

"How's trapping?" the chief asked over a mug of Joan's coffee.

"Pretty good," I replied. "Marten and fox, anyway. Not having much luck with wolves."

"Been up Ruby Creek way lately?"

"No. I get within about a mile or so and then turn around at my last set. What's going on at Ruby Creek?" I said.

"We think we found an illegal cabin, new, on Ruby Creek, and we wondered if you knew anything about it."

"Sure don't. Find it on airplane patrol?" They hadn't been up the West Fork on the ground. I knew every track in that valley.

"Yeah, about a week ago. We're headed up that way now to check it out, but the snow is so deep the dogs are having a hard time pulling. Wondered if you'd want to break trail for us."

"Sure. Have another cup while I get my gear together and warm up my snowmachine. Maybe Joan will fix some lunch to take with us." They declined the lunch offer, saying they had their own lunch in their packs lashed to the dogsleds, but she made a moose meat sandwich and a thermos of hot chocolate for me.

I broke trail all the way to Ruby Creek, and then returned to wait as the dogs struggled to catch up. We took a break at noon and ate lunch a couple of miles beyond the Colorado Creek cabin, which was now buried under the deep snow.

"You know," I said, "last fall I met a guy walking out of here who talked about Ruby Creek being a good place to build a cabin."

"Remember his name?"

"He said his name was Lawrence. I don't know if that was his first or last name."

"Yep, that's the guy. We've been checking around and were told that he had disappeared for a while and was probably up the West Fork in his new cabin."

"If he's not there, he left by way of Easy Pass and around to the headwaters of Bull River," I said. "I haven't seen any tracks coming out this way."

"We don't think he's there now, but we want to check out that cabin from the ground anyway. It's a long hike to Ruby Creek in the summer, and we're too busy with tourists then to bother with it."

We finished our lunch and I drove my machine to the confluence of Ruby Creek and the West Fork and headed up the creek. I tried to drive up a steep bank that nudged the stream into a shallow turn, but I got stuck. By the time I had dug out and turned around, the dogs caught up to me and the rangers decided that dogs could break trail better on that bank than my snowmachine could. I agreed, and watched them heave and tug until they broke over the top. I followed on snowshoes.

There, in a tiny clearing, sat a log cabin, well made, with notches that would make any cabin builder proud. The peeled logs contrasted with the spruce-green backdrop, but I had to admit that unless you knew the cabin existed you weren't apt to stumble across it. I was surprised that the rangers had spotted it from the air.

The chief ranger opened the cabin door and said, "Just as I expected." There, on the wall, were the un-tanned hides of a grizzly and a black bear and a wolf, all likely shot in the park. The cabin was neat, and if Lawrence had constructed it by himself in a month, he hadn't paused to sleep much. I suspected that he'd been at it for more than one season.

The cupboard contained no food, but the wood box was filled with split wood. The builder obviously planned to use this cabin again.

I wondered aloud at the senselessness of erecting a cabin on national park land. Was he dodging the law, which was an easy conclusion to reach? The rangers assured me they wouldn't allow the cabin to remain. "What'll you tell him?" I asked.

"To dismantle it and return the area as closely as possible to the way he found it," they said.

They searched the cabin, found little of further interest, confiscated the animal hides, and we drove and mushed the twelve miles back to my cabin.

☽

Spring in the bush is both welcome and frustrating. Once the snow softens under the strengthening sun, travel becomes difficult and then impossible. I loved to take a few final flights before the lake ice deteriorated and landing on it became unsafe. The time between breakup and open water grounded me for several weeks each spring. Once the ice had melted, I could use my floatplane again.

One day in April, a gorgeous blue-sky, perfect-for-flying day, I flew my ski plane east from our cabin, checking on a caribou herd and a pack of wolves that frequented Honolulu Pass. After an hour or so of watching animals and marveling at the beauty of the mountains that rose above my tiny plane, I decided to fly up the West Fork and see if I could spot any tracks that would indicate that Lawrence, the squatter, had returned to Ruby Creek. As I flew over a ridge near Bull River, I noticed a pillar of smoke way up the West Fork, about where Ruby Creek would be. I flew on, noting the snowmachine tracks below me that hadn't been there three days ago. Those tracks led straight upriver, straight toward the hard park and the creek. I wondered if the rangers had driven snowmachines up the river and burned the cabin.

Flying low, just barely above the river, I soared past two snow-machines parked where Ruby Creek joined the West Fork. I hauled back on the yoke to climb beyond and above the cabin. Below me, two men ran toward their snowmachines while the cabin blazed in the clearing. They had used gasoline or diesel to soak the logs, and flames shot fifty feet high and higher. Uneasy at the way the men raced toward their machines, I climbed out of rifle range and circled, high. When they saw me circling, they walked back toward the cabin, picked up some packs and toted them to their machines, loaded them aboard the attached and heavily loaded sleds and raced back along the trail on their snowmachines.

I reported the fire to the chief ranger and he thanked me for the information. "I guess they saved us the trouble of torching the place ourselves," he said.

The following fall I found the squatter again. This time Lawrence was hard at work building another illegal cabin in a valley that led east from Caribou Pass, perhaps fifty miles from the remains of the cabin he had built on Ruby Creek. He moved in and spent the winter in his new cabin, trapping and hunting. I flew overhead occasionally throughout the winter and during the years that followed, wondering at the working of a man's mind that drove him to move far from town and live alone in the bush. We were glad he hadn't built an illegal cabin on state land near our property. We preferred to live alone.

❰

Six miles from our cabin, at the end of a rough road that miners had gashed into the land more than seventy years ago, the log cabin at Colorado Creek slumped against one of the foothills of the Alaska Range. The old road forked a quarter mile short of the stoop-shouldered structure that sat on a gold mining claim.

The right fork rambled uphill toward the Silver King mine, a mine in name only because it had never been worked, merely staked and claimed. Two miles beyond the Silver King lay the deserted Dunkle coal mine, just past a rough gravel airstrip where I landed my T-Craft whenever I felt the urge. The Dunkle mine had ceased operation in 1954, when the Alaska Railroad began converting to diesel and Alaska's military bases switched from coal to natural gas to power their generators.

The left fork led to the old cabin, but saplings that had sprouted years ago concealed the final approach. A few spruces had grown in what had become an obscure trail, and patches of the savage thorns of devil's club discouraged further investigation. Most folks didn't know the cabin existed.

The Colorado Creek cabin stared hollow-eyed out at the river where leaning cottonwoods interrupted a clear view of the braided West Fork of the Chulitna River. The silty river toted ground-up terrain and glacier-melt that turned it a milky green. A smattering of saplings grew on the level bench on which the miner—some say Wesley Dunkle—had built his temporary lodging. No other standing buildings were nearby, unless you counted the sway-backed derelicts that sagged toward Costello Creek three miles away, up at the Dunkle coal mine. Between the cabin and the old coal mine, the land is folded, fissured by Colorado Creek and rumpled by foothills that lean onto the adjacent Alaska Range.

One sunny day in late August I hiked to the Colorado Creek cabin, wondering if the shelter that still stood on the gold claims that straddled the creek could whisper some of its history to me. I ducked my head and hunched my shoulders and stepped into the dim interior, letting my eyes adjust. Daylight chinked the slow-rotting logs, and sunlight striped the dirt floor in places. Human atmosphere clung to the old cabin, defeated, morose, the mood reinforced by the jail-bar sun stripes on the floor. I toe-nudged a rusty can, one that had likely held beans or lard. It clanked against a porcupine-gnawed table leg, spun, and again lay silent in the dust of the past. The tiny building was sinking into the land, trying to become one with it, but not in any hurry.

A rough board shelf protruded from the wall next to a rusted-out woodstove, and more shelves climbed the back wall, canted in lockstep with the sagging logs that supported them. A bed frame made of rough-sawn lumber and sprinkled with vole and porcupine droppings angled downward in a rear corner.

I sniffed. A damp, rotting smell tinged the air—the scent of age and history and an era that wouldn't return. Miners had been here, but had they lived here? No, I decided, they lived in hope, they lived for the future, but they only grubbed in the present; they didn't really live in it. Payday, provided they found a nugget or two or a thimbleful of yellow flakes, was a brief return to the present, then they returned to the future—at least in their dreams—to the fortune that would surely be theirs if they didn't wear out before their shovels and sluices did.

I turned and peered out the rectangular hole that was a window and watched a raven float overhead, quarking as ravens do. Nothing else moved, other than the milky green water of the meandering West Fork. I stepped out through the door, slit-eyed in the bright autumn sun.

Out back and to one side, in a gully now furred with willows, Colorado Creek tumbled and stumbled between steep banks as it rushed toward the river. Scant evidence remained of mining activity, other than the rusted remains of a shovel and a few scattered, rust-pocked nails that may have once lent their support to a sluice box or a rocker box. Gray, weather-eaten boards lay about. Farther upstream, where the water spewed from the confines of a steep-walled canyon, a boulder stuck up like a bullet, as if warning claim jumpers of the consequences of their trespass.

Defeat lay everywhere, or was it triumph? Was nature actually winning in its attempt to restore the land? If so, the celebration would be a long time in coming, and I wouldn't be around to drink a toast to the winner. Besides, I thought, as long as the possibility remained that gold flakes might tumble from the fissures that cleaved the canyon walls, nature would remain vulnerable. Not even the National Park Service could stop mining in Colorado Creek without condemning the land and compensating the claim holders. I think I was, for a time, one of the claim holders.

☾

On 2 December 1980, the United States Congress passed the Alaska National Interest Lands Conservation Act (ANILCA). The act was designed "…to provide for the designation and conservation of certain public lands in the State of Alaska, including the designation of units of the National Park, National Wildlife Refuge, National Forest, National Wild and Scenic Rivers, and National Wilderness Preservation Systems, and for other purposes."

When ANILCA passed, what is now Denali National Park and Preserve flung a portion of its eastern border eleven miles farther east and netted Colorado Creek in the process, including the Silver King mining claims and the Dunkle coal mine.

ANILCA refined the way federal lands in Alaska were managed. The act protected huge tracts of wilderness and other land from development or mineral and timber exploitation. One of its many provisions protected mining claim holders and property owners when federal lands expanded to surround their property or mining claims. Such was the case at Colorado Creek.

The eight valid mining claims that straddled Colorado Creek remained legal in-holdings within the park. The requirement that claim holders perform a certain amount of annual assessment work in order to retain ownership of the claims—although still on the books—languished. For a few years, in my opinion, no meaningful assessment work was performed on the eight Colorado Creek mining claims, although the person who held those claims might disagree.

Annual labor, the term miners use to refer to the annual assessment work they're required to do on claims, is a nebulous piece of mostly fiction, in my view. Rarely does the government check the claims on the ground, where miners supposedly spend $100 per year per claim "assessing" whether the claims may eventually prove profitable. Thus, although the public has the right to travel onto mining claims on public land, many people don't understand that right and avoid the claims, and some claim holders behave as if the claims are private property. Some miners' cabins become hunting cabins in the fall and recreation cabins at other times. As long as the claim holders submit the required paperwork each year stating that they have performed assessment work on each claim—whether or not any real work was done—the claims remain valid.

The mining speculator who held the eight claims on Colorado Creek came to me one day and offered me half ownership in them, no strings attached. I wasn't even asked to help perform the annual labor. I agreed, and he said he added my name to the claims, although I never verified that.

Why would he offer me part ownership?

I was elected to the Denali National Park Subsistence Resource Commission, and I served as vice-chairman of that organization for ten years. Our role was to help protect the subsistence rights of people who depended on wild fish and game for a large part of their diet and lifestyle. The ANILCA-driven Denali National Park expansion granted residents of Cantwell, Telida, Nikolai, and Lake Minchumina permanent subsistence rights to hunt and fish in certain expanded portions of the park, but not in the original park. The National Park Service didn't require them to apply for a subsistence permit.

People who lived outside a five-mile radius of those villages had to apply for a subsistence permit and had to list two witnesses who testified that the applicant had formerly hunted and fished in the area affected by the park expansion. The park superintendent issued permits to sixteen subsistence users, including me.

With my name as part owner on the Colorado Creek mining claims, the gift of part ownership in the claims comes into focus. Although he never made any comment to that effect, perhaps the claim owner thought that, with my links to the park superintendent and subsistence resource rangers, I'd be more likely to support mining activity on those claims.

❰

My "partner" in the Colorado Creek mining claims came to me several years after he said he had added me to the claims and asked if I planned to do anything with my share.

"No," I said. "I have no interest in mining."

He said that he would likely sell the claims to the National Park Service at the right time, and that the transaction would be easier if he alone owned the claims. Since I hadn't done a thing to earn any right to the claims, I relinquished any claim he thought I might have.

Several weeks later, I flew up the West Fork and angled toward the Dunkle mine. Below me, a fresh scar slashed upward along the old road that led to the Dunkle. What had been nearly resorbed by the forest and was previously nearly impassible and hard to find now became a magnet for ORVs and snowmachines. The claim owner had hired a dozer operator to carve out a new road right across a section of Denali National Park and Preserve. To hell with permission, just do it and dare the National Park Service to do anything about it. Once the new road existed, how could it be undone?

I suspect that the objective was to convince the National Park Service that he was about to begin mining operations, a ploy that would spur the superintendent to offer to purchase the claims at a handsome profit for the claims owner. They bladed the road to the tiny Colorado Creek cabin too. What nature had spent decades trying to restore, man destroyed in a few days. I flew over that destruction only once more before we left the bush. The sight sickened me and I didn't want to look at it.

That senseless act was just one more reason for us to leave the bush before greed and destruction transformed the surrounding wilderness into something ugly. Each year the wilderness shrinks, nibbled and gnawed from all sides by man. Something unsullied and uncomplicated becomes blemished and complex. Some call it progress.

Last Moose Hunt

A moose as big as a Clydesdale horse sloshed toward me, paralleling the willow-choked lakeshore. He grunted every few steps, as bull moose often do during the rutting season. Surely, I thought, he would see me at any second, canter from the lake into the thick brush, and bolt over the nearby ridge into the next river drainage. Two hundred yards, 150 yards, 125 yards—and he kept coming. I silently begged him to turn right, away from the lake and into the brush before he saw or smelled me.

My brain waves must have been tuned to his frequency. The big bull approached to within eighty yards, turned, and lumbered into the willows in the golden half-light of dusk, still grunting. He now attacked the bushes, thrashing them with antlers the width of a pickup truck. Branches the size of broomsticks snapped and

301

cracked as he stripped the velvet membrane that covered his head-gear. His mock battle also strengthened his neck muscles in preparation for the coming combat over the favors of cow moose. The racket and the violent whipping of the willow tops marked his passage toward the ridge. The lake captured, briefly, the reflected red of an autumn evening, then released its grip as darkness squeezed out what was left of the day. I relaxed.

I had stood there, tense, with a huge bull moose bearing down on me, but I couldn't shoot. In Alaska, hunting is prohibited on the same day you've been airborne. That regulation makes sense because it prevents hunters from spotting a moose from a plane, landing, and blasting away, which isn't really hunting anyway. The regulation helps equalize the contest by giving the animals a better chance at eluding a hunter.

Because this bull wasn't spooked, he might linger nearby until morning. Then I could shoot him. It was mid-September, late in the moose season, and he was the first legal bull I had found.

☾

Before I could harvest my winter's meat, I had to find a bull with an antler spread of at least fifty inches, or a small moose that had no more than two points extending from each antler. I could shoot a big bull or an immature spike bull or fork bull, but nothing in between. A spike bull has one smooth antler growing from each side of his head, with no other protrusions branching from the main beam. A fork bull has a single antler on each side that divides into two points near its end, making a vee, similar to a fork in a road.

The antler limitations seem strange, but a close look at the reasons for the rule reveals the logic. Alaska bull moose are in their breeding prime at middle-age, between three and six years old. Younger bulls, those carrying spikes or forks as headgear, can't compete successfully against their larger rivals. They also have a higher mortality rate from winter kill. Older bulls also tend to have a greater winter mortality rate. The big old boys don't recover from the breeding season as readily as the middle-aged bulls. The middle-aged bulls, in the prime of life, are the most likely to survive the winter following the stress of breeding season. If hunters were to kill these moose, weaker bulls would do the breeding. This would result in fewer breeding bulls the following year because of the weaker bulls' higher mortality rate. Therefore, the reasoning goes, it's better to harvest the bulls that are least likely to breed or survive the winter. That way the prime breeding stock survives.

☾

Not only did I have to locate a moose with the right-sized antlers, I had to shoot him within easy packing distance of a lake. I usually hunted alone, and toting 1,000 pounds of moose meat from the kill site to my plane took a lot of trips. Each extra step seemed to add an additional pound to my pack.

My favorite hunting spot, Shallow Lake, hadn't been productive this year. Several moose, including two legal bulls, browsed on willows that crowded the edges of boggy meadows, but the bulls had remained a mile or more from the lake. I couldn't pack meat that far through tangled willows, across lumpy tundra, and through muskeg that seized my hip boots and tried to pull them off my legs. When I was young and foolish I would have charged out through the willows, popped the first legal bull I came across, and worried about packing out the meat later. With age came, if not wisdom, the sense to know my limitations. Even with only two days left in the season, I wouldn't shoot a bull moose located more than a quarter mile from the lake. If I did, I'd be packing meat to my plane for two days, and I couldn't take that much time away from our woodworking business.

Our little Loon Country Creations company became so successful that it controlled our lives and seriously interfered with my hunting schedule. During moose season, I worked in my shop during the day and flew each evening, weather permitting. I scouted several lakes, looking for a legal bull close enough to a lake to meet my minimum-packing standards. That way, I could bag my year's meat supply and keep up with the demands of our business.

Cantankerous weather, even wetter than the normal moose season sogginess, had kept me on the ground for several days. Because we relied on moose for the entrée in many of our meals, I felt the pressure building as the season neared its end.

Eventually, on a golden evening as I circled above a willow-clogged slough, the legal, Clydesdale-sized bull plodded toward Shallow Lake. When he swung his massive head from side to side, strips of velvet dangling from his great antlers flapped to and fro, looking like brown strips of jerky curing on the sun-whitened roots of an uprooted tree. I estimated the spread to be at least sixty inches from tip to tip. Weather permitting, I'd set up my hunting camp tomorrow evening.

Working in my shop the next day, I thought about that big bull while I cut out little birch moose pins with my scroll saw. When I couldn't concentrate on wooden moose anymore, I took a break, gathered my camping gear, stuffed some food and other essentials into my hunting pack, and resumed work until dinnertime. After enjoying a delicious dinner of last year's moose roast and Joan's fresh blueberry pie, I climbed into my floatplane and took off for my favorite lake.

A dirty-blond grizzly dug for ground squirrels in a tiny clearing about half a mile from the Shallow Lake shoreline. I enjoyed seeing bears when I flew, but sleep comes more slowly in a small tent when you know a grizzly roams nearby. Grizzlies grow rapidly under those conditions. This one bulked up by at least one hundred pounds as I passed overhead. He'd gain another hundred, maybe more, after the sun went down. And in my dreams he would double in size.

Shallow Lake is about half a mile long, maybe three or four football fields wide, and no more than shoulder deep. A little longer than the lake and perhaps a quarter mile wide, the slough that feeds the lake provides brushy habitat for a large beaver colony and lots of muskrats. It shelters several species of ducks, and hosts a pair of trumpeter swans year after year. The feeder streams, slicing through the profusion of scrambled brush that grew in the slough, made hiking across the potholed, willow-and-alder-strangled ground almost impossible. The channels, deepened by the beavers, are waist deep in places. In all the years I hunted in the vicinity of that slough, I crossed it once. Lesson learned.

In the middle of that brush-clogged bog stood the bull moose. He slogged diagonally across it, angling for the shore opposite my favorite campsite. Good. I could fly home, load my hunting gear aboard my airplane, return, and make camp without spooking him. I banked away from the slough and flew back to Colorado Lake.

"Joan," I said after I landed, "please clean up the shop 'cause I hope to have moose meat to hang in it by tomorrow night." I made sure to say please because Joan didn't enjoy that job. Sawdust and wood scraps littered the floor, and sanding dust covered everything. Joan undoubtedly thought ahead to the two long days of cutting and packaging moose meat if I killed the moose.

"OK, I'll clean the shop," she said with a sigh. "Can you move the router table and scroll saw out from under the center beam before you go? When you come in with the meat, we can hang it up without having to move the saw and table then." I moved them.

An average adult moose can weigh more than a thousand pounds. After I killed a moose, we let the quarters, ribs, back, and neck hang and cool in our shop for a few days before we removed the bones, thereby taking less space in the freezer. Then we cut the meat into fillets, steaks, and roasts, and double-wrapped the cuts in freezer paper. We ground the trimmings into mooseburger and formed it into one-pound packages. Finally, we transported the moose meat to our freezer, located in Jack and Phyllis Folta's basement in Willow, more than one hundred miles away. The Foltas, old friends from my Army days, graciously gave us lots of support during our years in the bush.

"How close to the lake is the bull?" Joan asked.

"About a quarter mile and getting closer by the minute. By morning he should be right across the lake from my campsite." I didn't tell her about the grizzly. Women tend to worry about things like bear attacks and airplane crashes. So do men, but they seldom admit it.

"Good luck," she said, "and be careful."

I loaded my hunting pack and rifle into the plane and flew back to Shallow Lake. An hour or so of daylight remained, plenty of time to set up my camp before darkness reduced visibility to a few feet. I checked on the grizzly and wasn't thrilled to see him still grubbing in the clearing, but at least he wasn't shambling toward the lake. The grizzly owned the land. Maybe he'd let me use small portion of it. If my moose hunt were successful, I'd leave as rent a head, a gut pile, and four legs from the knee down.

To the south, the sky darkened to a tender purple near the horizon, and rain streaks stretched from the clouds to the shadowed landscape beneath them. Patches of sunlight dappled the tundra between the showers. The leaky sky, oozing northward, might or might not squirt onto my campsite.

The moose stood on the shore on the north end of the lake, just as I had expected. I landed on the south end so as not to scare him and taxied to my campsite—a knuckle-shaped sandbar that punched into the lake about 400 yards from the slough. I tied the plane to metal skewers that I screwed into the ground and began to toss my camping gear onto the shore. The site was perfect; I could pitch my tent next to the plane, and the sandbar intruded into the water far enough to offer excellent observation up and down the lake. I looked toward the spot where I last saw the bull before I landed, but I couldn't see him. No problem. I knew where he was.

Busy with setting up my campsite, I forgot about the moose. I was driving the last tent peg when I heard a muffled grunt coming from my side of the lake. I wondered if another bull, one I hadn't noticed, fed in the tangled willows.

As I looped a rope over the tent peg, the moose grunted again, sounding closer. I sneaked over to my plane, a mere twenty feet away, and hunkered behind the cowling, trying to locate the moose. I watched a pair of swans swim slowly past not more than the length of the plane from me, and then I spotted that big bull moose. He was about 250 yards away, plodding toward me.

When he turned and grunted his way up the small ridge behind my tent, unaware that I was nearby, I felt certain I'd be able to find him in the morning.

I hustled to finish setting up camp before full dark. I inflated my mattress, made sure my flashlights were near at hand, placed my rifle at the side of my bedroll, and, after a last look around, crawled into my sleeping bag. A light drizzle spattered onto the tent, and I drifted off to sleep.

Slap, slap, slap, slap, splash, splash, splash—what in hell was that noise? Thoughts of that grizzly loomed large. I yanked open the zipper on my sleeping bag, pulled on my boots, unzipped the tent flap, snatched up my flashlight, and grabbed my rifle.

Bounding outside into the darkness, not wanting to destroy my night vision by turning on the light, I heard *honk, honk, honk!* The pair of swans had decided to make a night takeoff, and the huge birds flapped and web-footed across the water as they step-taxied prior to lifting from the lake.

I listened for a while after the swans departed. The bull moose, sparring somewhere on the ridge above me, grunted and beat on bushes with his antlers. Shivering but satisfied, I slipped into my sleeping bag and went back to sleep.

Kersplat! Like a trout leaping for a fly, I boiled up out of my sleeping bag and was nearly out the tent door, still half asleep, before I realized that this time a beaver had awakened me. My heart thumped damned near hard enough to break a rib. Making its nightly patrol, a beaver objected to my floatplane blocking its normal route. The frustrated animal announced its disapproval by slapping the lake's surface with its tail, which startled me awake. I turned on my flashlight and stood in the light drizzle, watching. The beaver paddled to and fro in front of the airplane. At the end of each circuit, it slapped its tail and dove, bobbing to the surface a few feet farther on. The beaver repeated the performance, keeping me awake long after I crawled back into my sleeping bag.

I wondered what that grizzly was doing as I listened to that beaver broadcasting its location. I hoped beaver meat wasn't the bear's favorite bedtime snack.

☾

As I lay there surrounded by wilderness, my thoughts wandered back to another hunt on Shallow Lake several years before.

Mark and I had zipped ourselves into our sleeping bags at this same campsite. We had nearly drifted off to sleep when, through the thin nylon tent walls, we heard footsteps. The sour smell of fear joined the odor of wet woolen socks inside the cramped, dark tent. Footsteps plodded near the shoreline, paused, resumed, paused…

A large animal walked in the shallow water. I guessed that the beast was no more than thirty feet away. Close. The faint silhouette of willow bushes against the tent hinted at some minor degree of visibility outside.

"What's that?" Mark whispered, scrambling for his gun.

"I don't know," I said in a hushed voice, grabbing my rifle and a flashlight. I didn't turn the flashlight on.

When I slowly and silently unzipped the tent flap, Mark said, "Where're you going?"

"I'm going to see what's out there."

"You're going out there?"

Not having a lot of confidence in the security provided by the nylon tent, I had to know if we were listening to a grizzly's footsteps, which, although unstated, is what we suspected. I preferred to confront the bear where I had a little more maneuvering room. Mark, me, and a grizzly inside that tent would have been a bit cozy. It was a three-man tent, not a two-man-and-a-bear tent.

In my long johns, on hands and knees, I crawled slowly and quietly from the tent into the wooly darkness, keeping a willow bush between the noise of the footsteps and me. Mark crawled out behind me. Frost glistened on the sandbar and sparkled on the willow leaves, but we lacked a moon to illuminate the scene. I eased up to the willow, gun in my right hand, flashlight in my left, and slowly straightened up. Mark was content to remain on his hands and knees behind me, waiting for me to make the next move.

I peered over the bush. Vague shadows and indistinct shapes wavered and trembled in the blackness. The only sound was the gentle stroke of tiny waves soothing the shoreline. I strained to see, I needed to see, but under the thin, moonless overcast, darkness defeated me. If I turned on my flashlight, I would destroy my night vision. But without light, I couldn't see the animal. I also risked dropping the flashlight if I had to shoot. A large animal remained beyond my narrow circle of vision, and by now it had to be aware of our presence. It hadn't run away. Time for action.

I aimed the flashlight toward the water's edge and slid the switch forward, parting the darkness with a narrow light beam.

Something very large and dark brown moved toward me, followed closely by something small and dark brown.

A cow moose and calf stared into the light. Whew!

The cow walked to within eight feet of me, just on the other side of the willow. She snorted when she caught my scent, recoiled, ran parallel to our campsite, and crashed into a willow patch that backed up to our tent. The calf chased after her.

Mark heard the commotion, but from his position on the ground behind me he couldn't see the cause of the racket. He spun around and scrambled away, still on hands and knees, and disappeared around the opposite side of the tent from the two moose. Hearing the noise he made, and in the tension of the moment not realizing what caused it, I spun around just in time to see his long-john-covered butt disappearing around the tent corner.

At that instant, the moose calf tripped over a tent rope. I had tied one of the ropes to a nearby willow rather than driving a peg into the ground. The calf stumbled into that rope. That action caused an immediate reaction—the tent jerked sideways, away from Mark. Then, as the calf fought free of the rope, the tent snapped back to its original position. Mark, on the opposite side of the tent, decided he'd had enough of this excitement. On hands and knees, he scrabbled away from the tent.

Behind the tent, a mass of willows formed a green and yellow, ragged barrier. From a spring located on the ridge above our campsite, water seeped into the willow clump, turning the ground underneath the bushes into lumpy pudding. Mark dove headfirst into the willows, muck be damned.

That willow patch stood in the path of the fleeing moose. They charged into the bushes right in front of my hunting partner.

Mark reversed course in midwillow. In a half crouch, he dashed back toward me, mud dribbling from his long johns. He shined his flashlight wildly around behind him. His eyes were bigger than the lens of the flashlight.

"What in hell was that?" he demanded, listening to the fading sounds of the spooked moose crashing through bushes on the hill behind the tent.

Bent over from laughing, tears running down my face, I managed to blurt out, "Moose."

"Oh."

Several minutes later, when I regained control of myself, I asked, "Where were you headed?"

"I don't know, but I was getting to hell out of here!"

"Don't you know you can't run from a bear?" I said.

Mark muttered something about me having more guts than sense and began dabbing at the mud on his underwear.

We calmed down and went back to bed, but I lay awake for a long time. It's hard to sleep while you're laughing.

☾

Alone on this hunting trip, and having charged out of the tent twice already, I still chuckled at the memory of Mark's long-john-covered rump disappearing around the side of the tent.

The beaver finally tired of slapping its tail on the water, and I went to sleep for the third time that night.

Quacking ducks awoke me at dawn. I noticed that the drizzle had stopped, and I rose and pulled on my pants and shirt. Hot chocolate and freeze-dried eggs, heated on my backpacker's stove, warmed me in the early chill of the gray morning. I ate some canned peaches and stuffed a Granola bar into my jacket pocket. Eager to find that bull up on the ridge, I listened carefully but couldn't hear him.

A large flock of surf scoters squabble-shattered the still morning. The pair of swans glided out of the slough and paddled over to inspect the plane. I remembered their noisy takeoff run during the night. A flock of mergansers swam by, twelve in all, looking like a troop of sailors passing in review, one behind the other. A red-throated loon fished across the lake from my campsite. Wigeons, buffleheads, and Barrow's goldeneyes quacked at various locations around Shallow Lake. I had enjoyed a similar scene year after year.

I eased up the ridge through thick brush and around mature spruces, moving quietly over the rain-drenched ground. The smell of wet leaves and crushed blueberries rose from the slope as I carefully stepped over downed limbs and bypassed clumps of alders and thickets of willows.

Alaska willows are more bush than tree. They don't resemble the more familiar willows common in the Lower 48, the ones with the tall trunks and weeping branches. A moose in these man-high willow bushes can disappear in an instant, and the thick vegetation distorts the sound and therefore the direction of the animal's departure.

Suddenly I heard the bull grunt, the sort of noise a man makes when belly-punched—a deep, brief, explosive sound. I stopped. I turned slowly to look down at my tent and the lakeshore, about 250 yards away. The distance met my meatpacking standards.

Now began the best part of any hunting trip. To know there's a legal bull moose nearby, and to try to sneak close enough for an easy shot, is a challenge I enjoyed. Meeting the animal on his turf, with the outcome always in doubt, got my adrenalin pumping, and I looked forward to that aspect of the hunt annually. The kill distressed me more with each passing year, but I loved the stalk.

Hunched over, I sneaked to within seventy-five yards of the bull. At that point, an unobstructed depression, blanketed with low blueberry bushes and a carpet of spruce-green moss, provided a clear look at the moose on the far side. I watched from behind a bush as he slashed at a willow with his newly scraped antlers. Only a few scraps of the velvet that had covered them still hung from the bloodstained tines. I watched him for several minutes, dreading the moment when I would have to pull the trigger, but if I wanted to eat moose meat for the next year, I had to shoot.

He moved behind some brush. I stepped into the opening and sat down, rifle ready, waiting for a clear shot. He heard me, because when he emerged from the brush, he looked directly at me. He grunted. Without moving, I grunted back. The bull began beating the bushes with his antlers. He thought I was another bull moose, which was why I grunted, reinforcing his delusion.

He was a big bull, not the smaller size I preferred, but this late in the season I couldn't pick and choose. I aimed and squeezed the trigger.

Head-shot, he crumpled to the ground with his back wedged against a spruce tree, which made field dressing him damned difficult. I couldn't move him away from the tree because that direction lay uphill. Alone, it's tough to deal with more than a thousand pounds of moose. I did it for years, but never found the task easy. This situation presented a special challenge. I managed to gut him, but quartering him was more than I wanted to tackle. I needed a come-along. Better yet, I could use some assistance.

My friend, Jack Turner, had offered to lend a hand if I needed help. I flew to Jack's cabin and explained my predicament. Jack grabbed his hunting knife, climbed into my plane, and we flew to the lake. Together we finished skinning the bull. With Jack's help, I quartered the moose and began packing the meat to the plane, a distance of about 300 yards. Jack, ravaged by years of fighting cancer, insisted on packing the lighter loads in spite of my objections. He was a true friend. This was Jack's last trip to the field, and in spite of the hard work, he enjoyed himself. He died about a year later, fighting that cancer to the last.

❰

This turned out to be my last moose hunt too. The years were piling up, and we began to look for an easier way to spend the remainder of our lives. The winter following the moose hunt saw us seeking a warmer climate in which to spend our retirement years. We decided Arizona met our requirements, and we began the difficult task of saying goodbye to Alaska.

Meanwhile, during our final year in the bush, we enjoyed the steaks, roasts, and moose burger from the last moose I'll ever kill.

Farewell to Alaska

We were shouldering our packs when the phone rang, surprising me. I assumed the phone had been disconnected. I swallowed hard, took a couple of deep breaths, and picked up the receiver. "Hello?" I said. My voice didn't sound normal to me, or to the caller. Emotion changes one's voice.

"Lee? This is Hollis. I wasn't sure I could catch you before you left."

Hollis Twitchell, an old friend who was a ranger at Denali National Park and Preserve, was calling to thank me for my volunteer work on the Subsistence Resource Commission and to get my forwarding address.

I thanked Hollis for his thoughtfulness, said goodbye, and slowly hung up the phone. My eyes watered. I sighed. Picking up my pack again, I took one last look around our cabin, home for sixteen wonderful years. I attempted to capture—forever—each image. I looked at the old woodstove that had warmed us throughout so many Alaska winters, and the scarred wood box that held our firewood. I gazed at the 1996 calendar hanging on the wall next to the wood box, and the date—August 6—circled in black.

My scan continued, taking in the circular stairs leading to our upstairs bedroom, the old table where we had eaten so many meals provided by Alaska's bounty, the view through the picture window of the Talkeetna Range reflected in Ravenhead Pond. In the closet, the pale-yellow wringer washing machine, now old and battered, reminded me of difficult but satisfying chores, now a part of our past.

The gray jays, our companions for so many years, squabbled at the feeder on our front deck. I wondered if they would miss us. We would surely miss their antics, and those of the chickadees, magpies, and other birds who fed daily at the feeder.

Our decision to leave the bush didn't come easily or suddenly. Instead, the thought had always existed at the periphery of our minds, unfocused, indistinct. We didn't expect the years to pass so quickly, but recently they had accelerated, had become as fleeting as daylight in December.

No singular event caused us to start talking about leaving the bush. Rather, it was an accumulation of things; a slow wearing down, like the wear on a grindstone after generations of knives have chiseled its surface. We found ourselves questioning whether to remain out there until we perhaps became victims of injury or disease and no longer able to maintain the self-sufficiency we cherished. And the winters…

Darkness and cold are pervasive, each year's effects building, unnoticed at first, upon the previous year's. Those effects accumulate and eventually become noticeable, one aggravation piling atop another. At first, life without electricity was a challenge. After a few years it became a minor inconvenience, then it graduated to the annoyance category. Even after we bought a generator, the lack of full-time electricity was annoying at times.

Trips to Anchorage started and ended in the dark, at least for six months of the year. Loading and unloading our sleds in the darkness at twenty degrees below zero became monotonous. Bundling up warmly for trips to the outhouse, only to unbundle upon arrival, was tedious. Starting snowmachines by pulling starter ropes at cold temperatures affected my arms, resulting in tendinitis, which I aggravated daily when splitting wood. Little things, each on its own easily managed, came together relentlessly and bore down on us like the increasing weight of a February blizzard.

Our small woodworking business became too successful; it overwhelmed us with its demands. Probably the final aggravation was when, after a winter of minimal snowfall in other parts of Alaska's interior, snowmachiners discovered our abundant snow cover and told their friends. The following years saw an exponential increase in thoughtless snowmachiners trespassing on our property and disturbing our solitude with their powerful, noisy, air-polluting machines.

We had had the area pretty much to ourselves for all the previous years. It's difficult not to feel possessive in such a situation, and we didn't adjust easily to the influx of intruders. Perhaps rather than adapt, we should face the inevitable. With trepidation, we began to talk of leaving.

Many questions demanded attention, but the two paramount ones dealt with when and where. We debated whether we would move closer to Anchorage or Fairbanks, or even if we wanted to live inside the limits of either city. The answer was no. Life in the bush had removed any desire for Alaska city life, and why leave an area we loved to move to another rural Alaska location?

Finally I said, "There are numerous beautiful locations on this earth and we might as well live in one of them. Let's find a place that offers beautiful scenery and a warm climate." Joan agreed, and we began our search.

Costa Rica was our first stop, and we traveled throughout that country in search of the ideal location. We didn't find it, and returned to Alaska for another year.

In 1968, while in the Army, I returned from my first tour in Vietnam to an assignment at Fort Huachuca, Arizona. I served there less than a year, but we enjoyed the assignment and the surrounding area. We had never revisited the state, so the year following our trip to Costa Rica, we traveled to Arizona. There we found what we were looking for, and we decided to sell our bush property and leave Alaska.

We knew leaving would be difficult, but the finality of our departure was overwhelming. Nevertheless, with the decision made, we sold our property and our Alaska "toys" such as snowmachines, three-wheelers, boat, and all the necessary items that contributed so much to our enjoyment of life in The Great Land. Moving out of the bush was painful, both physically and mentally, and we worked long and hard at the process.

Two years before we left the bush, I sold my ski plane. The demands of our woodworking business had cut into the time available for winter flying, and I also wanted to do less shoveling to keep the wings free of snow. Still, I kept the floatplane.

When we decided to leave the bush, I advertised the floatplane and sold it within two weeks. The new owner, flown to my cabin by his friend in another floatplane, handed me the certified check and listened as I briefed him on the flight characteristics and idiosyncrasies of the plane. He climbed aboard. I couldn't speak when he taxied away from my dock, slowly cruising across the ripples to the south end of Colorado Lake. He turned the Taylorcraft into the wind, applied full power, and took off. I swallowed hard when he banked and flew that little plane out of my life. My eyes watered while I watched that tiny blue and white plane grow smaller and smaller, fading into the skies I loved so much.

Joan gave me a silent hug. She understood. I wandered aimlessly toward the slough, a favorite destination when I craved solitude. I sat on a rock, staring at the rippling water. Alone with my thoughts and with an ache in my heart, I turned the final page on one of the most satisfying chapters of my life. Perhaps the story began way back in Vermont, when I watched with envy as my friend's father piloted a Piper Cub over our two-room schoolhouse. The story ended in Alaska. I would no longer pilot my plane through Alaska's skies.

☾

Loons played a big part in our bush lives. They nested on Raven-head Pond, and we watched them throughout the summer months as they raised their families. We listened each time they announced their presence with their mournful calls. Years earlier we named our cabin "The Loon," and attached a plaque with the cabin's name on it to the outside wall, next to the door. We even named our wood-working business "Loon Country Creations," because we referred to our property as loon country. At the end of our years in loon country, a loon would become part of Alaska's farewell to me.

I finished packing on our last full day in the bush and went for one final stroll, alone, down the path to the slough. At 10:00 P.M., the low sun of the August evening highlighted the spruces around Ravenhead Pond with a golden glow. The Talkeetnas, reflected in the pond, seemed to rise from the pond itself, their sharp peaks cutting into the deep blue sky. The golden light spread slowly from the spruces to the steep slopes of the mountains, and I felt as if Alaska was bidding me farewell in the only way she knew how—with an overwhelming display of her matchless beauty.

As I gazed with moist eyes at one of the most beautiful scenes on earth, a loon flew low over Ravenhead Pond directly in front of me, uttered a long series of quacks, and slowly gained altitude, becoming smaller and smaller against the backdrop of the golden mountains. If I could have arranged a farewell ceremony, I couldn't have selected one so appropriate or so heart wrenching. I whispered, "Farewell, Alaska," and reluctantly turned back toward our cabin as the glow faded from the Talkeetna Mountains.

The next morning, after a final look around our cabin, I sighed again, went out the back door for the last time, and locked it. As agreed upon with the new owner, who wouldn't arrive for another month, I hid the key under the hinged plywood cover that protected the propane bottles. Joan waited tearfully nearby, and, hand-in-hand, we walked away from the Alaska bush life that we loved so much.

Epilogue

The Anchorage terminal slid past as the Boeing 737 gained speed. My vision blurred. I reached for my wife's hand when the plane angled sharply upward and the wheels disengaged from Alaska.

Below us, city lights winked in the dusk of an August night, heliographing the true sprawl of Anchorage. What a different city this had become since our arrival in 1971. Now, in 1996, development wandered across the Anchorage Bowl like a herd of migrating caribou. Lights, where none had existed twenty-five years ago, dappled the Hillside. That residential area clung to the sides of the Chugach Mountains—jumbled geology that prevented land-hungry Anchorage from devouring wilderness farther east.

The plane roared skyward, banked over Turnagain Arm, then banked again to settle on a course that would pass just south of Cordova, a fishing village on Prince William Sound. I craned my neck for a final look at Denali, which glowed raspberry pink in the sinking sun of Alaska's vanishing summer. I searched the darkening mountains and valleys to the northeast of The High One, trying without success to pick out Colorado Lake and our former home. I knew I wouldn't be able to see our old cabin across 180 miles of wilderness, but I tried anyway.

My gaze returned to Denali. Alpenglow had crept up the towering snowfields until only a hint of pink kissed the summit. The disappearing sun deserted Denali as I watched, changing the wilderness panorama into a dusky, indistinct tableau. The fading scene signaled the end of our life in the Alaska bush; we would break trail in The Great Land no more.

Tears trickled down my face as I shifted in my seat to look at Joan. Her eyes, streaming tears, met mine. The airplane turned again and erased our view of a darkened Denali. We squeezed each other's hand and remained silent as we sped south, away from the best years of our lives.

Acknowledgments

Several people helped to bring this book to fruition. Various friends read selected chapters, and I'm grateful to them for encouraging me to more clearly depict actions commonplace to a lifestyle that none of them have experienced.

My wife, Joan, made many recommendations and helped refresh my memory when I described events that weren't detailed in my notes about our life in the bush. Her encouragement, patience, and understanding guided me along the trail to my destination—the completion of this book.

Lorraine Elder, our daughter, designed the layout of the entire book, including the front and back covers. Her critical eye and sharp memory pointed out small details in the manuscript that I had overlooked or had used imprecisely.

Artist Anne Kelty transformed my rough sketches of Alaska and the Colorado Lake area into maps that made sense.

Finally, editor Kathy Bradley did a superb job of helping me organize and refine sections of this book. Without her patience, expertise, and attention to detail, I would still be endlessly rewriting and self-editing.

My heartfelt thanks to all who helped bring this book from dream to reality.

About the Author

Lee Basnar is a retired Army officer living with his wife, Joan, in Sierra Vista, Arizona. He is a columnist for the *Sierra Vista Herald/Bisbee Daily Review*, is active in community affairs, and serves as a director of the Arizona Heritage Alliance. He speaks to various groups about his Alaska and Vietnam experiences as well as topical issues. He is a member of Veterans of Foreign Wars, the Military Officers Association of America, the Americal Division Veterans Association, and several nonmilitary-related organizations such as the National Audubon Society and the National Parks Conservation Association.

His first book, *Vietnam Vignettes: Tales of an Infantryman*, was published in 2004. His articles have appeared in *Alaska* magazine and *Alaska Outdoors* magazine, and his poems have appeared in newspapers and on veterans' web sites.

Printed in the United States
40053LVS00004B/3

9 781591 137788